D1584111

HOUSING, SOCIAL POLICY AND DIFFERENCE

Disability, ethnicity, gender
and housing

Malcolm Harrison with Cathy Davis

only

The POLICY
P~P
PRESS

First published in Great Britain in April 2001 by

The Policy Press
34 Tyndall's Park Road
Bristol BS8 1PY
UK

Tel +44 (0)117 954 6800
Fax +44 (0)117 973 7308
e-mail tpp@bristol.ac.uk
www.policypress.org.uk

© The Policy Press 2001

British Library Cataloguing in Publication Data

A catalogue record for this book is available from the British Library

ISBN 1 86134 187 3 paperback

A hardcover version of this book is also available

Malcolm Harrison is Reader in Housing and Social Policy at the University of Leeds. **Cathy Davis** is a Research Fellow in Geography at the University of Leeds.

Cover design by Qube Design Associates, Bristol

Photograph on front cover supplied by kind permission of Mark Simmons Photography, Bristol

Contents

Preface and acknowledgements

This book combines an understanding of aspects of theory with an account of specific housing issues. Its aims are ambitious, as the hope is to offer a fresh way of looking at social policy in general which copes with agency and structure as well as with diversity and continuity, while also exploring important facets of housing. Much of this writing has covered new territory for housing studies, particularly when introducing a notion of *social regulation* to embrace social control, social support, and responses to difference. Some readers may feel that I have been too bold; for example in rejecting oppression as an analytical tool, or in deciding to give no coverage directly to the literatures on postmodernism or reflexivity (albeit partly due to constraints of space). On the other hand, I have also been conservative, drawing on ideas for theorising social policy systems which I have written about since the early 1980s.

Many colleagues and students, as well as other informants and friends, have contributed to the development of ideas that have found their way into this book. At the start of the enterprise I was fortunate in persuading Cathy Davis to take on the chapter related to gender. Thus Cathy wrote Chapter Seven, and made valuable observations on other sections of the book. Thanks are due also to the people who read or advised on parts of the volume at various stages: Pete Dwyer, Austin Harrington, Ian Law, Geof Mercer, Chris Oldman, Ray Pawson, Deborah Phillips, Mark Priestley, Alison Ravetz, David Robinson, Ian Varcoe, and Terry Wassall. In addition, I have a debt to Colin Barnes, of the Centre for Disability Studies at Leeds, for advice and encouragement as I have begun to try to take proper account of disability within my analysis of the welfare state. Direct thanks are owed to Stuart Cameron, David Naylor and Kesia Reeve for permitting me to refer to unpublished writings. Valuable comments were also provided by two anonymous referees. Above all, throughout the writing process Gill Harrison has provided a great deal of support and advice. Any faults in the text or arguments of the book, however, are errors of the authors alone.

Malcolm Harrison
October 2000

ONE

Introduction

This book brings disability, ethnicity and gender into the centre of an analysis of housing policies and practices. At the same time it offers a distinctive way of looking at welfare arrangements in a complex society. We explore interactions between human agency and institutional power, and examine how 'difference' is responded to and regulated in the modern welfare state. Touching on issues ranging from minority ethnic housing needs to domestic violence, we locate specific housing concerns in relation to a larger backcloth of dominant ideas, social changes, and challenges from the grass roots. The book acknowledges the significance of diversity of experiences and of household strategies, but also highlights the persistent influence of longstanding 'structural' factors shaping housing choices for many disabled people, minority ethnic households and women. We also try to connect manageable theoretical preoccupations with daily practice and experience, drawing on the record available in UK housing.

Our focus on housing issues is primarily from a social policy standpoint, with comments generally being about social trends and issues rather than matters of building design, physical environment or economic analysis (cf Clapham, Kemp and Smith, 1990). Social policy is not easy to define precisely, because most kinds of public policies have social implications, and the study of social policies overlaps with other fields of enquiry. For practical reasons, our boundaries are generally drawn to exclude analyses of governmental economic management policies, industrial policies, environmental policies, and policies on political processes, although these come into the background of the study. Analysis from a social policy perspective has come to imply an awareness of institutional strategies, rules, values, histories, discourses and practices related explicitly to distributional and household welfare concerns, an acknowledgement of questions of social division, order, conflict and cohesion, and an understanding of policy issues across non-governmental as well as statutory agencies. In looking at questions raised in housing by disability, ethnicity and gender, we are working very much within this social policy tradition. Our discussion also concentrates centrally on housing access, management and consumption rather than production. Policies and practices in construction clearly affect consumers, employees, and wider communities, but we cannot tackle here the housing industry as such.

We begin below with four sections offering signposts to our thinking as far as theoretical issues are concerned. The first three draw attention to the impact of 'difference' and diversity, point out the continuing significance of ongoing structural forces conditioning people's choices, and consider how to bring experiential diversity and the effects of structure together in a simple model. Two terms are introduced which are used later in the book: *social regulation* and *difference within difference*. Neither is entirely new, but both are worth developing. The fourth section then positions our analysis in relation to welfare state theory. This is followed by outline material on the policy context, briefly summarising UK welfare state changes since the end of the 1970s, and noting recent housing events. Finally, we outline the plan for the chapters that follow, and clarify some of the terms used.

Issues of 'difference' and diversity

Difference is on the agenda right across the social sciences, and is having a profound impact on areas of daily practice for professionals, politicians and grass-roots activists. The theme of difference is very important in our analysis, as the title of this book indicates. In using the term we are referring or relating to distinctions between people or groups of people, to diversity of outlooks or experiences related to age, gender, sexuality, impairment, ethnicity and so forth, and to social, cultural and identity divides that have had an impact on politics, policies, and academic analyses. In reviewing difference and diversity in housing we are especially interested in the conditions and experiences of households, and their individual and collective strategies, as well as what happens when households break up.

For some years social scientists have been accustomed to approach social divisions not only by thinking about class, social stratification, or region, but also in terms of divides between black and white, and between male and female. Somewhat belatedly, a distinction between 'able-bodied' and disabled people's experiences was also added to analyses of social divisions. Fuller acknowledgement of disability, 'race' and gender has enriched social science, including housing studies. Clearly, however, these broad categories have limitations when we look at identities, experiences, affiliations, housing conditions and preferences of smaller groups and individual households. There may be complexities or lines of fragmentation within as well as between disability, ethnicity, gender or class. Older assumptions about broad political solidarities and identities built around being black, female or disabled have been questioned, just as a similar critique developed not so long ago about class-based solidarities. People are acknowledged to have possibilities of multiple identities and affiliations, and highly specific forms of experience. For example, terms like 'simultaneous oppression' have been used to describe distinctive experiences of disabled black people, which may differ from both those of black people and those of disabled people in general. Some differences, while not in themselves new, are more visible than in the past. Sexual orientations in particular can be expressed more freely than in earlier decades. Similarly, issues of domestic violence are much more on the public agenda, so that there is more awareness today that 'the home' may have very different meanings for women in difficulties here than for those in more mutually supportive relationships.

The most obvious implication of recognising more fully the diversity which has always been present in human experience is that when we generalise we need to be cautious, and remember that individuals and groups are important actors in political and social processes. They may have strategies and experiences which cannot be read off simply from social class, age, disability, 'race', or gender. Acknowledging diversity, however, is not just important for researchers or writers. Variations in people's circumstances and preferences can be important for practical policy reasons. Knowledge of detailed household differences and their implications is relevant in community care, in the provision and management of dwellings, in health services, and so forth. One result of recognising diversity has been an increasing interest in what is referred to as 'cultural competence' among practitioners, the hope being that services can be made more sensitive to the specific traditions, identities or outlooks of diverse user groups. This is on the agenda for service providers in the UK and North America, with a developing literature on the issues (for ideas on a 'Cultural Assessment Framework' for health planning in the USA see Huff and Kline, 1999). The 'micro-politics' – or the interactions at localised levels – affecting definitions of need have altered, as more voices from users have been heard. Furthermore, debates about equal opportunities and fairer practices have been supplemented by concerns about claims focused on the wishes of specific cultural, ethnic or other groupings.

Structure, agency, and the regulation of difference

Although diversity is very important, people's distinctive experiences are nonetheless strongly affected by matters that are determined outside the spheres of household or locality. For example, an individual's housing strategies can be affected by laws, government policies, or the requirements of a financial institution. We need to chart the mechanisms, practices and influential assumptions through which people's varied lives and plans are constrained, confirmed, supported, conditioned, or even liberated. To provide an analytical reference point for this, our book draws on ideas about 'structure' and its relationships with human agency. The paragraphs below provide a starting point. Later chapters deal more fully with agency and with structural factors.

The term *structure* denotes factors which may help *to* structure choices, events, perceptions and behaviour or frame people's decisions. It may refer to institutional factors and forces which influence opportunities and outcomes, and which provide supportive or restricting conditions for human actions. Since some established ideas have persistent and widespread effects on freedoms of action, it is desirable to cater for this in the concept of structure as well. In many instances there are links to power in various forms (political, economic, cultural or ideological). The concept of structure implies elements of continuity over time and place, despite possibilities of change. Among the most concrete images of important structural factors relevant to housing are those that picture the operation of economic determinants or constraints at governmental level derived from external global markets in capital and goods. These might be portrayed as 'structural imperatives' binding a succession of individual governments, apparently making expenditure on social policies difficult, and pointing towards solutions dependent on private investors. Within societies there are also many specific hierarchies, economic dependencies, conventions, rules and limits in the operation of institutions, that can be seen as rather systematic across spheres of activity, and longlasting enough to be interpreted as structural. They may relate to patriarchy, to inter- and intra-class divisions, to successful major battles fought by groups of people or movements in the past, to the legacy of the imperial era or to capitalistic arrangements.

Given our specific focus, we do not explore general relationships in society between capitalistic forces, patriarchy, racisms and democracy, but we acknowledge at the outset some powerful pressures of markets, class divisions and profits (cf Ball, 1983; Dickens et al, 1985). Roles of state institutions and the social organisation of supply and consumption of housing in a particular society, may be influenced by the success and power of class, cross-class and intra-class interests, and the ownership or control of capital. The consequence in the UK (as in most Western countries) is that the housing system as a whole is primarily market-led, is influenced by ideas about the risk that some kinds of households bring to social conformity, property and investments, and is affected strongly by notions of rights cast in terms of the liberal model of full ownership (see Honoré, 1961; Harrison, 1987). Access to good dwellings in housing markets is influenced by income and wealth, which are themselves linked with inherited property rights and labour markets. Class, disability, gender, age, region, neighbourhood, and the black minority ethnic/white divide all remain significant markers of likely opportunities or difficulties, and access to financial and cultural resources (or 'cultural capital') is often crucial. Alongside 'free' market processes (themselves legitimated, mediated or modified by governments), public sector activities sift and supervise as well as support people. Despite claims that people today have far more choices than ever before, there are still influential financial and administrative systems which can hedge households in. Furthermore, some policies and practices affecting households have been influenced in the past by racisms and other deeply-entrenched discourses and ideologies (such as those linked to traditional ideas about the family). As later chapters indicate, for consumers at the 'sharp end' the agenda is both benign and oppressive, even though more liberal notions about diverse lifestyles have spread. In the very act of assisting or protecting, the welfare state classifies, deters and supervises.

The various facets of structure are difficult to disentangle, but for people at the grass roots they can be summarised in the notion of (relatively) ordered environments of constraints and options. The ordering is never complete or fixed, is not necessarily a direct or over-riding determinant of outcomes, and is challenged frequently, but remains important for life chances. For our study, this sets the scene for the concept of *social regulation*, a term which we will use flexibly but which is linked with structures and institutionalised relationships of power. Using the idea of social regulation helps us talk about the implications of structural forces in specific settings. As we explain in Chapter Three, the word *social* means that we are focusing primarily on particular aspects of societal relationships (and difference), and not directly on the management of capital, production and labour. We are especially concerned with the regulation of difference in the welfare state, and the practices and assumptions helping condition people's lives and plans. The highly differentiated experiences of being a citizen (through which some people have a better set of realisable citizenship rights or expectations than others) are part of wider patterns of division. People may be constituted differently from one another as far as the practices of institutions are concerned, and located in differentiated ways in terms of human relationships and social expectations.

Although processes of regulation in housing are linked with structural factors, practices are carried out and shaped through individuals and groups. Broad patterns of constraints and opportunities are not entirely fixed, but alter through human action. Our notion of social regulation must therefore include interactions and challenges, and have space for human agency. The social science term *agency* tends to refer to people in their roles as individual or collective actors, and is often contrasted with 'structure'. Agency in this sense, therefore, does not refer to organisations such as housing provider agencies. The term agency is linked with recognition that people have a degree of independence in their daily lives, and may change the course of events. This is clearly important in housing, whether we are considering individual household preferences, the discretionary power of a housing official, the whims of a government minister or the collective activities of campaigners such as tenants.

People certainly may resist a dominant set of ideas or practices. Indeed, increased recognition of diversity has provided a lever for challenges to negative treatment. For example, black and minority ethnic exclusion from mainstream housing policy networks has been challenged by organisations which have, in some cases, coalesced partly around claims about cultural specificity, ethnicity and religion as well as discrimination. Black and minority ethnic housing associations have been able to draw on and refer to diverse cultural heritages and local expectations (Harrison, 1991, 1995). Securing new legal frameworks can also be important in change. For example, despite its limitations, 1970s legislation on sex and 'race' discrimination in the UK has had a longer-term impact on practices across a range of housing organisations, and helped alter the intellectual climate within policy networks. Of course certain changes sought by activists may be very hard to secure. Restraints upon some women's housing choices have been caused or underpinned by the experience or threat of violence from partners, itself supported historically by a set of assumptions about male/female relations in 'the family', and unequal rights in the home. Although traditional attitudes have been increasingly challenged, the responses of housing provider organisations in dealing with needs remain gendered (see Chapter Seven). This is still contested territory, where issues are complex, and where contrasting or contradictory expectations may be found. Perhaps – both for material practices and in the realm of influential ideas – the 'rules of the game' conditioning choices in housing are best thought of as produced and reproduced through an ongoing complex interplay of agency/action with structure. Change, however, may sometimes be slow, and not by any means always in the interests of disadvantaged groups. This is hardly surprising, since structural factors to some extent reflect, confirm, embody, manifest and operationalise the interests of the powerful.

We have said enough to indicate the importance of agency, and the desirability of keeping it in mind when considering regulatory processes. Some social policy scholars claim that agency has been neglected in analyses. We suggest instead that there are specific questions about it which deserve more attention, and we touch on some of these directly or indirectly as the book proceeds. One question which social policy researchers might ask more often concerns how and to what degree certain people make their own histories against a backcloth of structural factors. A related question might concern the extent and ways in which diverse collectivities may form and operate in relation to structural constraints and opportunities. Perhaps social policy writers could also consider ways in which agency and structure are mutually implicated rather than opposites, and see what this means in specific contexts (in effect revisiting the framework imposed for analytical purposes, and amplifying its meanings and qualifications).

Difference within difference

Given the significance both of experiential diversity and of broad patterns of outcomes linked to structural factors, we need a simplifying image to depict the complex landscape of differentiation and action. People make their own histories as individual actors, negotiating their identities against particular settings, and experiencing housing in differing ways. They may occupy more than one position, and may deploy more than one identity (as has long been the case). For example, an individual might simultaneously be chair of a local residents' group, a member of an extended and powerful kinship network, a participant in a disabled people's organisation and an active trade unionist at work. Each role might have different implications in terms of personal identity, status, obligations, sense of solidarity or claims on public policy. An apparent fragmentation of constituencies related to the latter may be one of the most important political markers of novelty or 'newness' in the present period, reflecting diversity of affiliations and a decline in some traditional solidarities. Yet despite their supposed choices, individuals rarely act on ground of their own choosing, and power and resources strongly affect their leverage. State institutions have not withered away and neither have the distinctions between rich and poor, even if these appear more complex than before. Even the cultural dimensions of lives may be shaped by, as well as influencing or, to a degree, being a part of, structural conditions. (From some perspectives culture can be perceived as integral to structure.) Difference is not merely an expression of choice, but is itself developed and regulated through an intimate relationship with structure. It is a flexible concept, being something defined from within a group or projected onto a group, or both.

We could work with a notion of 'difference' as something that has been developed to counter externally-imposed categorisation, to convey respect for diversity and to resist pre-determined orderings in status (cf Williams, 1996, p 70). This is only part of our perspective, however, for differences are socially constructed. Perhaps to some degree people can be 'recruited' into identities by weight of traditions, material practices, networks, or official sanctions, influencing perceptions. Neither our identities nor our sense of our interests floats entirely free of contexts (we say a little more on this in Chapters Two and Three). In any event, difference is asserted or applied in numerous ways. Society frequently distinguishes between women and men, but also sometimes between gay and heterosexual men, and often between 'able-bodied' men and those with physical impairments. As subsequent chapters indicate, regulation is multifaceted and often potentially contested, as well as being both supportive and disciplinary. There are varying and overlapping modes of regulation which are consciously pursued, challenged, resisted and adapted politically, as well as operating and developing in a less visible or overtly political way. Our understanding needs to be sensitive not only to the visible mechanisms of finance, law or administration, but also to the pressures of social conformity and expectations.

To help relate difference to regulation in housing contexts, and to provide a backcloth when considering grass-roots claims and the responses of provider institutions, we can think of overlapping domains, patterns or levels of aggregation. Thus we deploy the idea of difference within difference (see Chapter Two for a fuller discussion on this). This implies that there can be more than one domain of differentiation, and that *diversity of household experiences, strategies and identities occurs alongside or within a broader and persisting pattern of differences* related especially to power, property, discourses or ideologies, and entrenched citizenship practices. This analytical approach is not about prioritising structure within one domain and agency within another, but about patterns of effects and their persistence over time and, to a degree, space. There are big divisions and potential persisting commonalities of material interests related to class and property, disability, racisms, gender, region and age, despite the multiplicity of positions individuals occupy (we comment further on 'interests' in Chapter Two). Of course, domains of this kind are not distinctly separable in the real world. Academic schemes are essentially organising devices, to help with analysis (this applies also to the agency/ structure distinction itself).

Furthermore, the processes, influences and practices embraced by our term *social regulation* are not confined to one or other domain. For example, regulation over time reflects, confirms and helps modify broad patterns of inequalities, but also responds to and provides context for differences in the strategies of households.

Theorising welfare systems

From the point of view of welfare state theories, this book is a contribution to placing diversity of experience, action and agency within an account of parts of the state. We are describing a situation of regulated difference and differential incorporation rather than of unconstrained private choices. One conclusion is that 'social exclusion' should not be viewed primarily through a focus on an ever-increasing range of disadvantaged categories of people, or on 'deprived neighbourhoods'. There should rather be a confirmation of old concerns for processes and institutional practices, albeit measured and given meanings to an extent through their interactions with diverse households. Furthermore, for activists wishing to pursue political programmes, particularistic strategies (such as those focused around distinctive group preferences) probably require underpinning or circumscribing with universalised systems of citizenship rights and access to resources (Harrison, 1995; cf Lister, 1997a, 1997 on 'differentiated universalism'). A society may accommodate diversities in the domain of individual or group choice but it will do so most productively if broader responses to difference are tackled too. The development of more sensitive responses at the 'micro-level' can parallel moves towards greater equality at the broader level or be used to legitimate inaction there. In addition, as Chapter Eight indicates, those who assert their cultural or lifestyle preferences should be aware of the case for subordinating parts of their claims, in the interests not of assimilation but of mutuality, security, equality and universalistic citizenship.

There are many overlapping modes of regulation, whether supportive or restricting, but our emphasis is especially on institutional behaviour and policies. It is often through institutional power and practices that entrenched discourses and ideologies take on their force, and that political or economic interests may be operationalised or find expression. It is also in their institutional contexts that practices have been challenged and amended. In looking at regulation we hope to contribute to understandings of how differentiation *in general* is managed, noting processes, power and patterning over time and place. Despite the confines of our study, this is a rather significant aim. Scholars who develop overviews of welfare state systems and their impact may privilege certain lines of social division and marginalise others. This problem can affect even highly sophisticated accounts. For example, Duncan and Edwards (1999) refer critically to the work of Esping-Andersen (1990) on *welfare-state regimes*, and show conclusively the benefits of acknowledging the gendering of policy rather than relying solely on models rooted in capital/labour divisions. Yet disability, age, racism and sexual orientation are not especially emphasised in their own discussions (Duncan and Edwards, 1999, pp 216-52). When referring to the Esping-Andersen model as 'largely gender blind' (Duncan and Edwards, 1999, pp 218, 220), Duncan and Edwards are perhaps unaware of the irony of their terminology. Although restricted to housing, our own approach offers starting points towards complementing such studies, by examining processes and practices in ways that might illuminate institutional relationships with differentiation in general (even though we too cannot be comprehensive).

Social policy and housing

It is now time to leave theory and introduce the policy terrain that provides illustrations throughout the book. (We return to theory in Chapters Two and Three.) The account below summarises points that will already be familiar to students of housing or social policy.

Welfare state arrangements in many countries have undergone significant changes in recent years, connected with alterations in populations and households, ongoing economic restructuring, political change, and developments in the global economy. The social policy agenda facing governments has shifted. In Britain, national and regional differences and north/south distinctions have complicated matters. Nonetheless, in general terms, divisions built around access to resources, decent jobs, wealth and incomes seem to have intensified in the last two decades, and this effect is manifested clearly at neighbourhood level (see Social Exclusion Unit, 2000, p 22; see generally Hills, 1998). The rising importance of homelessness has been one indicator of increased risks facing households (for recent studies see Burrows, Pleace and Quilgars, 1997; Hutson and Clapham, 1999; Kennett and Marsh, 1999; Bhugra, 1996). Governments cannot control most long-term demographic and social trends, or developments in lifestyles (although taxation and subsidies affect these), and neither can they decisively determine how pressures from the globalising external economy affect the work opportunities of households. Even so, national policies play mediating roles, albeit shaped by obligations to conform to external requirements (such as those derived from membership of the European Community).

As is well understood, from 1979 onwards Conservative governments aimed to facilitate labour market flexibility and competition by reducing the influence of trade unions (and some professions), by encouraging competitive tendering, and by privatising many assets and services previously managed through state-owned corporations or local government. There was an emphasis on trying to reduce direct state costs. The central reason for welfare state restructuring and cuts was not the sense of an overwhelming need for fiscal prudence to compete in a global marketplace, although that no doubt played a role. Rather, the weakening of organised labour, a fragmentation of traditional political interests and the changing face of the world of work provided political opportunities to create new sources of private profit through contracting out and privatisation, to refocus (or narrow) support for the poor, to undermine the main opposition party (including its local government base) and to attack trade union practices. Local government, seen earlier as an appropriate vehicle for expansion of service delivery, now became a target for privatisation of workforces and assets (including council houses and land stocks) and, by the end of the 1980s, political rhetoric was referring to the 'enabling' rather than providing local authority (see Goodlad, 1993). Housing made a large contribution to asset sales, through the 'right-to-buy', which gave most sitting council tenants (and some housing association tenants) the option to purchase their rented homes at discounted prices (for comments see for instance JRF, 1998g). Conservative goals of privatisation and increased selectivity in social policy were supplemented by ideas about marketisation and producer competition within public services, by reliance on organisations outside direct local electoral control (including the Housing Corporation), and by new institutional frameworks to manage organisational performance, budgets and service delivery across a range of fields. In some public sector settings the term *quasi-market* was applied (see for example Bartlett et al, 1994).

The trends of the 1980s and 1990s were highly significant for many in the groups with which we are particularly concerned, both in terms of employment prospects and social welfare. Losers in the more flexible job market would be likely losers in terms of long-term welfare too, since privatised services and financial supports (such as private pensions or health care) relate best to people in better and more secure jobs. Nonetheless, state support did not disappear, despite images of welfare cuts inspired by fiscal crisis (cf Mooney, 1997, pp 231-2). Indeed, some tax reliefs blossomed under Thatcher, so that parts of the real welfare state particularly valuable to the better-off (and designated *fiscal welfare* in the 1950s by Titmuss) were still growing at a time when direct investment (especially in housing) was being reduced (Wilkinson, 1993; Titmuss, 1958).

Housing policies, 1979-97

Since the private sectors require state sanction, with laws to frame their operations, even the most 'private' parts of housing activity are influenced by government, with numerous effects for differing groups of households. All tenures are affected by public policies: whether on taxation; planning and building regulations; health and safety; inheritance of wealth; public sector investment in building; income support; equal opportunities; rights of householders and owners; or regulation of the financial sector. In Britain, support for a 'property-owning democracy' has been manifest in policies that have helped owner-occupation become dominant. McCrone and Stephens say that the UK owner-occupier sector "is exceptionally large by the standards of other similar countries" (McCrone and Stephens, 1995, p 273; but cf Bramley and Morgan, 1998, p 570), so public policies affecting it are very significant. Given their lower average earnings and disadvantaged labour market positions, women, black and minority ethnic households and disabled people probably benefited less than 'able-bodied' white men generally did from the tax reliefs ('tax breaks' or 'tax expenditures') that in recent decades facilitated owner-occupier house purchase (see for example Smith, S., 1989, pp 53, 61).

Despite the growth of owner-occupation, Britain has been distinctive in the priority given to large-scale direct investment in housing built by or for local authorities, and managed by them. As Balchin, Isaac and Rhoden indicate, one feature distinguishing the UK from elsewhere in Western Europe is that the UK still has "proportionately the largest stock of local authority or municipal housing", whereas housing companies, associations and "other forms of social housing" constitute much of this sector elsewhere (Balchin, Isaac and Rhoden, 1998, pp 95-6). UK social policy debate about housing has often revolved around financing and managing council (municipal) housing, supplemented by consideration of more specialised accommodation for vulnerable households, and (in certain historical periods) of slum clearance and redevelopment by councils. From the mid-1980s onwards, housing associations became increasingly important for public policy, but in some ways their activities came to mirror those of local authorities, although funding and accountability were different (see Cope, 1999). In the Conservative period the term *social rented housing* became customary as a description primarily denoting council and housing association stock.

For housing policies the 1979-97 period was radical. To some extent the Conservatives recast the framework of national governmental assumptions. They emphasised the ideal of individual consumer choice, increased reliance on means-tests and selective (targeted) support, engineered a large shift away from council housing, and began restructuring renting in the direction of greater competition and more encouragement for private landlords and investors. It has been suggested that their policy was "obsessed with housing tenure, rather than the broader shape of the housing system" (Cole and Furbey, 1994, p 207; cf Hamnett, 1999, p 54). Malpass indicates the importance of continuities in policy development (Malpass, 1990, pp 4, 158), and council housing as a tenure was certainly in difficulties well before Thatcher became Prime Minister. Cuts in spending had begun in earnest, the tenure was catering increasingly for poorer households, and subsidy support had changed so that more costs fell upon tenants (or at least the better off ones) (cf Cole and Furbey, 1994, pp 2-3, 72-6). Yet the Conservatives did make major departures from the immediate past. The most radical point was that one crucial conception of consumer choice for the Conservatives was in terms of routes out of council housing. Ideas about raising physical standards and quantifying needs now had less priority, and the objective of promoting council house building to achieve specific targets was certainly no longer a "recurring motif in housing programmes", as it had been in earlier times (see Cole and Furbey, 1994, p 71; for a 1979-97 overview see Malpass and Murie, 1999, chapter 5). The right of council tenants to buy individual dwellings was supplemented by encouragements to transfer entire council estates to new landlords or developers, as strategies for changing ownership and management of the stock developed (see Mullins, 1998). Housing associations became the primary vehicles for providing new social rented tenancies, and the chief recipients of transfers. There were specific schemes for regenerating council housing estates, but expenditure was modest in relation to the scale of problems, and gains and sustainability were uncertain (for observations on limitations of past regeneration strategies see Social Exclusion Unit, 2000, pp 7-8).

Although social renting has never been a universalistic alternative to market provision, it had, at certain periods, a broad brief to meet general needs or the needs of working households, giving it status as a potential collective rival to individualised ownership. Gradually, enlargement of owner-occupation undermined this potential, making it increasingly easy to depict social renting as a 'safety net' rather than an honourable alternative to owning. A key feature of the post-1979 period was that the downgrading of the role of council housing was made politically explicit, with its function increasingly cast as a service for the poor. One government aim was to divert support from general investment towards more selectively focused spending. Direct housing investment was reduced by restricting finance available to local authorities for building rented homes ('bricks and mortar'), and 'newbuild' (new housing construction) levels fell. This retrenchment was offset by an increase in the overall costs of providing means-tested assistance to households via housing benefit, tied in with increased rents for council tenants (for an account of trends see Malpass and Murie, 1999, pp 88-97). By emphasising the use of means-tested support to make rents affordable for individual households (rather than keeping general rent levels lower), government confirmed the dependent and distinctive position of poorer consumers, and made access at a manageable price conditional on measurement of circumstances and on effectiveness (or otherwise) of administrative procedures for handling vulnerable households. As time passed, life on estates itself became a subject of increased official concern, as worries about social order fuelled measures to control 'anti-social behaviour' (see Chapter Four). Meanwhile, although investment via housing associations had grown, it had not made up for the decline in council programmes and had been accompanied by pressures on associations to bring in private monies, adopt a more commercial stance and raise rents.

The Conservatives' shift towards high council rents (and away from the principle of bricks and mortar funding) was eventually partly reversed (see Malpass, 1996; Secretaries of State for the Environment and Wales, 1995, p 26; Lund, 1996, p 56). Nonetheless, their strategy had reflected faith in tighter targeting and greater selectivity of support, in line with economic liberal ideals, which also found expression elsewhere (notably in means-testing for improvement grants). It was felt that assistance should be restricted to specified households where need could be proved. The sale of council houses through the right-to-buy, conferred on many sitting tenants from 1980 onwards, reflected the notion of the superiority of private ownership for those who could (with a certain amount of help) afford it. Apart from their impact on the character of the owner-occupied sector, sales reinforced pre-established tendencies for council housing to move towards becoming a low-quality stock targeted heavily on the poorest. The implications for specific groups of consumers could be very important. As we note in later chapters, many disabled people and single parents rely on non-market provision, as do substantial numbers of minority ethnic households from certain communities. One interpretation is that, at the same time as the sector's status and relative quality declined, it also became more receptive to these groups (albeit not necessarily in an unproblematic or even way). Although UK events in social renting may not be unique, there are differences in institutional arrangements and specific policies between countries that are "rooted deeply in political culture and historical circumstances" (Kleinman, 1997, p 155). Thus Murie notes that the extent of tenure polarisation in Britain in recent years has been significantly greater than in other comparable countries which developed substantial social rented sectors (Murie, 1997, p 97).

As far as the day-to-day practices of housing providers were concerned, there was increased encouragement for service user participation during the Conservative period, and some growth in awareness of differences in culture and needs. The Conservatives' emphasis on serving customers strengthened the case for formal rights, access to information and participation for individual council tenants, with the onus on competitive providers offering better services. Collective participation also received some encouragement within council estates, while the community care dimension of housing saw more recognition of user preferences and diversity (see Chapter Five). Housing Corporation support for black and minority ethnic associations was further evidence of changing thinking, acknowledging connections between disadvantage and difference, as well as responding to pressure from the grass roots.

Conservative strategies in the market sectors were mixed, but dominated by preferences for competition and growth as well as for expansion of private sector functions at the interface with non-market provision. With an interest in financial deregulation, government facilitated building society diversification (and conversion into banks), while there was an end to the sheltered circuits of capital which had underpinned societies' growth and the stability of owner-occupation in earlier years (for developments see Kearns and Stephens, 1997). For owner-occupiers, policy was initially encouraging (with the right-to-buy, continuing tax relief and so on), but in the 1990s government began to withdraw some financial support (see Secretaries of State for the Environment and Wales, 1995, p 16; Wilcox and Ford, 1997, pp 26-7). Government also gave an impression of lack of long-term commitment to large-scale maintenance and repair in the private sectors, and a confirmed preference for more selective targeting, although there was assistance for elders to 'stay put' in their homes (for an overview see Leather, 2000). For private renting the Conservatives enhanced landlord rights and attempted to build up the sector, but with substantial costs through rising commitments to income-related allowances or subsidies focused via the tenants (see Mullins, 1998, p 130). Some rent levels remained "bound to the administrative rules and rent determination procedures that govern housing benefit", with private renting partly subject to support and supervision rather than a 'free' market (Marsh and Riseborough, 1998, p 121). For the groups we are particularly interested in, the crucial feature of Conservative market sectors strategies was the absence of much to moderate the dominance of wealth and risk as determinants of outcomes as owner-occupation grew, although there were schemes to encourage low-cost home ownership (see Bramley and Morgan, 1998; Cope, 1999, chapter 10).

New Labour: how much changed?

The Labour government brought changes but also continuities (see Kemp, 1999; Brown, T., 1999; Malpass and Murie, 1999). Matters have been complicated by devolution leading to or enlarging significant policy differences between UK countries (see for example Goodlad et al, in Brown, T., 1999; Barnden, 2000; also *Roof*, September/October 2000, pp 30-3). There is also an impact from strategies covering local government, regional administration, urban regeneration, social exclusion, and child poverty (for the significance of the latter see Blair, 1999, pp 16-17).

Following the General Election, Labour fairly soon amended

homelessness arrangements (see Cowan, 1998), and approved substantial local authority housing investment backed by capital receipts accumulated from previous sales of council houses. The government appeared less concerned with the tenure balance than were the Conservatives, and committed to provision of services through the sector best placed to provide them and meet performance targets (see Kleinman, 1999, p 230). There were changes affecting local authority management of services, including a move away from imposition of compulsory competitive tendering, and creation of an alternative built around achieving 'best value'. This approach has been described in terms of a "cultural revolution for local government" (M. Reid in *Housing Today*, 11 June 1998), pointing to more dialogue with customers and partners as well as aiming for effectiveness of provision. Labour also gave approval to building regulations taking more account of impairment (see Madigan and Milner, 1999), developed proposals on support services for vulnerable people (*Supporting People*; see DETR and DSS, 2000, p 123), and endorsed a new policy statement from the Housing Corporation for meeting black and minority ethnic housing needs and further supporting minority ethnic housing associations (for recent supportive comments here by the Minister, Raynsford, see report in *Housing Today*, 26 October 2000).

Recently a major Green Paper has appeared for England as well as an important Social Exclusion Unit report (DETR and DSS, 2000; Social Exclusion Unit, 2000). (For some Scottish developments see *Roof*, 2000; also debates in *Roof*, March/April, 2000, pp 27-9.) The Green Paper seems to have been fairly well received among housing commentators, one observing that it was "delivering much of what housing thinkers have been wanting for years" (Simons, 2000, p 17). Holmes notes the stress it places on greater investment in affordable housing, with goals including elimination of the £19 billion backlog of disrepair in council housing over the next 10 years, and a 'starter homes' initiative for key workers (aimed at helping those on lower incomes become owners). There is also proposed extension of the protection of homelessness provisions to more groups at risk, expected to result in more access to social rented provision for vulnerable 16- and 17-year olds, care leavers, ex-offenders and single people escaping violence (Holmes, 2000, p 18; DETR and DSS, 2000, pp 86-9; Dwelly, 2000). In a summary of its own, government includes the following among eleven of its key proposals listed: a stronger strategic role for councils; the starter homes initiative; new approaches to help poorer homeowners maintain their homes; a mix of voluntary schemes and licensing to raise standards in private renting;

higher rates of stock transfer; a new investment option for the best-performing local authorities (involving management through 'arm's-length' companies); lettings policies giving tenants 'real choice'; stronger protection for the homeless; and rent reforms in social housing (DETR, 2000). On housing benefit the changes envisaged are to be "improvements to the current system rather than a great upheaval" (Simons, 2000, p 17). Here the Green Paper emphasises improvement of customer services, reduction of fraud and error, improved work incentives, but also (looking further ahead) explorations of other 'reform' options (DETR and DSS, 2000; see Kemp, 2000, and Weaver, 2000, for political background). Of course, although changes appear modest to government, they may have significant effects at grass roots. The Green Paper covers a great deal of ground, although it remains to be seen how far it is implemented. At the time of writing it seems that substantial increases in expenditure for new affordable homes in high demand areas are being promised, with an increase in the low-cost home ownership programme, and efforts to bring existing social housing up to standard (*Housing Today*, 20 July 2000; *Planning*, 21 July 2000). The new resources have been welcomed, although precise implications for social renting are not yet clear (see for example *Housing Today*, 27 July 2000).

Despite changes after 1997 there have also been marked continuities from the Conservatives, notably on investment levels in Labour's first years of office (see Balchin, Rhoden and O'Leary, 1998, pp 309-10; Malpass, 1999; *Roof*, September/October 1998, pp 5, 40). According to Dwelly, writing in a critique of low levels of investment in new social renting, the message of the 1980s, "that it is better to subsidise people than buildings", is still "holding sway", while the release of capital receipts from right-to-buy sales "only just rescued investment from a very deep trough" (Dwelly, 2000a, p 8). Given the dominance of owner-occupation, explicit interventions to meet affordable housing needs through public investment in building are inevitably less central to government's agenda than they once were. This does not mean that housing policy has ended or has no future (cf Malpass, 1999; with Kleinman, 1999; and Williams, P., 1999), but political interest in financing more rented, affordable, publicly-owned new dwellings has diminished. Although there is a commitment to substantial investment following the Green Paper (see N. Raynsford, in *Axis*, August/September 2000), there has been no return since 1997 to any wholesale faith in directly municipally-run housing. Government asserts, as the then Housing Minister, Armstrong, argued in 1998, that "a plurality of landlords is better than a monolithic landlord" (H. Armstrong, in *Housing and Planning Review*, October/November, p 8). The Green Paper supports further stock transfers from councils to other social rented housing landlords, and mixed tenure in new social housing projects "to help create sustainable communities" (see DETR and DSS, 2000, pp 11-12, 17). It will be interesting to see what share is taken of transferred assets by "tenant-led organisations" (DETR and DSS, 2000, p 17; cf Scottish experience prior to Labour; D. Robertson and M. Taylor, *Roof*, March/April, 1996, p 15). So far, despite Labour's democratic socialist roots, the government does not seem to have placed much emphasis on developing any alternative vision of social housing based on well-funded packages for co-ops and mutual organisations.

Labour's stance on transfers reflects financial considerations. Unlike local authorities, social rented housing landlords outside public ownership (including housing associations) have been able to borrow private monies to invest in refurbishment or new building, against the security of their housing assets and rents, without this appearing as part of the public sector borrowing requirement (for discussion see Hawksworth and Wilcox, 1995). Involving such 'alternative landlords' rather than councils remains attractive under Labour because it looks like a means of improving or increasing stock while closely containing direct public investment. Indeed it has been made clear that the commitment to an extensive social rented housing repairs and modernisation programme will only be delivered if there is a "significant injection of private finance" made possible by transfers (N. Raynsford, in *Roof*, May/June 2000, p 18; see also *Housing Today*, 19 October 2000; P. Williams, in *Axis*, October/November 2000; V. Jackson, in *Housing Today*, 26 October 2000). The new landlords might include housing associations and not-for-profit companies or corporations. (For alternative approaches via councils and 'arm's-length' companies see DETR and DSS, 2000, pp 67-8; also P. Jenks and D. Butler in *Housing Today*, 13 April 2000, pp 12, 19; and P. Hebden in *Housing Today*, 21 September 2000.)

That Labour is encouraging more transfers suggests significant structural constraints, but as much in the domain of dominant ideologies as financial realities. For, as Burchardt and Hills indicate, although capital finance raised by housing associations from private funders is referred to as 'private finance', insofar as the cost of this borrowing is passed on to tenants and then covered by housing benefit, "it looks more like indirect public finance" (Burchardt and Hills, 1999, p 17). Costs (and private profits) will still be carried by the public purse. At the same time there has been some continuity about restraining social housing rent levels, holding rents "at an affordable below-market level" (DETR and DSS, 2000, p 93). The effect of high rents on the national housing benefit bill remains of concern (for governmental acknowledgement of difficulties of change on benefits see A. Eagle, reported in *Housing Today*, 13 July 2000).

Other continuities include concerns with management of social rented housing and with concentrated interventions for estate renewal. There has been further encouragement for tenant participation (with 'tenant participation compacts' introduced for council housing), and support for neighbourhood management. Labour is also concerned with behavioural issues and potentially deviant households, within its broader law and order interests. Given our focus, it is important to note government's commitment to initiatives "to help stamp out racism", including changes in the law (Social Exclusion Unit, 2000, p 33). More generally, Labour's approach to assisting households is crossed with notions of conditionality (implying that people must earn the help they receive through approved behaviour), operationalising the view that duties accompany rights (see Dwyer, 1998). Labour politicians have stressed the work ethic as a foundation for welfare practices, implying an emphasis on responsibilities of adults to take work if they can, to obtain dignity and to escape from dependency (for a summary of development of New Labour ideas see Powell, 1999). Blair has asserted that duty is crucial, and defines the context in which rights are given (for example see Blair, 1995). This stance has implications particularly for those whose access to paid employment is unsatisfactory, including many single parents and disabled people who rely on non-market provision. Unsurprisingly, incentives to work feature in housing policy rhetoric (see DETR and DSS, 2000, pp 39, 112).

On the social order front, 'bad behaviour' is not perceived as confined to tenants, since the Green Paper refers to an 'unholy alliance' of bad private landlords and bad tenants (DETR and DSS, 2000, p 49). It suggests that housing benefit could be reduced "for unruly tenants", while the method of direct payment could be denied "for landlords who failed to do what they could to control the behaviour of their tenants" (DETR and DSS, 2000, p 52), although there is recognition of the desirability of proceeding with great care in this area. Perhaps these particular ideas will not be pursued, but Labour does give an impression of a moralistic stance linked with a belief in social engineering, with housing expected to play a role in achieving goals ranging from "strengthening the family" to "meeting welfare to work objectives", and from renewing neighbourhoods to building "sustainable and cohesive communities" (Armstrong, 1999).

There is little will, however, to touch levers that might influence the key disadvantaging trends experienced in particular localities. As far as regional and locality economic differences are concerned, government appears to accept as given (as its predecessor did) those ongoing processes, practices and trends in economic restructuring, labour markets and private business investment and disinvestment, which help shape variations in job chances, local services, house values and demand for social rented housing.

On private renting, convergence with the Conservatives means that although the parties are not in complete accord there is "broad agreement" about need for the sector (Marsh and Riseborough, 1998, pp 112-13). Perhaps convergence has as much to do with the diminished political significance of these tenants for Labour, and the temptations of involving private capital in provision, as with supposed advantages the sector offers in terms of flexibility. There has been commitment, however, to some further supervision of private landlords (DETR and DSS, 2000, pp 44-52; cf Secretaries of State for the Environment and Wales, 1995, p 24).

For owner-occupiers Labour initially brought few obvious gains and soon followed the Conservatives by cutting mortgage interest tax relief (although see DETR and DSS, 2000, pp 30-43). Dwelly (2000a) suggests that since taking office the government has saved £10 billion from cutting support to and raising tax on homeowners. There have been pressures to improve the treatment which lenders give to owners, moves to assist certain leaseholders, and some developments in regulatory frameworks for home ownership. Gurney indicates, however, that there has as yet been no "joined up thinking" (a Blairite term) on home ownership (Gurney, in *Housing Studies Association Newsletter* editorial, vol 28, Winter 1999/2000). Apparently, ideas for a benefit or cross-tenure allowance applicable to low-income homeowners as well as tenants have not found favour with parliamentarians (*Housing Today*, 15 June 2000, p 11). There is no effective overall strategy for sustainability, stability, support and flexibility (potentially especially important for some minority ethnic communities and women). The National Housing Federation has observed that a more strategic approach is needed on sustainable home ownership, "rather than a series of tools" (NHF, Update, Green Paper response, *Housing Today*, 10 August 2000). From our perspective, Labour's policies appear to reflect important political and ideological constraints conditioning governmental involvement with the dominant owner-occupation system. For the moment it remains largely shielded from further explicit and substantial supervision designed to protect or enhance household welfare. Unless governments develop more comprehensive approaches to household needs, risks and strategies here, many people within the groups that especially concern us will continue to lose out.

The plan for subsequent chapters

The book is effectively in three parts. Chapters One to Four touch on the interplay between difference, agency and structural factors, and note broad features of housing trends, policies and experiences. Chapters Two and Three are theoretical in orientation, but connect with specific housing concerns, including the meanings of *home*. Chapter Four investigates housing practices, relating these to structural factors and the ensemble of modes of regulation. Running through this part of the book is the belief that structure can be considered not only through reviewing institutions which exert social control and manage consumption, but also through thinking about the realm of ideologies and discourses.

The second part of the book contains chapters covering disability; ethnicity and 'race'; and gender. Each highlights specific selected issues, to amplify our broad ideas. We draw conclusions particularly about *self-management and citizenship* when reviewing disability, about *diversity and needs* when discussing ethnicity, and about *organisations' practices and assumptions* when discussing gender. Chapter Seven includes some new case study material illuminating current housing management practices.

Chapter Eight draws general conclusions. Housing experiences, preferences and strategies are diverse, but regulatory practices nonetheless constrain and facilitate people's choices in powerful ways. 'Social welfare movements' operate in situations where diversity must be understood alongside continuing commonalities associated with patterns in resources and power. As far as policies are concerned, relationships between the universalistic, selective and particularistic in housing systems remain important, as does the relationship between assistance and support on the one hand, and social control on the other. A comprehensive housing dimension to citizenship would embrace claims and consumer issues across the tenures, and include property rights.

Use of terms

Although we refer to racisms, we write *'race'* rather than *race*, because we are doubtful about distinctions drawn on the basis of supposed physical or biological groupings. In Western societies racist or racialised practices help construct distinctions between people, and may pick out supposedly important characteristics such as skin colour as a means of so doing, but this is a social construction rather than a marker of major human differences (cf for instance Lewis, 1998; Anthias and Yuval-Davis, with Cain, 1992). In many contexts we use the terms *black minority ethnic* or *black and minority ethnic* (or occasionally minority ethnic), following current practice in the housing field, for reasons of brevity and effective communication. This usage refers to a range of 'non-white' minorities, but should not be taken in any way to imply that white people do not have ethnicities, since everyone can have an ethnic location. The word *black* is sometimes used in a similar inclusive way to vary the text (or when this is how people describe themselves), but occasional less inclusive use may also be made of *Black* in line with census analyses. The terms *African/Caribbean* and *Asian* are also deployed, signifying a widely understood distinction drawn in current practice in the UK (despite overlap in reality), but with several smaller distinctive groupings embraced by the two terms. Chapter Seven's terminology reflects acknowledgement that minority ethnic communities sometimes instead distinguish *Asian* and *black*, and it mentions *African Caribbeans* to mean people who came from the Caribbean and have African ancestry.

The word *community* is used in this book primarily to refer to collective groupings, often at local level, but without specific theoretical connotations (see Harrison, 1995, p 10). The term *disability* is used generally to imply limiting circumstances created by social and environmental barriers and arrangements, rather than being treated as synonymous with specific impairments. We usually avoid the phrase 'people with disabilities', as it can imply that disablement means biological and physical limitations, and may implicitly deny positive identities associated with impairment or disability (see Barnes, 1999, p 578; cf Oliver, 1990, p xiii). The term *domestic violence* is generally shorthand for violence predominantly inflicted by men on women in personal relationships. The man may be the woman's partner, family member, friend or acquaintance. The violence may involve physical, sexual and/or psychological attacks, abuse and injury. Children may witness the violence or become more involved in it, accidentally or by the volition and planning of the abuser. Other terms – including *gender and class* – may have contested or varying meanings, but we hope that usages will be clear from the contexts.

Citing of sources

Limitations of space mean that some important studies are not referred to. Our purpose is not to create comprehensive literature reviews, and readers can easily obtain fuller pictures elsewhere (for example in Tomlins, 1999a). With certain topics (including citizenship, community care and social movements) we have referenced writings very selectively. To simplify presentation some sources are cited by initials; notably the Joseph Rowntree Foundation (as JRF), the Commission for Racial Equality (as CRE), and government departments (Department of Environment as DoE and so forth). Some brief press reports are referenced in brackets in the text, but others are included under specific authors in the bibliography. For Rowntree-sponsored studies we frequently cite the *Findings* series rather than full-scale reports, given the accessibility and excellence of the former for students.

TWO

Difference within difference

This chapter focuses on individuals, households, and larger groups, to review the character and impact of difference in housing. We consider how people relate to the home as well as their housing strategies. Background is provided by a summary of some socioeconomic and demographic trends, and we also keep in mind the constraints bearing upon households. Consequently we take up again the agency/structure relationships introduced in Chapter One. Nonetheless, it is agency which now mainly preoccupies us, since fuller discussion of structural factors and regulation comes in later chapters.

Dwellings, households, and socioeconomic change

The overall quality of housing has risen greatly since the Second World War, and provision of internal amenities (baths, toilets, central heating, and so on) has much improved. Lee points out that the number of households exposed to poor housing conditions "showed a major decline in Britain" by the mid-1970s, and problems faced by those people with least choice and bargaining power in the housing market are "very different today" from what they were in the past (Lee, 1998, pp 59-65). Of course, many limitations persist in the housing stock, including shortages of suitable dwellings for disabled people, or continuing deficiencies in internal amenities within private rented housing (see Lee, pp 60-5). Indeed, despite images of steadily improving conditions, the increased impact of homelessness has suggested a housing system with acute pressures and shortfalls. In any case, disadvantage in housing has several dimensions (cf Goodlad, 1993, p 128), revolving not only around a shortfall in physical standards, but also around exclusion from expectations of secure possession and comfortable environments widely enjoyed by others. Variations in housing experiences and the need for housing assistance continue to be related to income and wealth. As McCrone and Stephens observe, the "better pensions and unemployment relief are, the less need there is for housing subsidies" (McCrone and Stephens, 1995, p 3).

While general housing quality standards and economic disadvantage remain important, the housing agenda has been increasingly complicated by household and allied changes that seem to have undermined some of the policy assumptions of earlier post-war years. It seems that we now live within much more diverse households, with greater variety of outlooks and needs. Traditional conceptions of council housing and owner-occupation appeared to fit well with ideas of a two-adult household, following a conventional 'British' lifestyle and (for a particular historical period at least) enmeshed within relatively protective employment and welfare systems. Whether or not images of traditional families were realistic, they were tied in with a "hierarchy of inclusions in the welfare state", whereby some groups could be more effectively catered for than others (see Hughes, 1998a, p 4). What is sometimes referred to as 'the welfare state settlement of the post-war years' encompassed assumptions about ways of living and needs, and about whom the welfare state was primarily for. Perhaps the character of the housing to be provided seemed, before the 1970s, a relatively technical and predictable matter, when jobs and wages appeared relatively stable, when work was "spread more evenly across the population", and when "full time work was associated typically with a male breadwinner" (Forrest and Williams, 1997, p 202). Lund goes so far as to argue that in the mid-1960s "almost all discussions of housing" assumed that the "patriarchal family" was the household form to which policy should be directed (Lund, 1996, p 143). More generally, it is sometimes suggested that there was far more homogeneity of lifestyles and identities than today.

Of course, impressions of a far simpler past may mislead a little. There have long been divisions of region, religion, age, custom, dialect, class and occupation, as well as less visible differences concealed by the outward form of conventional family. Nonetheless, the traditional two-parent household was very important, and was expected to be headed by a male breadwinner committed to (and able to find) full-time employment at an adequate 'family wage'. Before the 1960s families had less control over when and whether to have children, and it was likely that the female partner might be assumed to play rather unquestioned caring and supportive roles within the household, even if also in paid employment elsewhere. Older dependents might sometimes remain within or return to an extended household built around the two-adult couple, depending on variables such as income, property, health, social class and ethnicity.

The context for housing provision has changed gradually through labour market trends, other developments in economic life and an increasingly visible and extensive complexity of household forms and expectations, with a widened diversity of identities, solidarities and strategies at household level. Divisions may have grown between dual and multi-earner "work rich" households, and "work poor" ones (Buck et al, 1994, p 2). Households may more frequently operate around a different sexual orientation, or simply contain a single person. Single person households seem to have become more important not just in terms of numbers, but as a group within the lowest category of household incomes and in the worst dwellings (Lee, 1998, p 62). Meanwhile, divisions of labour and status have not been static within the traditional family, and women are more likely today to hold tenancies or share in legal ownership of homes. Nonetheless, although some men may take more home responsibilities than in the past, or spend considerable time on maintenance (for recent history see Ravetz with Turkington, 1995, pp 219-20), caring for children or helping older relatives still falls primarily to women. Yet men's position as the main breadwinners through formal regular employment has – especially in some localities – been undermined by labour market changes (for changes see Green, 1997). This affects expectations and options. We might anticipate that within today's 'traditional family', individuals will negotiate and plan quite diversely (for instance over delaying child-rearing), influenced by many variables of social class, ethnicity, education, occupation, personal preferences and so on. Although the conventional family form may suit some people, others find it unsatisfactory, and a traditional familial ideology can still create obstacles in access to, or use of, dwellings for people who do not conform to it.

Marsh refers to contemporary debates about coping with the "rapid growth in the number of households" over coming decades (Marsh, 1998, pp 2-3), but this is only one of several issues raised by trends in populations, households and their resources. Spatial differences in prosperity and housing demand have been subject to ongoing change, with pressures such as 'gentrification' and colonisation by middle class households in some urban or rural areas contrasting with declining demand for social renting in specific localities (for the latter see Cole, Kane, and Robinson, 1999). One of the most significant factors affecting housing is increased life expectancy (see JRF, 1989, for some implications of an ageing society). There are now large numbers of older people on their own, often in unsuitable conditions, sometimes experiencing frailty or loss of mobility (although elders are not a homogeneous group). Some have dwellings lacking appropriate design features, adaptations or affordable heating, and many have low incomes (for an introduction see Malpass and Murie,

1999, pp 113-14, 122-3). Writers highlight elders' difficulties within more general accounts of housing (for example Rhoden, 1998, pp 107-12) and there is extensive coverage in specialised literature on 'care' issues. A major change is the "significant ageing of elderly people", with increases in numbers over 75 (Harrison and Means, 1990, p 6) and there are also distinctive concerns related to ethnicity (see Blakemore and Boneham, 1994). Elders living alone – the majority women – are more likely to occupy housing in poor condition than elderly couples. As Sykes noted in the 1990s in discussing older women and housing, while there had been some improvement in "reducing the number of elderly households which lack basic amenities", the "overriding problem of large numbers of elderly people in poor housing remains" (Sykes, 1994, p 79). Writers note housing implications arising from the greater longevity of women (for example Clapham, Kemp and Smith, 1990, p 76), which needs to be considered alongside low incomes and the impact of impairments. Although we associate poverty in old age with women more than men, not all older men are in good accommodation, some being found in unpopular dwellings such as difficult to let sheltered housing schemes (Tinker, Wright and Zeilig, 1995, pp 59-60, 65).

Another crucial change has been growth in numbers of single-parent households, overwhelmingly headed by women, many dependent on low wages or income support and reliant upon social rented housing (for homelessness issues here see Smith, 1999). This reliance on social renting is shared with many disabled people, who also frequently experience low incomes. Ideas about care in the community related to disabled people and elders have been significant for housing, since depending less on residential institutions implies appropriate accommodation and support outside (see Chapter Five). Black and minority ethnic households have also become more important on the housing agenda (for issues see Chapter Six). Their cultural expectations and experiences of racisms can affect perspectives on where to live and the desirability of social renting, while their households, family forms, employment patterns and outlooks may be distinctive (see for example JRF, 1999b, 1998c). Minority ethnic tenure and settlement patterns may not fit neatly into any general model we have. Although social rented housing has catered increasingly for "the least well-off and least powerful sections of the population" (Harriott and Matthews with Grainger, 1998, p 250), many low income minority ethnic households are also found elsewhere. Furthermore, it is increasingly difficult to generalise about the housing circumstances of minority ethnic groups. Certain problems are widely shared, but there is also evidence of divergence. Some communities are growing in contexts of housing shortage, low incomes and overcrowding, while others are successfully climbing the owner-occupier ladder.

Lastly, we should mention younger households. Maclennan refers to a "fundamental shift" occurring in "housing market careers" for the UK young (Maclennan, 1997, p 53). Certainly, prospects of securing good rented accommodation or of entering owner-occupation may have altered, affected by changing labour markets, housing demand and prices. Among some younger single people there have been changing attitudes towards leaving home, obtaining work or lifestyles, with implications for specialised accommodation and support services. Carlen notes that "the expectations of 1980s youth were both much higher than, and qualitatively different to, those of the young poor of previous eras". She also points to the political hostilities aimed at some people who departed from established expectations about lifestyles (Carlen, 1996, pp 4, 23-4). More generally, it seems that becoming an independent adult is taking longer because of changes in housing, education, labour markets and welfare benefits, and the average age for leaving home has been rising (see Clapham and Dix with Griffiths, 1996, p 39).

Increased interest in difference and experiential diversity

The societal changes mentioned above have helped stimulate increased interest in diversity. At the same time the character of struggles over rights and resources within societies has altered, against the backcloth of the declining sociopolitical significance of organised labour based in male-dominated workplaces. Although it is hard to measure the extent of political changes in any simple way, activists and movements concerned with social welfare have put the claims of particular groups onto the agenda directly and visibly (see for example Fagan and Lee, 1997). Disabled people's organisations, minority ethnic organisations, women's organisations, and gay and lesbian groups have all influenced debates and perceptions about social issues (cf Williams, 1999; see also our later chapters). Paternalistic and professionally-determined definitions of needs have been challenged, opening the way for more culturally sensitive provision (for a housing example see Penoyre and Prasad et al, 1993). Localised or specialised networks, communities or solidarities have also developed – not a new phenomenon but a shifting one – sometimes involving ethnic or religious identifications (for example see Eade, 1989).

Meanwhile, provision of services by public agencies has increasingly been cast by governments in terms of responses to clients, consumers, customers, citizens or users, creating some opportunities for people to make their particular experiences and preferences known. It has become more difficult for practitioners and politicians not to show an interest in diversity. Formalised citizenship practices have begun to accommodate difference more, providing in some respects for equality of opportunities at the level of individual treatment along with some recognition of diversity in law and its interpretation (for analyses see Poulter 1986, 1998). The position on UK formal citizenship has contrasted positively with that in some other European countries, although there are places where recognition at the level of formal intent has apparently gone further than in Britain (see contributions in Özüekren and Van Kempen, 1997, pp 43-5, 55-6, 207, 223, 233; cf Kvistad, 1998).

Scholars have responded to change by analysing and theorising differentiation in increasingly sophisticated ways. Beyond the initial concerns with acknowledging disability, 'race' and gender, new themes have been developed around multiple identities, sexual orientation, ethnic divisions, diasporic identities, transnational communities, and so forth. Initially, older assumptions about solidarities or identities based on class and occupation were supplemented or displaced by notions of political or social solidarities and commonalities built around being black, female or disabled. These in turn have come to be questioned or re-evaluated, as recognition of further fragmentations and distinctions has developed. In 'race relations' for example, the 'black/white dichotomy' seems to have been de-emphasised, as "Blackness defined as the common experience of oppression" for non-whites has "given way to a myriad of externally imposed or self-asserted ethnicities" (Ranger, 1996, p 1; see also Ballard, 1996, 1998). Ethnicity here may be about culture, religion or origins, but its practical expression is in terms of the construction of boundaries, mutual identifications and shared activities.

One feature of change has been a diversification of debates about ways forward. For women, for instance, varied strategies can be advocated. Woodward suggests that although feminists might agree on the existence of gender inequalities and seek to highlight women's experience, yet "both empirically in their research methodology" and in deconstructing "gender neutral" categories, they do not agree "on the causes of gender differences and inequalities", nor on "the form which commitment to change and strategies for effecting change might take" (Woodward, 1997, p 90). As well as varied interpretations about women's roles, there have been differences related to sexual orientation, age, personal relationships, 'race' and disability. Whereas many women might feel that a right to abortion is a matter of controlling one's own body, a disabled person or member of a black minority ethnic group – especially given the history of sterilisation as a method of removing the right to reproduce – might also see the control of fertility as having a threatening potential that should be viewed warily. Of course, disabled people themselves are diverse, and this has been acknowledged. While debate has criticised the medicalised individualisation of disabled people which can separate them as the objects of medicine from their individuality as humans, this has not displaced recognition of differences as perceived by individuals and groups. Thus specific impairments remain important, and there can be no denial of personal experiences of physical or sensory circumstance, illness, or the fear of dying (cf Morris, 1991, p 10). Some people with significant impairments may not wish to be included as 'disabled', or may have reservations (see Hughes, 1998, p 86).

One implication of recognising diversity more fully is that the varying standpoints of individuals may be paid more attention. In research this fits well with participatory approaches, involving community informants and potentially helping to empower local people. A little too readily, however, the reasonable step of acknowledging diversity can be used as justification for asserting (much less sure-footedly) that there is a sharp discontinuity with past ways of thinking or previous social conditions (captured by inserting the word 'post' in front of a variety of terms), that all standpoints have equal validity in complex societies, that universalistic (as against relativistic) ideas of need are inevitably unsound, and that it is enough to focus primarily on people's specific cultures, identities, negotiations and desires, independent of contexts. Critics may disagree with such propositions (see for instance Doyal and Gough, 1991, on needs), but the specificity of individual or small group experiences does seem to have moved up the academic agenda in such a way as to undermine attempts to elaborate meta-narratives (see Stones, 1996, pp 23-6), to pursue universalistic policies (see Thompson and Hoggett, 1996), or to analyse and assert the importance of widely-operative structural determinants of conditions (see Malik, 1996 for interesting criticisms).

Doubts and reservations

Scholars should be cautious about neatly periodising historical change, casting the past in simplistic terms and highlighting present novelties in social relations without analysing continuities such as inequalities rooted in property and the distribution of resources. Each person's situation is different, arising from "a unique conjunction of factors" (Abberley, 1997a, p 161), but the apparently heightened capacity for individual reflection and choice today can be exaggerated (cf Giddens, 1994, p 192). Focusing on the 'politics of self' downgrades concerns for ordered inequalities of power and position that some scholars feel might be confronted through collective struggles (cf Anthias, 1999, p 178). Identities themselves (individual and collective) are not formed in a vacuum, but reflect established societal divisions, friendships, associations and commitments formed by earlier generations, the practices of institutions, and images in the mass media, political debate or popular discourses. Identity may be 'positional', and located in more than one set of discourses (cf Hall, 1996, p 135), but is not independently invented. Furthermore, myths about a supposedly much more homogeneous past can be used to falsely inform views of the present. Cultural diversity is not necessarily as novel as it is made out to be (for interesting comments on Germany and the USA see Parrillo, 1998).

Particular problems arise from overemphasising experiential diversity or 'micro-differentiation' (Harrison, 1998a). Difference can be a basis for hostility or supervision as well as a source of strength or foundation for assistance. While people may develop and embrace their own or their group's distinctiveness, differentiation is also an attribute of processes of labelling and marginalisation. In housing history, the terminology used by officials and politicians has often conveyed strong judgements about so-called 'problem people' or 'problem places', and specific categories of households have been included: gypsies; households headed by single parents; homeless people; families with children taken into care; black minority ethnic households; unemployed people; those dependent on benefits; or those with rent arrears. Practices in slum clearance sometimes divided households from the slums from others, and some research gives an impression of humiliating procedures applied to slum-dwellers or 'slum-clearees' (Damer, 1974; Barke and Turnbull, 1992).

Ideas of the outsider, the stranger, or the alien 'other' provide images to project onto people, classifying them and potentially depriving them of individuality and of status as members of a wider social forum. Stereotypes about 'race', gender or disability may work in this way. Negative images of black people have contributed to their being allocated inferior social rented dwellings. Yet at the point when such broader racist practices are retreating, the same forces may work in relation to more specific categories and identities too, with dangers of pathologising particular groups, and of adopting managerialist strategies which sidestep wider commonalities of situation. It is a very easy step from acknowledging difference to denigrating 'others' as deviant or a threat to social order. We can illustrate with ethnicity. Meanings applied to this vary from 'primordial' formulations associated with ties of religion, blood, language, region and so forth, to treatments of ethnicity as a sociopolitical and cultural resource for differing interest or status groups, and something socially constructed (see Hutchinson and Smith, 1996, pp 8-10). In any event, it is certainly possible for observers strongly to associate specific traits (including culture) with groups around which boundaries are assumed to exist. Benson (1996, pp 52-3) gives cause for reservations about the implications of scholars' cultural emphasis on Asian communities and assumptions that Asian groups and African/Caribbean groups differ broadly. She indicates the danger of a perspective in which "If Asians have culture, then, West Indians have problems: an opposition which denies both the vitality and interest of Afro-Caribbean cultural practices and the impact of racism upon the lives of Asian populations". Relationships between ethnicities, identities, cultural practices and interests are complex, but ethnicities can be to a degree manipulated or 'constructed' for groups as well as within them, and there is often a danger of thinking that ethnicity is primarily a characteristic of exotic, non-white outsiders (rather than – more accurately – something we all participate in).

Sometimes, radically differing ethnic groups may have a roughly identical 'racial identity' imposed upon them (see Ballard, 1996, p 21, discussing Marable), just as the presence of a 'community' may be assumed by officials or policy-makers in a particular place. In practice, households' commitments to ethnicity may be context-dependent, with specific ethnic mobilisations establishing boundaries of both inclusion and exclusion. Rather than overstating or privileging ethnicity, some scholars might prefer "a more modest examination of how power, resistance and knowledge operate in the construction of constituencies within the context of specific struggles involving policy makers, community and political representatives and those they claim to represent" (Eade, 1996, pp 64-5). People engage with very specific issues or incidents; identity, affiliation and the resources available to them vary according to contexts. Nor is descent by any means "coterminous with ethnicity" (Ballard, 1997, p 189). We might argue for a flexible notion of identities, negotiated against a variety of settings and histories and linking the human subject with the social environment (including its patterns of power and resources).

Individual events may affect identifications, as Drury reveals in discussing the impact of events in the Punjab on young Sikhs in Britain (Drury, 1996, p 110). Commonalities or affinities may emerge or find expression in particular economic, political or civic contexts, where shared identities may be confirmed or renegotiated, or where some aspect of common interest or experience may be incorporated into an individual's sense of identity. The notion of a localised community may shift in relation to external as well as internal forces, and may have varying boundaries or periods of existence.

This flexible but contingent view of individual (and collective) identities contrasts with ideas of the autonomous individual, and with a notion of an independent 'life politics' built around relatively unbounded choices about self-definition. Perhaps some components or layers of identity for individuals are more likely than others to reflect external categorisations that affect substantial groups (for discussion distinguishing between 'ontological' and 'categorical' identities see Taylor, 1998). Our position does not deny that individuals can be creative contributors to their environments. Yet because identities can be multiple, dynamic, situational and complex, constructing a lasting politics around them can be more vulnerable than building a strategy around specific commonalities of long-term *interests* linked to policies, power, resources and options. For activists, this is why a focus on institutions and practices remains vital, however fragmented identifications seem to have become. There is, however, a qualification about 'interests'. We should not lapse implicitly into a contrast between what we take to be 'authentic' understandings of needs, and perceptions shaped for people in such a manner as to create 'false' understandings. Our concern is primarily with interests that may readily be perceived by and influence actions by people, that have been perceived in the past by households, or that might be expected to be a basis for action without a dramatic shift in how people view their housing worlds. While perceived interests may be constrained in a similar way to identity, they offer distinctive bases for collective actions, and for building bridges across identity divides.

Turning to the managing and regulation of difference, we can note that even apparently benign assumptions about difference which affect the activities of provider organisations hold potential difficulties. People's needs may be managed in accordance with predetermined or over-rigid ideas about their memberships and identities. Stereotypes may draw on cultural determinism, placing too much weight on a particular aspect of heritage, or with assumptions that culture is something fixed and independent of other social and economic factors. It is hard not to blur culture and religion, overstating the role of the latter. Writings note, for example, the 'over-Islamicisation of Muslims', with Ranger actually referring to the "respect accorded to Islam in British official ideology" as one of the factors producing "British ethnic Islam" (Ranger, 1996, pp 2, 19). There is thus an ethnicisation of religion, with religion over-identified with a group of people of specific ethnic or geographical origin. (It is worth remembering that in principle Islam is not about origins or ethnicity.) Furthermore, gender issues may cut across as well as sustain aspects of a cultural tradition, raising questions about whether ethnicity is something men deploy over women, whether women are key bearers for ethnicity, or whether there is a complicated mixture of the two.

In any event, sometimes people might be assumed to need access to services primarily as members of a predetermined category related to origins, religion, impairment, household form or culture. They could be thought to look towards solidarities within this specified group, and to have identities in which this affiliation would be central. It might be assumed that they would wish to live near other 'members' of the same category. Sometimes an identity might be projected onto people, or they might be represented in a way that reflected only parts of their own understandings of their social, cultural or economic locations (for very brief housing instances see Harrison, 1998a, p 797). When policy makers are involved, their assumptions help set the stage for interactions with consumers, and may influence how identities, cultures and affiliations are manifested or negotiated. Official recognition of ethnicities, for example, may bring expectations about collective needs, and help sustain a provider response that relies on facilitating or managing ethnic differentiation (for ethnic managerialism see Law, 1996, 1997). Parallels may be drawn with specific impairment. Yet this differentiation cannot be assumed to be the most significant dividing line in people's lives, and for some it may be a troubling rather than fruitful one. Furthermore, it may indirectly serve an unfortunate political purpose if it obscures broader patterns of inclusion and exclusion.

Looking again at agency and structure

Given the problems noted above, we need a balanced picture in which experiential diversity and differences in household affiliations or strategies, can be placed alongside broader societal patterns of differentiation. Before sketching this, however, we must consider further the emergence of these patterns. The agency/structure contrast provides a good way in. We have selected this because we think it productive, although agency and structure are not easily separable. Structure refers to ongoing effects of the aggregation of human actions of the past, in intended and unintended consequences of such actions, and is manifested through agency in the present. Some agency/structure debates and formulations might be better interpreted as ways of sensitising sociological thinking and language to the need to overcome any structure/action impasse within theory, rather than as immediate guides to empirical investigation[1]. There is difficulty in trying to translate preoccupations or languages of theory from a 'meta' level into a policy forum. To avoid terms becoming mere jargon we must pursue, amplify, interpret, and perhaps disaggregate them, in concrete settings. *Our notion of social regulation is one means for bridging the gap between 'meta-thinking' and empirical territory.* Nonetheless, the agency/ structure frame can also be seen as a general point of reference to which we can return when weighing up particular events and outcomes.

Agency is a vague term, and should not be used as a substitute for detailed accounts of social relations. Within general theorising, agency embraces various dimensions, of which human action is one. In looking at specific contexts we may decide that some particular 'components' or dimensions of agency preoccupy us, but the potential contrast with structural factors nonetheless remains generally important. As Chapter One indicated, agency often tends to refer to people in their roles as individual or collective thinkers and actors. Giddens cites a dictionary definition of an agent as one who exerts power or produces an effect, and he also highlights people's capability of doing things rather than their intentions (Giddens, 1984, pp 9, 14). Seen from his perspective, resources are "structured properties of social systems", drawn upon and reproduced "by knowledgeable agents in the course of interaction" (Giddens, 1984, p 15). We suggest that access to forms of power and to resources are highly differentiated and patterned, while regularised relations of advantage, disadvantage, independence and dependence are evident in the systems and practices with which we are concerned. Thus a contrast can reasonably be drawn between the importance of agency and the impact of longstanding institutional or structural factors which provide a setting. Social interaction is structurally conditioned, although not structurally determined, "since agents possess their own irreducible emergent powers" (Archer, 1995, p 90). There is a real danger, however, that the terms are used so broadly as to embrace almost everything important in human action and societal arrangements, and the term structure is (like agency) potentially contested and confusing. Alternative terminologies may be used; such as 'capacity' (implying constraints and particular possibilities) and 'choice' (implying freedoms of action), but this may not solve all the problems of vagueness. Archer refers to two qualitatively different aspects of society, the social and the systemic, or if preferred, 'action' and its 'environment' (Archer, 1995, p 11).

An important concern has been that structures themselves may potentially be confirmed, validated or reshaped by the conduct of actors, as well as conditioning or framing that conduct. (For a well-known account of theoretical issues, and the theory of 'structuration', see Giddens, 1984; for housing see Sarre, Phillips and Skellington, 1989, chapter 2.) Or we might say that structural factors or tendencies are to a degree activity-dependent. Thus dividing lines between agency and structure can be unclear, and the 'rules of the game' (structural) may be produced and reproduced partly through a complex interplay of agency/action and structure. This is not a particularly unexpected discovery. Practical examples show that some rules or frameworks may be altered by people's actions in the short term, others only in the more long term. For instance, a single court case may change the immediate effects of a body of law, moderating the outcome of previously-established rules for a particular litigant. Yet this might have much less certain impact on the broad orientations of that part of the law covering the case. Collective action may likewise seek to reset assumptions, institutional frameworks or rules affecting behaviour. For example, in her study of squatters in the 1968-80 period, Reeve notes that in one place in London squatters established for a time an apparently democratically-organised 'people's court', to deal with conflicts within the community or 'anti-social' behaviour (Reeve, 1999, pp 121, 234).

A more extended housing example will show interconnections further. Divisions among council house tenants provide an historical illustration of the intersection of household preferences or status expectations with the needs and values of organisations. Longstanding divisions of interests between 'respectables' and 'less respectables' helped validate and secure discriminatory institutional practices that were themselves linked with persistent 'structural' influences of social control, selectivity, rationing and social order tied to traditional models of behaviour, work, citizenship and family. Daily practice was in turn influenced by individual officials and their particular political and organisational settings, and by the reactions of those who were seeking accommodation. Thus, in council house allocation and management structural factors played a crucial role, but not in a way that was independent of 'agency', in several distinct manifestations. This simple example, however, cannot imply that nothing was in place before individual actors entered the social rented housing arena. Far from it. Intra-class divisions grounded in generations of economic and industrial experience (see Mann, 1992), racisms tied to imperial history, and ideologies of work, risk and family, were all entrenched factors that could shape choices. Agency historically had a hand in their emergence (and in each period helped influence the agenda passed on to subsequent tenants). Yet having continuity over time and place, and longstanding, regular impact, such factors are distinct enough to analyse as qualitatively different and relatively autonomous from agency in the short term, and likely to have specific kinds of causative effects in the present. Adding to this in terms of Archer's approach to realist social theory, "structure" (in some senses or interpretations) "pre-dates the action(s) leading to its reproduction or transformation" (Archer, 1995, p 15); people encounter a "structural inheritance" (Archer, 1995, p 72). This does not imply subordination or neglect of agency; only that it has to be set in specific historical/structural contexts. In that sense *structure is very much about time*. Experiences are shaped by interactions of agency and structure, but people bring very diverse histories and resources into their present arenas of choice.

The contrast between agency and structural factors is a useful shorthand reminder of important dimensions in the way that we can look at power, action, time and change and of distinctive properties or characteristics that the two terms can be read to imply. In one sense it points to the choice between emphasising methodological individualism or voluntarism, as against structural determinism. On the other hand agency may also be a matter of collective actions, and of challenges to structures, and need not entail an 'atomistic' conception of agents. It would therefore be a mistake to cast agency in housing too strongly in terms of individualism, as an intellectual side-effect of our having acknowledged diversity. At its most extreme, an assertion about the increased choices of individuals and their lack of commonality might thereby lead to a stress on individualised 'life politics', as opposed to collective emancipatory politics. This could mean treating issues like racisms in much too personalised ways, and seeing them in the limited time space of the immediate present, without historical context.

Perhaps the important point is neither to become too committed to particular parameters ascribed to the agency/structure debate (cf Anthias, 1999, p 158), nor to be immobilised by overlaps between the two sets of elements. It is specific interplays between two qualitatively different kinds of elements that are worth looking at (elements that might be distinctive in their relations to time, and sometimes perhaps to place). Some factors may be amenable to being described either as part of agency or structure: culture in general, for example, is difficult to place (although perhaps 'dominant cultural factors' or 'cultures of resistance' might not be). Meanwhile, we should stand firmly by an acknowledgement that differentiating patterns and important continuities in the socioeconomic and ideological realms are crucial to understanding policy fields and outcomes, however strong may be the demands for adjusting our view to accommodate 'the individual'. Some scholars imply that agency was seriously neglected until recently in accounts of the welfare state or parts of it (see Deacon and Mann, 1999; Thomas, 1999). It is doubtful that this applies in a broad sense for housing, as there has been good research on preferences and grass roots experiences, and several specific studies touching on collective action with housing dimensions (for instance see Dobash and Dobash, 1992; Stewart, 1981; although note comments in Bowes, Dar and Sim, 1997). Furthermore, conventional pluralistic accounts of welfare state development have frequently attributed a great deal to human agents, particularly specific politicians and representatives of interest groups, sometimes to the neglect of structural influences.

Perhaps it is not so much that 'agency' in general has been neglected, but that particular key issues concerning agency are worth investigating further. Restating a question noted in Chapter One, we might ask how and to what degree people make their own histories against a backcloth of structural factors which offer them enabling resources or generate profound barriers. Parts of later chapters provide some 'data' on this (for example in discussing disability and housing). Again taking up a point from Chapter One, we could ask a linked question about the focuses of collective groupings in contexts of diversity, where commonalities of interest might potentially form in relation to structural constraints and opportunities, despite particularistic concerns. This is something we return to briefly in our concluding chapter. Chapter One also mentioned the mutual implication of agency and structure, pointing thereby to the significance of bringing together aspects of each in accounts which consider how the structural shapes or confirms particular outcomes and experiences. One might need to consider, here, *who in particular* makes history, and *how stable* are the differentiations which privilege some rather than others. In housing we see diverse material and cultural interests and strategies being pursued by households and other decision-makers, and many ways in which human actions influence outcomes day by day, so that agency is very complex. Meanwhile, structures and institutions change over time and place as a result of human agency in many forms. Put in general terms, actors may reproduce or transform social systems for the next generation, "remaking what is already made" (Giddens, 1984, p 171). Social practices are ordered across space and time, but this is not unchanging. Some changes in institutions and power distributions may incorporate grass roots interests, or amend them. Housing history is made by millions of households, but some are much better placed than others to help make it in ways that benefit them. This is by no means random.

As was indicated in Chapter One, this book sometimes deploys an idea of 'domains', 'levels' or 'layers' to help review differentiation. There are dangers here. Distinguishing between analytical tasks in terms of 'micro-analysis' and 'macrosociology' has been subjected to critical comment (see discussion by Archer, 1995, pp 6-12), and implicit notions of hierarchy and boundaries can be problematic. For example, the idea of levels creates difficulties when related to ethnicity and 'race'. We might identify certain ethnic and religious groupings in Britain with a notion of locality-based community networks, apparently on a more disaggregated basis than the racialised divisions around being black or white, or than class divisions. There is thus a useful sense of layers of differentiation added to a traditional model of social divisions or differences. Yet focusing on localised Islamic networks we find them parts of something much wider, a religious community going far beyond national boundaries. Clearly, people have complicated affiliations and identities, and are located in a variety of ways over time and place. One way of tackling this might be through envisaging overlapping networks of interaction (some more extensive and lasting than others), but this does not quite meet our needs.

Despite reservations, therefore, we have built the notion of domains into our concept of *difference within difference*. As developed here, difference within difference refers to 'micro-social' or experiential difference within broader and *more persisting* patterns of differentiation and resources. In one domain we observe the diversity of individual households, the grass roots or small groups, but there is another domain beyond or around this where powerful organisations, widespread entrenched practices and earlier struggles have shaped and conditioned broader patterns of experience, or at the very least the ground upon which more complex differentiation occurs. Thus in one domain (or at one level) broad and persistent differences may be projected onto people as excluded 'others', while their commonalities of experience may bring them together. Within this they have more diverse conditions and identities, also capable of generating mobilisations where interests are shared and manifest. Our approach is essentially a simplifying device, conveying a sense of overlapping but nonetheless distinguishable sets of patterns and characteristics of difference (or perhaps configurations), one being less amenable to the short-term effects of diversity and choice than the other. It is important not to confuse this device with the structure/agency distinction, since structure/ agency interactions and processes of social regulation permeate all domains. Rather, we have more than one pattern of differentiation in which we can locate people, and agency/structure interactions may be distinctive in the two domains.

Five manifestations of agency in housing

Given the dangers of vagueness noted above, we should emphasise specific examples of agency. There may be a capacity to produce effects in at least five overlapping important ways in housing. First, individuals using dwellings have space in which they develop and pursue their individual strategies; for example they may make choices (albeit constrained) about tenure, neighbours, the composition of their households, the costs they will pay, savings, and so forth. (A similar circumstance may apply also to households and kinship groups.) Second, households and their representatives or advocates may act collectively to pursue explicit housing goals. This has been the case with squatting, tenant campaigns, environmental campaigns related to residential areas, the Black Voluntary Housing Movement and many other instances. Third, there may be effects within and among organisations or enterprises as personnel shape, interpret or resist change and daily practice. This has several facets. For instance, there are developers, landlords, property agents and exchange professionals who participate in housing and finance markets, and there are people operating within public and voluntary sector bodies (some of whom participate in professional organisations or trade unions, attempting to secure the interests of occupational groups and to influence or challenge consumer/producer relationships). There may be resistance within housing organisations to changes or to trends in management (see Jacobs and Manzi, 2000). Fourth, individuals and groups with direct power and influence in public policy making may contribute to formal policies and the goals of practice, with personal wishes, policy communities, networks, and party programmes playing roles.

Finally, there are less visible collective effects of agency which concern constituencies and interests that are reflected or politically represented, although they may not necessarily become overtly mobilised. This is a more difficult category to propose, but is meant to cater for the situation because of which politicians and others 'reach out' to gather or build support – as they have done from owner-occupiers – anticipating actions and interests on behalf of those whom they claim to represent. Discussing agency, Archer refers (more generally but not dissimilarly) to collectivities whose very presence has an effect, consequential either for society or for some social organisation; this concerns the capacity to "make a difference" (Archer, 1995, pp 118-20). It is important to try to include something beyond immediately visible 'housing agency' here, especially to cope with political processes of differential incorporation within the welfare state, and with the agenda setting and bias that may connect deeply with perceived material interests at household level. Non-housing actions, such as voting against the Conservative Party in the 1997 General Election, may have reflected housing concerns, such as the experience of negative equity, and this is part of a pervasive set of political relationships. Acknowledgement from politicians confirms or confers power. If we are considering tenure or residential choice, it is worth remembering that one group's exclusionary priorities may well be "the principal source of another's external constraints" (Ballard, 1998, p 36), but that this need not require specific actions of defence or exclusion (although it may). Markets in owner-occupation help facilitate exclusionary preferences by virtue of the segregation that arises through price mechanisms, but gradations within this tenure and between it and social renting may have significant political connections and consequences. Although the point is not explored further here in theoretical terms, the 'less visible' agency of the better-off may be a crucial obstacle to the agency of others, and if it takes a consistent direction and has powerful effects over time, it can be construed as part of the structural constraints those others face.

There are a couple of additional observations to add about developing more general accounts of human agency in social policy. Agency should not be over-identified with disadvantaged groups, or with positive transformations in the welfare politics and culture landscape. As we have indicated, there is far more involved. Certainly, agency cannot be assumed to have primarily anti-oppressive or emancipatory effects. Indeed, active agents at grass roots as well as higher up the stratification ladder may help make or maintain social divisions in an exclusionary manner (cf Mann, 1992, p 3).

The home: meanings, constraints and strategies

Each household brings something distinctive to housing, has individual requirements of a dwelling and has a specific relationship with tenure. A way to highlight these things (and to connect with some of the manifestations of agency mentioned above) is to focus on the home. This involves looking into meanings and functions of the home, the impact of tenure, and the strategies of households.

Meanings, localities, and functions

The meaning of home varies, depending on the occupier's circumstances, networks, and use of a dwelling, and on tenure, design features and resources. A dwelling is not necessarily a home, since the latter term implies more than mere shelter, and measurable physical qualities of a dwelling may not always be a good guide to the satisfactions derived from it or to the roles it plays. The home may be a strong reflection, or source of, identity or a place where identities are expressed without fear of censure. Individuals' personal relationships may be crucial, especially if these – satisfactory or less so – incorporate or give meanings to 'home'. For some people perception of home may also relate to a wider sense of group identity (cf Somerville, 2000), or might be linked to peer-group ethnic allegiances based in notions of territory or 'turf' (for a USA study see Pinderhughes, 1997).

There has been considerable debate about the home, its meanings, and its benefits (see for example Saunders, 1989; for very recent comments see Kearns, Hiscock, Ellaway and Macintyre, 2000). Gurney suggests the idea of a hierarchy of meanings, with the home existing at a variety of different levels of experience (Gurney, 1990, pp 1, 40-3). It has also been suggested that 'being at home' might mean something quite different in recent times from its meanings fifty years ago (for historical analysis see Ravetz with Turkington, 1995, chapter 10). One thing affecting this in the UK could be the strengthened association between the idea of home and support for owner-occupation. Households themselves also pass through 'housing stages' or phases, during which there may be various changes in outlooks on (and needs from) the home, with age and the presence of dependent family members being crucial factors (Donnison, 1967, pp 215-16, 276-8; cf Bowes, Dar and Sim, on Pakistani families, 1997, p 82; and Rowe, 1990, p 6 for 'three stages of retirement'). Sometimes adaptations to dwellings are part of an ongoing response to changing needs (see Oldman and Beresford, 1998, p 50, for disabled children). Having dependents, caring responsibilities or additional contributing adults can affect housing opportunities, attitudes to dwellings and costs. Some people are more dependent upon the environment of home and immediate locality than are others: this may be more likely to be the case for many women with children, perhaps for people long-term unemployed, and for people with chronic illnesses or severe physical impairments. This can make matters particularly painful if abuse within personal relationships renders home a place not of security and affection but of danger. In addition, dwellings may be places of economic activity, affecting perceptions. Homes may be places of refuge, defence or autonomy, as well as constraint (cf Donzelot's example, 1980, p 41). They may also be places of heavy financial or psychological investment. At the physical design level, features of buildings may affect the sense of security, autonomy, or privacy (as in the case of thin walls allowing noise to travel readily).

The wider local residential environment can have an impact on meanings of home. A locality may provide or lack networks of kinship, friendship, support or even disapproval and constraint. Historically there is some evidence that among the poorest households 'neighbouring' was mainly carried on outside the home, and between women rather than men (Ravetz with Turkington, 1995, pp 211, cf 214). Today women may play a very important role in social networks within local residential areas, leading McCulloch to argue in his analysis of estate activity that active young women often carried a 'triple burden', of household, community and work. He suggests that working class men and women live in sharply different social worlds, and have very different commitments to their communities and localities; when men do take up community activism, they often "mop up any paid work" (McCulloch, 1997, pp 66-7). Such findings cannot be transferred simply across localities, ethnicities or social class, but we might expect a high level of commitment to some local networks and interactions from women with a strong stake in them (cf Andersen et al, 1999). For some women housing and estate life might have different connotations than for men (but cf Saunders, 1989, pp 179-82), and women may be particularly active locally in unpaid capacities. Women may be more interested than men in taking part in improving their estates, since much daily community activity is centred around children (for example see Clapham and Dix with Griffiths, 1996, p 28). Alterations in culture and daily customs for youth also affect neighbourhoods, along with trends in crime (again see McCulloch, 1997 for insights). Worries about the safety of oneself or one's children may be especially pressing for women and minority ethnic residents, influencing preferences about where to live. Religious divisions may have effects too. We learn that in Northern Ireland (in Belfast) Catholic household search differs from that of other households, and is consistent with black minority ethnic search in segregated urban areas of the USA (McPeake, 1998; see also Doherty and Poole, 2000).

There is a view that the development of prosperous estate living encouraged a more family-centred or even house-centred rather than people-centred existence. The spread of new equipment (televisions, telephones, washing machines, and so on) has contributed to changes, alongside differences in transport, internal layouts, space, water supply, heating, lighting, and gardens. Many earlier routine household tasks associated with women's work in the home have become obsolete, although it is difficult to generalise about changes in the division of household labour (Ravetz with Turkington, 1995, pp 217-24). It is likely, however, that some traditional male/female divisions of tasks remain rather robust, and that expected domestic 'service roles' interact with physical space limitations to reduce the sense of privacy or relaxation attached to the home, primarily (although not only) for women (cf Munro and Madigan, 1993). Relationships with children, and their specific needs, may also strongly affect adult or family perceptions of home, as in the case of a disabled child needing better facilities. On the other hand dwellings may reflect primarily the needs of non-disabled family members, and some disabled people living with parents may lack independence or privacy.

Stereotypes about meanings people give to the home must be treated with care. It has been argued that male and female relations with the home differ significantly, Darke suggesting that women value their homes in a particular way (Darke, 1994, p 11; cf Saunders, 1989). This difference, though, will not be universal or consistent. While a contrast might be drawn associating men's involvement in the home with status and investment, and women's with domestic commitments, this is unreliable (for relevant discussion see Dowling, 1998). Women or men may make a strong identification with familial needs, with financial security, or with status. Each may in certain circumstances move "between degrees of relative security and insecurity", and experience "both freedom and confinement at home and on the streets" (see Wardhaugh, 1999, p 97). For each, in addition, social class may affect relationships with home. Nevertheless, there is greater likelihood of women experiencing certain restrictions, burdens or violence at home (for economic or cultural reasons), and it is no surprise that some of the constraints of isolation in new estates have been expressed historically in the phrase the 'captive housewife' (see Ravetz with Turkington, 1995, p 204). Nonetheless, although the home may be a place where some women experience disillusionment and distress, for others it may be vital in an individual or shared enterprise of building a preferred lifestyle. Ravetz with Turkington note, for example, that a large bulk of evidence has shown that married women in Britain have strongly identified with the marital home (Ravetz with Turkington, 1995, p 208). Of course, a positive orientation to the home may be as an individual living alone, as a partner with a man, as part of a larger group (including children, carers or dependents), or in a lesbian relationship. As Smailes remarks, "home can be the only safe place to be a lesbian" (Smailes, 1994, pp 153-4).

For some minority ethnic households too, the home may be one of the places where there is the greatest security and chance to feel a full person, as well as a place where cultural practices best conform to preferences (albeit that these practices may suit one member of a household more than another, and could in some instances be oppressive as well as comforting). Avoiding stereotypes is important, as it is all too easy to construct views of Asian extended households in particular that are simplistic, or that even assume them to be "organized in a manner closely akin" to that which could be observed "among the native English during the last century" (Ballard, 1997, p 190). There is actually a mix of choice and diversity, with constraint, culture and tradition. One assumption is that certain communities will cater for needs of elders through the extended family, so that (say) a Pakistani community will use housing differently from a white community, and have less need for separate elders' accommodation but more need for large dwellings. This might well have some truth, but needs verifying in specific times and localities. At a more fundamental level, religion may make specific requirements of the dwelling. A Muslim may believe that, ideally, 'my home is my heaven', implying particular physical arrangements but also a commitment to an appropriate ordering of family and community life (Hamzah, Harrison and Dwyer, 2000, p 22). In any event, housing preferences for minority ethnic groups appear complex, with issues of locality choices, experiences of racisms, costs and opportunities difficult to disentangle. Some conventional wisdoms – such as the expectation of a widespread preference for ownership – need careful disaggregation, and may be conditional on particular markets and income levels.

Finally, we must not overlook disability, where disabled people may wish to assert their right to live at home rather than in a large institution (cf Morris, 1991, p 165). On the other hand, a 'family home' may become unsatisfactory for a proportion of younger disabled people (just as it does for other young people). The ideal of independent living may carry differing meanings for young people depending on contexts, and being able to live on one's own can be less crucial for some than being able to make decisions and do things oneself, perhaps especially if loneliness follows from living alone (see JRF, 2000a). Although there may be a belief that nearly everyone prefers to live in ordinary housing rather than institutions because of the former's greater capacity to be a 'home', this is not the route to independence for everyone. Means cites the instance when achieving citizenship may require a younger physically impaired person to leave the parental home in order to have an independent lifestyle; yet for some this might necessitate "the level of help and companionship made possible by supported housing schemes" (Means, 1996, p 228).

A home can perform many functions: as a place of refuge; a place of conflict or an imprisoning environment; a means of capital gain or source of income; a place to conduct a business; a badge of status; a basis for subsequent mobility; a store of memories; and so forth. Not only the house but also a garden may be a place of recreation, display or where something valuable is produced (exotic vegetables for example). Some purposes (such as keeping pets, running and parking a car or carrying on economic activity) can be constrained by the type of dwelling or by rules attached to being a tenant rather than owner-occupier. Certain positive functions can be inhibited by insecurity. Dwellings also bring burdens and responsibilities affected by tenure. The joys of DIY (do-it-yourself) maintenance for an owner-occupier can turn in older age into difficulties that having a good landlord would resolve (burdens accompanying the valued status of independent resident are noted in JRF, 1999c). Home also may be the basis from which an inheritance can be planned for the next generation, although this might be specific to one cohort more than another. Thus economic functions may be integrated with cultural values and expectations (for discussion see Dupuis and Thorns, 1996). Apparently some older home-owners are "incensed by the thought that they may not be able to hand their hard-won asset on to their children" because of what they see as "the policy requiring them to sell their home to pay for institutional care" (JRF, 1999c, p 4). It is also possible that some houses may be seen as growing assets which will facilitate owners' early retirements through 'trading down' and realising capital sums; a reversal of the common direction of causal links between labour markets and housing circumstances. Generally, dwellings may be perceived as resources affecting people's opportunities beyond the home, advantaging the better off. As Morris and Winn put it, housing situation is "an expression of inequality", but also has an effect on other inequalities (1990, p 2). This may be a matter of your address influencing chances of credit or a job interview, or of having enough room to work from home. More directly, for disabled people a particular dwelling may facilitate or constrain independent living.

The only effective way to discover the meanings that home has for people is to consider their voices, expectations and behaviour. Nonetheless, meanings and uses are contingent on social circumstances, and shaped by income and economic situations, popular cultural wisdoms, and "the kinds of emotional and familial experiences that occur within the bounds of a dwelling" and which themselves are influenced by "dominant discourses concerning home and family" (Dupuis and Thorns, 1996, p 486). Insights into some societal expectations might be read from images attached to being without a home. Passaro suggests, for instance, that homeless men are viewed both as "hypermasculinized and emasculated", while homeless women are "seen as the apotheosis of Woman – dependent, vulnerable, frightened" (Passaro, 1996, pp 1-2). She goes further to argue that the homeless adults who will be rehoused are those who return to or recreate normative 'homes', and the gender roles they imply (Passaro, 1996, p 3). Perhaps we might learn much about social constructions of home, and how these interact with household diversity and choices, by looking at homelessness (cf Tomas and Dittmar, 1995). In any event, the meaning of home may reflect not a simple identity, but several different strands or aspects of a person's activities and orientations, within a context influenced by external effects. Tenure is important here.

Tenure and the meanings of home

We have already begun mentioning tenure, and Chapter Four deals with it again. For present purposes, however, we need to emphasise that tenure may amplify, modify or reflect aspirations and meanings people attach to home, and can set limitations or constraints. Perhaps some relationships people have with home are filtered through tenure, although this is contingent on variables such as income. Historically the tenures have had varying relations over time with class, although ownership has often implied independence, including the independence to oppose one's employer without losing the home (see Daunton, 1987, pp 72-86). Recently it has been argued that housing tenure has come to "usurp even location" as a "criterion of residential and social status" (Ravetz with Turkington, 1995, p 206), while a preference for owner-occupation has become widespread, albeit somewhat dependent on circumstances of period, place, finances, housing markets, state support and other tenure options (cf Cole and Furbey, 1994, pp 69-82). There are important and apparently positive relationships between being an owner and possessing a home, and people may be strongly attached to the status and identity of owner-occupier (JRF, 1999c). Gurney (developing an analysis derived from Foucault) refers persuasively to home as a "discursive practice which normalises ownership" (Gurney, 1999, p 175). Tenure change may have been encouraged by discourses about ownership as the norm to which all home-seekers would aspire.

We might attribute the success of these ideas partly to the form of property rights that is dominant, and to the confirmation that economic liberal property ideologies receive in the daily lived experiences of buying, borrowing, possession, inheritance and capital accumulation. By contrast with owner-occupation, however, the private rented sector appears to offer little beyond a flexible capacity to house a variety of households (to some extent distinguishable by price levels, locations and degrees of dependence on housing benefit). While 'up-market' renting may bring satisfactions for those who select it, some people have 'chosen' private renting in the past because of being unable to secure priority in social renting. Private landlordism's record has been unimpressive. For example, Muir and Ross indicate that affordability has been a major problem in this sector in London as far as women are concerned (Muir and Ross, 1993, pp 22-4), and apart from cost there have been additional problems of discrimination and insecurity affecting a variety of potential tenants. Thus it is not so much its marketised character that gives owner-occupancy its favourable images, as the assumed advantages and bundles of rights accompanying ownership itself. The significance of occupiers' rights is confirmed by the political battles that have taken place (and continue) over the positions of long leaseholders, who may feel entitled to the status of owner-occupiers, yet have lacked some of the key rights associated with ownership.

Owner-occupation, however, has differing meanings or purposes for different users, is achieved in differing ways and with varying degrees of risk, and is somewhat fragmented (Forrest, Murie and Williams, 1990). To some it is empowering, to others a struggle. For households in financial difficulties, home ownership's demands can erode rather than sustain feelings of control and satisfaction in everyday lives (cf Gurney, 1990, p

10), while not all households enter the tenure without reservations. For example, a recent Scottish study indicates that minority ethnic home owners there appeared to have had less choice than their white counterparts about whether to enter owner-occupation, and 25% said that they would have preferred an alternative tenure at the time of entry (Third, Wainwright and Pawson, 1997). Four times as many minority ethnic as white owners in the study had at some time been in mortgage arrears (Third, Wainwright and Pawson, 1997, p 48).

Many women achieve owner-occupancy, or share it, but circumstances vary among them. Becoming or remaining owner-occupiers may depend on women being in relationships with partners, given the commitments to children and the likelihood of lower incomes and different career trajectories of many women by contrast with men. As Gilroy puts it, the woman may still have "to find her prince before she gets her palace" (Gilroy, 1994, p 54). This is mainly due to economic relationships, a fact captured in the title of a study by Muir and Ross: *Housing the poorer sex* (1993). The best rewards from owner-occupation, including security of possession as well as dwelling quality, have remained dependent on households' income and wealth. Women may run a greater risk of losing their home if a relationship fails (Muir and Ross, 1993, p 3; cf Greve 1997, p xv, on lone parents with dependent children being particularly at risk of homelessness). They may also experience poorer quality dwellings or financial difficulties if remaining in owner-occupation (see for example Lund, 1996, p 146). Perhaps the key general point from our discussion so far is that for some households ownership is aligned positively and easily with creating a home, while for others this is not so.

Social renting also has varying implications for perceptions of the home, depending on age, gender, occupational status, ethnicity, financial resources, dwelling characteristics, locality, and so forth. Some tenants might see renting as permanent, others as a transition stage on the way to ownership, perhaps through the right-to-buy (offering extra options for those with enough resources). Social renters include particular categories heavily over-represented in a statistical sense, low income households and single parents among them, lacking the resources to acquire adequate private sector accommodation (see Lee and Murie, 1997). A social rented home today in some localities may have connotations of segregation or lack of choice, while the tenure's general image has been affected by reductions in newbuild, in renovation, and in numbers of good quality re-lets in preferred locations. Landlords may project limitations on the meaning of home onto their tenants (see for example Chapter Five for the notion of 'underoccupation'). As far as minority ethnic households are concerned, some council dwellings have been seen as inappropriate homes, given the worries about harassment and the difficulties faced by those allocated properties away from family, friends and facilities (although council housing nonetheless may have become more a part of the 'culture' of some groups; Bowes, Dar and Sim, 1997, p 82). Despite such reservations, however, large numbers of households (black and white) depend upon social renting, and parts of the sector remain sought after. Writing about the problem of homelessness faced by many women, Smith refers convincingly to their "special need for low-cost permanent social housing" (Smith, 1999, p 108). It has been the case that "for every family type other than married couples, women are more dependent than men on renting from the local authority" (Clapham, Kemp and Smith, 1990, p 73), and Lund writes of the 'feminisation' of public housing (Lund, 1996, p 147). Dependence on social renting and the chances a household has within the sector might affect meanings attached to home.

Interests and strategies related to the home

In practical terms, although we may all become victims of circumstances, and are influenced by widely-established ideas in society, we think and act in ways which are individual and not predetermined. Even though we may be under constraints, we may take what we can best secure from the action space we are offered. Even people who have little leverage with housing providers may have options to subvert, divert, obstruct, resist or simply refuse to participate. People's actions range from efforts to 'normalise' their lives – as in the case of some households responding to racist harassment – to collective campaigning. At the same time there are decisions made on the composition of the household itself, for instance in respect of including somebody needing support. Human agency may play a role through political channels and private decisions in influencing the demand for external institutional alternatives, an important issue in relation to development of residential or community care (see Oliver, 1990, pp 38-9). Housing consumers are not passive receivers of consumption experiences (cf Dickens et al, 1985, p 203), although individuals may be unaware of or isolated from the struggles of others experiencing similar problems. As Ballard points out in relation to ethnicity, people subjected to constraint and "exclusionism" do not become "helpless pawns", unable to negotiate the terms of their own existence, and there is a creative capacity to circumvent oppression and exclusion, and devise "moral and spiritual strategies", alongside "more concrete and physical" ones (Ballard, 1992, p 485).

Strategies may aim at achieving very specific housing objectives, and reflect people's diverse situations and ideas about their homes. Consequently it may be difficult on occasions to perceive commonalities of interests among households with apparently similar needs. Even though we all probably want to be well housed, our particular expectations and wishes depend on exact circumstances. Some can pursue housing aims easily as individuals, creating successful housing careers, producing the home as desired. Others cannot. Indeed there may be divisions of interests within some households (with unequal practices rather than joint planning). Certainly, households' material interests may diverge. Nonetheless, specific factors can generate collective concerns. People rarely build their lives in a vacuum, and may have personal, kinship, cultural or community commitments, with a sense of what might be appropriate or safe for group members as a whole. One response to feeling disadvantaged is to join with kin or community members, perhaps arranging mutual financial assistance, sharing costs, and so forth. Another strategy is to act in directly political ways, to secure more sensitive services, more spending, or a greater degree of self-management. Collective responses to minority ethnic housing needs may affirm shared cultural or religious affiliations, or seek to create new channels for provision less affected by the common experience of racisms. Shared identities may be a means for "levering spaces open" (see Hall, 1996, p 132). Yet it is *perceived commonalities of interests which are crucial* (even though the sense of 'interests' is not arrived at independently of social contexts and influences).

The practices and institutions of social regulation affect group mobilisation, providing ground on which battles for resources may be fought out. At the same time, such interactions can be an expected adjunct to (or part of) regulatory processes. People may coalesce in response to a threat, opportunity or action space created by public expenditures, policies, or an invitation to participate. Chapter Four refers to officially-encouraged tenant participation in social rented housing, but there has in any case been a long history of council tenants collectively resisting events affecting them, or campaigning about the imposition of unfair costs (for a recent example see C. Parr on the Daylight Robbery Campaign, in *Housing Today*, 9 December 1999). Voluntary and community housing organisations have also been focuses for (or results of) campaigns and actions, the outcome sometimes being independent housing enterprises controlled collectively by households themselves (see for example Rosenberg, 1998). There is another dimension to the impact of social regulation, apart from the material effects of institutional practices. The way the home is perceived in popular or official discourses, and in counter-discourses (or those of resistance), may be important in strategies and for the making of common cause. The rise of owner-occupation as an ideal may have reinforced general tendencies for home to be linked as a goal with privatised rights exercised by individual residents, and with notions of protected space.

The idea of social movements or 'social welfare movements' – a slightly narrower term – is potentially applicable in housing (and will be touched on again later). The notion of a movement implies collective activity organised around favoured goals, which in housing may have important material dimensions. For instance, among issues addressed by the Black Voluntary Housing Movement has been the shortage of certain kinds of affordable accommodation managed by black people and accessible to particular communities. Movements may also be concerned with rights, a matter highly salient for collective action. Pursuit of even the most individualistic strategy depends on rights or financial arrangements that are affected by politics and collective actions. The celebrated pre-war struggles of owner-occupiers, challenging the then oppressive practices of building societies, combined the collective and individual. Challenges were made through mortgage strikes and campaigns, as well as through actions around individuals' legal rights (Craig, 1986).

Collective action raises numerous questions; concerning the combination or separation of housing, political and cultural issues for households, the interactions between aspects of regulation and mobilisations, processes of incorporation of groups by official institutions, and the roles of property rights. Conceptions of the home may play important parts (implicitly or explicitly) when individuals or collectivities make claims and plan actions.

Conclusions

This chapter has reviewed differentiation, exploring its implications in housing by looking at the array of possible understandings and strategies linked with the home. In the 'micro' domain of households and small groupings there is considerable fragmentation beyond well-used distinctions of 'race', gender, class, and able-bodiedness/disability. Household and 'family' embrace variation that fits uneasily into traditional UK housing provision. Tenure is at times an uncertain guide to distinctions.

Dwelling quality and costs vary greatly within sectors, and no simple correspondence occurs between outcomes in terms of the tenure divide and socioeconomic position. Although there are broad relationships between tenure and relative wealth or poverty, deprivation is not confined to social renting. Owner-occupation is diverse, fragmented by income, wealth, locality, gender, ethnicity, and age.

Yet experiential diversity, and differences in household affiliations or strategies, need to be understood alongside broader patterns and effects allied to persistent structural factors. There is much variety in how the home is approached by households, and even in difficult settings there is a capacity to develop independent and conscious courses of action. Nonetheless, choices about home are regulated through finance and bureaucracies, through class and labour markets, and through the defining and stereotyping of differences and tenure forms in popular discourse and official and market practices. Social stratification influences housing opportunities, although housing resources also contribute to ongoing development of social divisions. Furthermore, disability, gender, and racisms help structure the meanings of home and residential areas, and affect paths into housing. There are persistent patterns and characteristics of difference, not greatly amenable to the short-term effects of the diversity and individual choice that we have noted, and justifying our use of the phrase *difference within difference*. Various factors help maintain patterns of achievement and limitation, *framing the diversity of daily living*. It is now time to trace more explicitly these factors and their potential impact.

Note

[1] Thanks are due to Ian Varcoe and Terry Wassall for observations here.

THREE

Structural factors and social regulation

We now move towards a fuller account of regulation, exploring factors and features that shape choices. First we discuss structural factors and oppression and explain why we favour the idea of modes of regulation. This builds on comments about structure in the preceding chapters. The next section then reviews social control, support and the management of consumption in the welfare state. Third, we address briefly the topic of ideologies, discourses and language. There is then a discussion of citizenship, followed by a short concluding comment. This chapter focuses less specifically on housing than Chapter Four. Although it is important to connect with particular material relevant to social policy and housing rather than becoming mired in a long discussion about vocabulary and meaning (cf Giddens, 1984, pp 16-37), the present chapter is theoretically inclined. An assumption is that structural factors can be traced in a range of specific settings, and through looking at regulatory practices in particular. Processes of *social regulation* (the term adopted here) reflect various influences and forces connected with the broader economy, social stratification, racisms, patriarchy and so forth. Regulation also responds to grass roots agency in several manifestations, including social welfare movements.

Structural factors, oppression and social regulation

Chapters One and Two noted the positive or supportive potential of structural factors as well as effects in terms of constraints. By writing about structural matters in the social policy arena we are usually implying significant social, political and economic features which enter into daily events with a measure of continuity over time and place, and may influence, constrain or facilitate a range of actions. They are factors which help to structure choices, events, perceptions and behaviour, or frame decisions. They include institutional factors which influence some outcomes in housing, and forces which order relationships, set, operate and are manifested in rules, help maintain popular stereotypes, and even condition identities. Structural factors to some extent reflect, confirm, embody, manifest and operationalise the interests of the strong more than the weak.

In Chapter One we mentioned economic constraints at governmental level derived from external global markets. These could be portrayed as 'structural imperatives' restraining a succession of individual governments, apparently making expenditure on social welfare difficult. We also referred to hierarchies, economic dependencies, conventions, rules and limits in the operation of institutions, which can be seen as rather systematic across spheres of activity, and longlasting enough to be interpreted as structural. Some relate to patriarchy or to inter- and intra-class divisions, and many are tied to economic liberalism, markets, private property rights systems, or paternalistic traditions. The organisation of housing in a society may be influenced by the success and power of class, cross-class and intra-class interests, the control of capital, and the importance accorded to profits. The UK housing system is primarily (although not by any means solely) market-led, is influenced by ideas about minimising financial and other kinds of risks, and is affected strongly by notions of rights cast in terms of the liberal model of full ownership (cf Clapham, Kemp and Smith, 1990, pp 26-8). Racisms and other deeply-entrenched ideologies (such as those linked to traditional conceptions of family or impairment) have permeated practices of housing provision and of citizenship in relation to welfare. The experience of being a citizen is differentiated, although this is frequently contested, and some people have a better set of realisable citizenship rights than others. Drawing on Chapter One we can summarise structural factors through the notion of (relatively) ordered environments of constraints, facilities and options. While the ordering is rarely complete, unchanging, consistent, or free of contradictions or tensions, it remains important for life chances. Thus freedoms of action are set within frameworks of opportunities, ideas and resources that have considerable continuity, even though structure is not necessarily an overriding determinant of precise outcomes, or independent of human agency.

Oppression: a limited concept?

The word oppression is used frequently to characterise the diminishing of the circumstances or experiences of particular social groups through various conscious or less visible means, and the idea may be used as a key concept in general accounts of societal organisation or injustice (see especially Young, 1990). It may be seen as a product of both "cultural values and material relations of power (such as political economy, patriarchy or imperialism)" (Priestley, 1998, p 86). Some activities – such as physical violence against lesbians, gays or Asians on housing estates – certainly have very oppressive effects. Indeed, the anticipation of violence or the possibility for it may restrict many people's plans and encounters, the routes they choose when walking, and so forth. Violence against women may be seen as threatening to bodily integrity, restricting the potential for action, with consequences for women's freedom to exercise active citizenship: restrictions are shared by all women who experience domestic violence or feel the potential for it (cf Lister 1997a, pp 112-13). This is part of a larger set of oppressive constraints allied to a sense of physical limitations experienced widely across society, although often differentiated in significance along lines of gender, frailty, impairment, ethnicity, age, or economic resources. It might also be potentially oppressive to be excluded from the chance of jobs open to others. More universally, hierarchical relationships have potential for oppressive exercise of power and creation or confirmation of disadvantage. Likewise, some firmly established values, such as those concerning family or nation, may be viewed as oppressive from certain perspectives. Traditional family values, for example, have served to affirm unpaid domestic responsibilities accorded to many women (although such values may also imply rights or supervision for children or elders that are the counterpart of the assumed duties of younger adults). Nation has served as an exclusive device, where an assertion of 'English values' denies the validity of membership claimed by black people, while racialised boundaries rest on categorisations of groups according to which they may be inferiorised, excluded or subordinated (see for example Anthias and Yuval-Davis with Cain, 1992). Oppression may also be linked with the theme of the body, where physical signs of 'natural' differences can lend apparent legitimacy to popular assumptions about significant distinctions between groups. Thus, for instance, colour or impairment can become used as bodily signifiers for classifying particular groups as superior or inferior (for an introduction to embodiment see Saraga, 1998, and particularly Lewis, 1998). This must be seen in context, however, for although attributes assumed to arise from our physical characteristics may become defined as keys to understanding or placing us (and thus become important in constructing us socially) the socioeconomic, historical, cultural and physical intimately overlap.

In fact oppression is a term variously applied, drawing attention not only to laws and money but to language and images. Abberley refers, for example, to a theory of disability as oppression, and to the stereotype of the disabled person which a "particular social formation produces and acts towards real disabled people in terms of" (Abberley, 1997a, p 171). He goes on to say that for disabled people the body is the site of oppression, "both in form, and in what is done with it" (Abberley, 1997a, p 172), giving examples of prohibitions applied to disabled children. For him, "oppressive theories of disability" systematically "distort and stereotype the identities of their putative subjects, restricting their full humanity by constituting them" only in their "problem" aspects (Abberley, 1997a, p 174). Construction of a 'deviant' and relatively powerless status as 'other', distinct and apart from the supposedly 'normal' and 'natural' majority (Hughes, 1998, p 51), marginalises many disabled people, even while it appears to sustain them by focusing on their medical requirements. Abberley suggests that as with racism and sexism, a theory of disability as oppression must at some point face the question of who benefits from oppression, and he identifies "the present social order, or, more accurately, capitalism in a particular historical and national form" (Abberley, 1997a, pp 174-5). One implication is that, historically, particular categories of 'disabled people' were constituted as a product of the development of capitalism and its concern with the compulsion to work (see Abberley, 1997a, p 175). Barnes has recently chronicled the legacy of oppression in relation to disability, and the contributions made from within disabled people's movements in combating and laying it bare (Barnes, 1997; also 1999; and Hughes, 1998, pp 77-87).

In considering oppression in general, we can say that the term captures important aspects of histories and relationships, and has material, cultural and ideological facets. The disability example can be paralleled by looking at gender and 'race'. For the latter, the deployment of the very term 'race' may be interpreted as part of an oppressive discourse which draws unreal 'biological' divides and constructs social categories to legitimate the exclusion of people 'of colour'. More particular images have denigrated groups on the basis of supposedly 'deviant' lifestyles or cultural traits (for example gypsy and traveller lifestyles). Perhaps, however, there are important distinctions between disablement and other forms of oppression (Abberley, 1997, pp 38-9; cf Oliver, 1990, pp 69-70). Within ideology, a work-based model of social membership and identity might involve a value judgement upon the undesirability of impaired modes of being which goes beyond (although it parallels) what arises in relation to ethnicity or gender.

Unfortunately, as a basis for developing a theory about differentiation and power, oppression is vague, too universal in its incidence within human interactions, and yet not comprehensive enough. We are all likely to feel ourselves oppressed in some way or other at some point. For instance, the dividing lines between able-bodied and impaired are themselves uncertain, most of us will be impaired to a degree during our lifetimes, and there is a continuum of physical/mental capacities along which we are all located differently. So, sooner or later, anyone may be subjected to patronising or off-hand treatment from a medical professional, or assumed to lack powers of judgement because of old age. Of course, some people are much more likely to experience such treatment frequently, and the important questions are about how and why this happens, and the roles that hierarchical institutions perform. For any individual, specific social and economic factors bring into play a myriad of kinds of oppressions, affirmations of status and contradictory messages. Social constructions apply to everyone, and may have positive and negative facets. While some men revel in the aggressive 'macho' masculinity constructed for them through violent films and military institutions, and acquire inspiration from it in their dealings with women, other men may feel oppressed and damaged by it. At the same time we all have dependencies in our relationships with other people, and these are often capable of becoming oppressive or supportive (or both at once), and may involve reciprocities (for an overview of interdependencies see Twine, 1994). The processes and mechanisms of domination and differentiation are crucial. Structure is not merely about various kinds of oppressions, important though these are. Structural factors may advantage and support some people, facilitating rather than constraining their liberties and positive options (cf Giddens, 1984, pp 25, 169, 173, for references to structure as both enabling and constraining). Structural forces are also contested and sometimes contradictory in effects. The concept of oppression cannot easily embrace or elucidate the variety of circumstances and distributional issues that need to be considered, including processes of differential incorporation, empowerment and exclusion of which we must be aware (see below). An approach via regulation offers more, although it must acknowledge the presence of oppression.

Modes of social regulation

Reviewing what we refer to as social regulation moves a structural account in the direction of specifics, and towards our particular interests. The word 'social' here does not imply real-world separation of the social, environmental, political and economic, but rather that we are focusing especially on particular aspects of societal relationships (and difference), and not on the management of capital and labour, or the grander agenda found in interesting academic writings under the title of 'regulation theory' (for an example of critical commentary here see Byrne, 1997, pp 29-33). We locate our analysis mainly on the terrain of 'welfare', social policy and consumption, rather than of employment or capital accumulation (although these stand in the background to our picture). The word 'social' is also a reminder that we are not writing about the particular regulatory responsibilities of organisations like the Housing Corporation, where 'regulation' describes administrative processes of monitoring, feedback and supervision (but cf Mullins, 1997). We are concerned with the regulation of difference in the welfare state, embracing (as noted earlier) mechanisms, practices and influential assumptions through which people's varied lives and plans may be constrained, confirmed, supported, conditioned or even liberated. There are various overlapping facets or modes of social regulation, and forces of institutions and ideas. Some kinds of regulation are more visible than others, evident manifestations of relationships of political or bureaucratic power, money, property or markets. For example, access to good dwellings in housing markets is influenced visibly by income and wealth linked with inherited property rights and labour market positions (for housing/labour market connections see Allen and Hamnett, 1991). Class, disability, gender, age, region, and the black minority ethnic/white divide are all significant here. Alongside 'free' market processes (always legitimated, mediated or modified by governments), direct governmental interventions have visible effects on who lives where and at what costs.

Other kinds of regulatory process may seem more subtle, operating through shared or dominant ideologies or value systems confirmed in practices within markets and mainstream official, administrative and political networks. Various overlapping, reinforcing or competing discourses condition housing activities, helping to establish or challenge the arenas of constraint and opportunity for people's housing choices and actions. For instance, ideologies and discourses about family tended historically to divide public and private spheres, locating many women in the latter, and confirmed the domestic (private) environment as a focus for unpaid personal support work (alongside other things). This connected with the notion of adults' duties exercised towards children, and to a degree towards older non-employed people or household members with severe impairments, within the context of family. These duties co-existed with ideas about the desirability of state entry into this territory in order to deal separately with some types of support or supervision, and to handle them collectively (in sheltered housing, institutions for disabled people, and elsewhere). Alongside assumptions about women's supportive roles were others about behaviour, permitting many men to exercise a degree of physical violence within that private sphere, a matter which remains extremely important for housing.

Although structural factors interconnect, there are benefits in disaggregation, categorisation or tracing of specific features (cf Allen's approach, 1997, pp 87-90), and in looking at regulation we might perhaps focus on types, levels or clusters of constraints or facilitating factors. We approach social regulation more simply, however, by working under two main overlapping headings below. The first mainly covers institutions, policies, and practices, and the second chiefly ideas. We take it as given that the two are intimately connected, not least because ideologies are strong when rooted in or confirming 'common sense' daily practices that in turn connect with institutional power and social differentiation. After these two sections, we turn to the issue of citizenship, approaching some of the same concerns from a different perspective.

Social control, support, and the management of consumption

There is a scholarly tradition which has long challenged assumptions that welfare systems simply concern assistance or security for people. One particular matter analysed has been social control, connecting with the theme that development of welfare states has created new forms of domination and subordination, and that bureaucracies, markets and professions may all contribute to the management, 'colonising', and control of clients, service users, and marginalised groups. From this perspective the apparently supportive apparatus of institutions and personnel may sometimes be the reverse. In some respects, even family itself may be interpreted as an instrument of government (see for example Squires, 1990, p 30), alongside its potential as a base for private comforts and resistance to state and corporate institutions. Social policy writers have considered how poverty is regulated, how the poor are disciplined, and how policy ideas in 'race relations', social security or allied fields reflect or stimulate pejorative assumptions about marginalised groups. There is material about the history of surveillance and 'respectability', acknowledging the potential of official and legal discourses and practices to help in the 'construction' and delineation of distinct categories of people (see for example Saraga, 1998a, on prostitution). Such themes have resonance for students of housing, given the history of council house allocation or the practices of segregation which were so important in relation to accommodation for disabled people (see later chapters). While social policy may have become better-informed about consumers' needs, the supposedly deviant have never disappeared from the governmental agenda, despite the spread of liberal notions about behavioural diversity. For households at grass roots, that agenda is both benign and oppressive.

A widely referenced North American study in this field is by Piven and Cloward, who cover "relief-giving and its uses in regulating the political and economic behavior of the poor" (Piven and Cloward, 1972, p xiii). They suggest that relief policies are cyclical, being "liberal or restrictive depending on the problems of regulation in the larger society with which government must contend" (Piven and Cloward, 1972, p xiii). In their analysis, expansive relief policies are designed to mute civil disorder and restrictive ones to reinforce work norms. For them, relief arrangements have a great deal to do with maintaining social and economic inequities (Piven and Cloward, 1972, p xvii), the chief function being "to regulate labor" (Piven and Cloward, 1972, p 3). They observe, too, that the regulation of civil behaviour is intimately dependent on stable occupational arrangements, and that mass unemployment breaks bonds, loosening people from "the main institution by which they are regulated and controlled". If mass unemployment persists, it may diminish the capacity of other institutions to bind and constrain people (Piven and Cloward, 1972, pp 6-7). This is an important proposition, certainly for UK housing scholars. It raises questions about surrogate systems of regulation for those who cannot work, and about conditionality implicit in systems of provision. We may note, also, that Piven and Cloward assign significant roles to collective resistance from marginalised groups within their account of historical developments in 'relief'.

Pursuing similar concerns, Dean points out that several eminent writers on social policy have observed that social security (and especially the administration of benefits) appears to have "as much to do with controlling behaviour as with meeting need" (Dean, 1991, p 1). He looks at the history of disciplinary techniques here, and considers the sense in which the "phenomenon of modern poverty has been created or constituted through the social security system" (Dean, 1991, p 2). Dean's analysis draws on several theorists (including Foucault and Donzelot), and notes the terms 'surveillance' and 'normalisation', the latter defining a "form of penality not confined to penal institutions", but which imposes (in Foucault's terms) "a ladder of normalcy, the rungs of which, while indicating membership of a homogeneous social body, themselves serve to classify, hierarchise and distribute social rank" (Dean, 1991, p 31, citing Foucault). He suggests that through a "myriad of minute interventions", every-day institutions exercise a system of "continuous normalisation", and by thousands of tiny individualised rewards and punishments, "effect the substantive control of individual behaviour". Commenting on social security, Dean notes change historically from the brutal repression of the poor to "gentler and more subtle forms of discipline" as well as the importance of regulation by the imposition of self-discipline (Dean, 1991, p 51). Clearly, the exercise and techniques of power change over time, and state activity can be influenced by contradictory or emergent discourses, such as those focused on self-help, individual needs, citizenship rights or duties, self-management, empowerment, and so forth.

Approaches focused on social control can present a very forceful view of the state and its welfare policies. Squires, for example, refers to the "disciplinary 'welfare state'" (Squires, 1990, p 1; also Jones and Novak, 1999; cf Foucault, 1979, for the 'disciplinary gaze' and 'disciplinary society'). Some scholars suggest strongly that repressive forces, discourses or practices increased in the 1980s and 1990s in some spheres (cf Dean, 1991, pp 180, 183-4), and this is especially important for debates about crime, youth, single parents and racism. Jones, for instance, refers to a decisive shift from the late 1970s onwards in the practice, language and ideology of state welfare towards "brutalism and ruthlessness" (Jones, 1998, p 6; see also Jones and Novak, 1999). He deploys the term 'social violence' to include the damage done to people who are compelled to rely on the state for all or part of their incomes (Jones, 1998, p 10) and also points to the rapid expansion of imprisonment which is "targeted quite deliberately at those who are deemed to be the most troublesome, namely young black men" (Jones, 1998, p 20). This kind of analysis can be linked with the centrality of labour markets, whereby an individual's position in relation to the world of waged work is a crucial factor, especially when there is widespread unemployment and low pay. Mirroring the notion of 'failure' for men who cannot secure satisfactory employment and (therefore) be adequate fathers has been the association of women with 'family failure'. Squires suggests that historically the notion of the 'problem family' stood typically upon the "implied culpability of women as inadequate mothers" (Squires, 1990, p 169).

Interestingly, under the Blair leadership, moral codes have stressed obligations to work or contribute to society rather than engage in 'welfare dependency', with political spin-offs such as welfare-to-work themes (for the general tone see for example Blair, 1995, 1999). This appears to be in tension with established ideas about the necessity of direct involvement by mothers in child-rearing, and the desirability of supportive personal relationships involving disabled people and male or female carers. Clearly there may be contradictions in Labour's emphasis on pushing people into work or training on the one hand, and "the importance attributed to parenting in maintaining social order" on the other (see Levitas, 1998, pp 5, 140-7, 169). More generally, conditionality has been heightened as an adjunct to having to manage and finance growing numbers of households with economic difficulties, an authoritarian stance being facilitated by the political weakening of such households through the decline of traditional working class voices within the Labour Party.

Dean's conclusion on social control is that it is not a unified design, but a nonetheless "palpable process of subjection occurring under capitalist social relations and penetrating every aspect of human life and existence" (Dean, 1991, p 33). He argues that discourses of debate and limits to state action are "fashioned and constrained through the essential form of capitalist social relations ... one of exploitation, not co-operation" (Dean, 1991, p 34). Under capitalism, he writes, "the necessary regulation of our social lives is not so much a matter of policy ... as a matter of untheorised and often unintended strategies of domination" (Dean, 1991, p 176). An important aspect of outcomes is the tendency to partition and label populations, thereby helping to define and constitute households in certain respects, perhaps affecting their self-definitions and identities as well as the perception others have of them. The partitioning of populations has been an extremely important issue for the groups with which we are concerned, given the history of the involuntary segregation of many disabled people, and the limitations on residential choices experienced by minority ethnic communities.

There is much to be learned from analyses of the kinds cited above, but some danger of losing sight of the *multi-faceted nature of social regulation*, and the interactions between human agency and the supportive and facilitating aspects of welfare state operations. First, it has to be emphasised how closely the supportive and repressive can be locked together. This is true for aspects of law and order activity, where protection for people's lives goes alongside surveillance and restraint. For example, laws offer protection for children through constraining activities of adults, and inhibit freedoms of expression or action in order to protect potential victims from racist hostilities. Donzelot, in discussing the "policing of families", refers among other issues to the longstanding theme of the "preservation of children" (Donzelot, 1980). Clearly many laws and policies have reflected attempts to safeguard and manage childhood and, while there is social control here, there is also protection and encouragement for development. Priority for children, however, has not been allowed to over-ride social stratification linked to parental labour market status and inherited wealth, as is clear from Britain's continuing extensive childhood poverty (see Hills, 1999, pp 41-2). Furthermore, in the hierarchy of work, unpaid domestic activity (including childcare) comes far lower down than paid work by an employee, largely because of the "structural dominance of the market" (see Levitas, 1998, pp 147, 169). Nonetheless, children are a focus in competing discourses, a matter evident in housing, where some priority is offered to households with children while at the same time youth is a target for social order strategies.

A second point concerns the genuine intent to assist disadvantaged groups that underpins many official policies and practices in social work, housing, community care, and health care. This is not completely distinct from social control, but differs in quality and in the degree and manner in which it reflects grass roots interests. Sometimes, however, it leads into procedures of assessment and classification which are meant to measure relative needs and priorities, and in so doing come to label, define and place households. Furthermore, the nature of support defined as a gift to the disadvantaged is frequently very different from assistance or approval focused around the idea of households' rights. The interlocking of the supportive and controlling is not universal. Acknowledgement of rights claims is highly significant, connecting with citizenship, and cuts across hierarchical social control. In Britain we do not tend to associate the universally-targeted parts of the health services with oppression, and the feeling that there is a general right to use services tends to dispel the drawing of distinctions on grounds of status (although it cannot eliminate distinctions completely). By contrast, those who appear to receive a gift or handout are sometimes assumed to need supervision, while drawing boundaries around selectively targeted groups possibly entitled to receive the gifts brings into play mechanisms of policing or qualifying (with means-tests, interviews, penalties for being less deserving, and so on). In effect, *oppressive practices are contingent* to an extent on the particular sets of relationships that develop around the provision of services through institutions, and especially around forms of selectivist support.

In any event (as our health services example suggests), some aspects of the welfare state are less easy to construe primarily in social control terms than are others. Municipal housing in Britain has undoubtedly had social control implications (see Chapter Four), but it has also been perceived as a collective enterprise dedicated to improving people's lives in practical ways. This rarely figures prominently in the kinds of accounts we have mentioned above. In welfare state analyses, boundaries between control, incorporation, paternalism and concessions to grass roots pressure are not necessarily hard and fast, and over-reliance on a notion of control implies too deterministic a model of power and a narrow view of structure. Our view does not preclude interpreting some helpful responses to needs as persuasive practices which confirm particular identities or expectations among recipients, or contribute to processes of subordination. We simply argue for caution.

In addition, social policies that restrict some categories of people may serve the interests of others, unjustifiably or justifiably. A current example concerns the issue of crime and neighbour behaviour. Controlling such behaviour from certain households may help other residents. As Clapham and Dix with Griffiths point out, though "anti-social behaviour may be a result of being powerless and excluded from society it reduces the rights of people affected by the behaviour"; consequently housing organisations are increasingly "having to deal with balancing the rights of those affected and the potential rights of those excluded" (Clapham and Dix with Griffiths, 1996, p 25). Research can reveal strong local worries about behavioural issues and crime, and people can be very concerned to see a reduction of anti-social behaviour. These kinds of preoccupations became very clear, for example, in 1999/2000 Leeds University focus group meetings in Bradford convened from minority ethnic households to discuss housing. Diverse participants raised worries about local behaviours such as break-ins, drug abuse, litter, unacceptable activities of children, bad neighbours and so forth. One man discussed a particular 'nightmare neighbour'; the housing association landlord had been slow to act here, but eventually the transgressor had been evicted (from unpublished material gathered by D. Phillips and M. Harrison). Housing organisations will respond to some extent, as they have long been accustomed to do, to expectations of would-be respectable residents, although capacity to react constructively depends on resources. There can be a point, of course, where such responses blur into unfair labelling and discriminatory practices, or over-forceful constraints (see Chapter Four). For the moment we need to acknowledge that social order practices are not simply a product of the power or needs of employers, ruling elites, or capital, but reflect social divisions within class groupings, as well as the interests and actions of those who feel the need for defence or confirmation of their life-styles. Thus grass roots agency should not be overlooked.

It follows that in locating social control we should consider how repression, constraint, *and* empowering processes manifest themselves in policy and practice. Empowerment may reflect people's efforts to influence events and practices in their own (and others') favour. There is more than one player in the development and practice of social control, an array of differing resources available to groups seeking to defend their interests, and many different beneficiaries as well as losers. Of course, while there is a degree of popular approval for practices that control or segregate, agency here does not operate in a vacuum, but is tied in with institutional traditions, differentials in power, influential discourses and fragmentation in welfare systems. The latter brings us to a vital strand of work on the welfare state, the set of ideas associated with the notion of a social division of welfare. The thesis has been advanced here that welfare is delivered through a variety of visible and less visible routes to a wide range of consumers, and that the receivers of assistance through differing routes are, to an extent, differentiated within the wider social stratification system (Titmuss, 1958; Sinfield, 1978; Mann, 1992; Harrison, 1995). A key theme in this tradition of analysis has been its casting of welfare systems broadly, to include not just obvious services and benefits provided directly by state institutions universally (like the National Health Service) or selectively (like housing benefit), but also mechanisms helping households through tax concessions, support for occupational 'fringe benefits', and so forth. The thesis alerts us that many forms of assistance disproportionately benefit the better off and that patterns of welfare access and infrastructure provision are linked to work-related social stratification. Particular kinds of household structures also attract specific forms of support (cf Jarvis, 1999, p 502). Furthermore, some channels of assistance may stigmatise consumers or clients, while others are associated with assumptions about rights and independence. For example, whereas means-tested support for tenants to pay their rents has been associated with a degree of stigma or conditionality, help for owner-occupiers through the tax system, improvement grants or right-to-buy discounts has had an image as assistance to help maintain or reward sturdy independence.

What is being argued here is that while social control in a negative sense is important, it is not the only issue. Institutional and financial arrangements reflect pressures for empowerment and self-management as well as for repression and exploitation. Success in securing acknowledgement or official sanction for consumers' rights claims can be crucial in shaping the quality and style of provision or treatment by organisations. Institutions may pursue strategies of inclusion, accommodation or incorporation as well as exclusion, supervision and marginalisation. Of course being incorporated, and thus to a degree catered for, may bring with it loss of autonomy as well as possible gain. Indeed, there is an argument that development of consumption in society itself deepens labour discipline and dependence, putting people in positions where they feel a need to acquire and consume and must earn to do so, unless they steal and risk punishment (see Corrigan, 1997, pp 20-1, discussing Baudrillard; but cf Bauman, 1998). This could run alongside, or form part of, the "hegemonic force of disciplinary discourses which permeate society as a whole" (Dean with Melrose, 1999, p 33). Rather less generally, we can see that side-effects of being incorporated into the better parts of the labour market may include compulsory forms of savings or investment (such as pension schemes or insurance). In any event, outcomes of interactions between institutions and households, individually and collectively, include and reflect patterns of differential incorporation, which have multiple implications and effects. *Analysis via differential incorporation is much superior to an account phrased in terms of an exclusion/ inclusion dichotomy.* The latter might focus on 'solutions' for the excluded via efforts at 'social integration', yet ignore existing complex patterns through which differential incorporation and empowerment already take place constantly.

Our approach makes proper space for agency, since it caters for mobilisation of bias and the setting of the agenda on behalf of the better off as well as the poor, for political and administrative pursuit of middle class interests as well as resistance from the marginalised. In earlier work, reference has been made to patterns of differential incorporation within a system of organised or managed consumption and political representation (for example Harrison, 1995). Incorporation strategies may be pursued from within official agencies or political parties, and from movements.

Institutions and the regulation of difference

Envisaging a set of welfare channels and opportunities intermeshed with mechanisms of social order is a reasonable entry point to looking at the intersection of regulation and difference. Channels or routes to welfare involve institutional practices which both influence the social construction of differences and respond to social distinctions. The ways in which the channels operate reflect underlying structural factors, including the dominance of private property rights assumptions and the importance of market concepts of the relative risks that people represent. At the same time professionals and politicians help define groups as suitable for assistance, draw boundaries, and focus attention on (and measure) what they feel are key problems. The character of professional involvement, however, has been changing (see for instance Shaw, 1990). Under the Conservatives, and now under Labour, some professional groups have become more liable to vilification and tight direction from government, so that the 'measurers' themselves are subjected to more time-consuming (and often counter-productive) appraisal and control. This affects relationships with service users and clients, while the managerialist obsessions that it reflects are important indicators of authoritarian and market orientations within New Labour. Methods of governance have shifted, with less reliance on occupational group authority within social regulation processes.

In any event, for consumers, access to support and achievement of status may require individuals, households and larger groups to meet specific criteria in terms not merely of funds (in market settings) or of needs, but also of respectability and behaviour. Thus notions such as the 'problem family' and the 'problem estate' become badges of 'failure' calling for therapeutic or repressive strategies. Conditionality is important, not merely in traditional ways such as being 'available' for work in order to be a 'legitimate claimant', but in relation to conformity to social order expectations in housing. In addition, dependence on public funds, or the wish to bid for such funds, may affect how interests coalesce under banners of community, ethnicity, religion, black people's needs, women's needs, disabled people's needs, and so forth. Public policies might reward some kinds of commonality rather than others, might potentially privilege some aspects of culture or tradition, or might offer services built around a particular expectation (for example that people will form a group on the basis of a specified impairment).

Institutional and political practices can also fragment groups. What might be perceived as overt attacks on African/Caribbean men may appear combined with some encouragement for African/Caribbean women, exacerbating division. As Hylton suggests, while young men are excluded from school, criminalised, diagnosed as schizophrenic, sedated with powerful drugs and classified as 'unemployable', African/Caribbean women "have emerged as the individual 'winners' in their private and public realms of activity in the family home, the work-place and community organisations" (Hylton, 1999, pp 55-72). People are not inert victims of such processes, and efforts can be made to overcome potential divisions here (see Hylton, 1999), but the example is a reminder of the forceful impact of relative exclusion and incorporation on everyday life. There is confirmation or encouragement for particular identities rather than others. This in turn can link with another facet of regulation, that it frequently connects with longstanding practices, values or traditions (including racist ones) that are themselves supported by specific groups of people, especially those who are well represented politically. Regulation is the product or manifestation not merely of institutional activity but also of established discourses and ideologies that are sustained or rooted in daily experiences, material interests or expectations of well-placed consumers and participants.

Ideologies and discourses

Ideologies and discourses are not easily separable, but the former may include sets of values, justifications and beliefs, while the latter may be taken to refer especially to particular ways of organising social knowledge through talk and writing. Practices and actors can be influenced by specific discourses, and the role of language may be important in underpinning 'common-sense' assumptions. At the level of conversation or description, not only are definitions 'value-soaked' – as Wootton put it forty years ago – but the way that words are used can be significant (for comments see Wootton, 1959, pp 220, 315-17). Going further, it may be justifiable to talk of discourses of power, helping to create or sustain social norms about people's relationships, roles or status, and legitimating organisations' interventions. From this perspective, we can see how discourses contribute to social regulation and connect to structural forces.

Clarke and Saraga say that when terms like the "normal, able-bodied and employable" are juxtaposed with "the impoverished, elderly or disabled" we are dealing with the consequences of processes of social construction. "These divisions", they continue, "are not natural, inevitable or intrinsic to the people being so described". Rather, they are "the result of ways of thinking about, defining and interpreting the social world" (Clarke and Saraga, 1998, p 1). Labelling, and approaches to 'pathologies' (see Wootton, 1959), have been tied in with the representation of people in particular ways in discussions (a tradition which certainly continues in the racialisation of crime or discussions of the so-called 'underclass'). (See Macnicol, 1987 for historical continuities of the latter.) Such thinking may be challenged or subject to competition from alternative ideas, but its prevalence is not unconnected with the interests of better-placed groups in society, with economic arrangements within marketised systems, and deeply established ideologies of welfare and work. Differences between people may be interpreted and constructed as social problems which then get 'managed', while dominant groups remain apparently unproblematic. The way a group is perceived can offer other people justification for its material positioning. For example, Smith comments succinctly that "In the crudest sense, racial ideology may be seen as a system of beliefs which legitimizes not only the identification of racial attributes but also their alignment with dimensions of inequality" (Smith, S., 1989, p 7).

None of this means that a specific group does not have some characteristics that are distinctive (along with many that are not), or that a social problem does not have features of pain or tension. Instead it means that although there are many different ways of thinking about people and their lives, some ways take on particular weight, and bear heavily on certain individuals and groups. For instance, it is fairly easy to move from the thought that specific households living on run-down estates have problems, to the assertion that these estates are reservoirs of 'problem people' who must be disciplined or treated (for an example of distortion in media stories about estates, see the 'babies on benefit' case, in Clapham and Dix with Griffiths, 1996, pp 33-4).

A particularly striking account touching on the construction of social problems is provided by Waddington, in a discussion of immigration. He refers to the theme of the burden to the taxpayer of illegal immigrants obtaining social housing, noting that "there is practically no evidence of any such housing problem" (Waddington, 1998, p 213). His analysis indicates that the previous government created an artificial problem, "revived a long-standing moral panic", and "tagged concerns about illegal immigrants onto the back of the furore about asylum-seekers" (with housing officers being brought into line with the rest of the welfare state in the handling of immigrants) (Waddington, 1998, p 231). This example reminds us how exclusive boundaries are re-asserted, developed, refined, and managed around difference, and also of the implications for rules, and for staff involved with resource allocation.

Ideas and identities

One concern of recent debates is the formation of identities. Hall suggests that identities are constituted within, not outside, 'representation', and are constructed within discourse, being understood as "produced in specific historical and institutional sites" (Hall, 1996a, p 4). For him, identities are seen as "points of temporary attachment to the subject positions which discursive practices construct for us" (Hall, 1996a, p 6). If differing discourses "cross and recross the social world, sometimes intersecting, sometimes competing, sometimes merging" (Chadwick, 1996, p 32), then identity construction is indeed a very complex process. We may locate ourselves, but are also located by other forces, both in the realm of ideas and of material relationships of kinship, money, administration, and so forth. Hall refers to identification, the process whereby groups, movements, or institutions, "try to locate us for the purpose of regulating us; try to construct us within symbolic boundaries in order to locate us, to give us resources, or take resources away from us" (Hall, 1996, p 130). Self-perceptions are not our concern, but it is worth noting that some negative perceptions or assumptions might affect the view people take of themselves. Definitions and wider systems of meanings in language may not merely label people, but even contribute to constituting their identities and maintaining relations of dominance. Liggett, for example, draws on Foucault's ideas to discuss what disability is, and "how it is produced as part of the contemporary political order" (Liggett, 1997, p 185). She refers to practices which produce and manage identities, and to the perpetuation of disabled identities, ensuring that "the disabled participate in the normalizing society as victims without crimes" (Liggett, 1997, p 192). As Chadwick indicates, perhaps the individualised model of disability – itself linked with the disabling power and knowledge of medicalised approaches – can "become a part of disabled people" (Chadwick, 1996, p 34). Putting this differently, an effect of the medical model may have been to help turn some people into recipients of 'care' who could be persuaded that they were deskilled and dependent. Nonetheless, as developments discussed in Chapter Five prove, there is scope for challenges, and for counter-discourses which reconstruct what has been previously socially constructed in an oppressive way. Oliver indicates that while "the disabled identity is not formed simply through internal psychological processes but may be externally imposed", the implications are "that this process is not fixed but can be changed by challenging dominant cultural images" (Oliver, 1990, p 77). Perhaps, nonetheless, the prior narrowing of opportunities for constructing a positive concept of self or group remains particularly important, something that might be relevant to the constituting of black men, in the context of gender relations and family (although again one must not discount the role of resistance or effective counter-discourses).

Structured selectivity

Ideas about the significance of language and culture can be connected up with concepts about dominant ideologies or discourses, or with the theme of *hegemony* (for a widely known treatment of these matters in relation to disability see Oliver, 1990). One possibility is that the values and beliefs which have the strongest and most persistent effects on how issues are perceived are integrally linked to capitalistic economic arrangements. A balanced view is necessary. On the one hand, the realms of culture and ideas have some independence from economic factors. Putting this in Marxian terms, perhaps it could be said that although ideas do not operate independently of economic forces, the realm of ideology cannot simply be reduced to an immediate reflection of those economic forces, while popular beliefs and similar ideas are themselves 'material forces' in society (see Gramsci, in Showstack Sassoon, 1987, pp 188-9). Yet it can be argued from the same kind of perspective that "the mode of production" may have "a determinant influence on cultural values and representations and not the converse" (see Priestley, 1998, p 88). While language may be a crucial aspect of culture, the latter is not itself an independent variable. Whether or not we wish to accord significance to the mode of production in this way, we need to place culture in material settings.

Discourses are at the most only relatively autonomous, even though public policy trends may be affected by competing discourses which help to constitute "ways of acting in the world" as well as offering understandings of that world (see Levitas, 1998, p 3). More specifically, while it is clear that differing and alternative discourses are propagated or sustained by various groups and political interests, there is a *structured (or structural) selectivity* which helps accord some of them more recognition than others (for different use of similar terminology by Offe and Hirsch, see Jessop, 1982, pp 104-7). Some ideas may be received as 'common sense', and enter widely into people's definitions of themselves or their surroundings, yet are legitimated in rather specific and selective discourses. This is especially clear in relation to property rights claims and concepts, where discourses around the liberal concept of full ownership have become increasingly dominant, and can readily be sustained, because of the day-to-day operation of markets and legal processes that accord primarily with economic liberal ideologies. This is very important for housing experiences and policy (see also Chapter Eight). Furthermore, although discourses may influence identities, self-perceptions and roles, this is generally alongside or within specific mechanisms and institutions that may transfer and reproduce ideas. It cannot be independent of political, administrative, financial and legal practices in social policy, the news media, medicine, or the world of paid employment.

The revision of conditionality

Before leaving the terrain of ideology we note a particular issue. In political history, and within religious beliefs past and present (see for example Dean and Khan, 1997; Hamzah, Harrison and Dwyer, 2000), duty was often seen as something owed by the fortunate to the less so. Possessors of goods and land held these resources conditionally, subject to good stewardship, and with moral and political obligations. In western societies this ideal was eroded through the advancing of beliefs that those who have the most are deserving, that they have earned what they possess, and that ownership of assets is best conceived of in terms approaching a very unrestricted set of rights (cf Harrison, 1987). At the same time the issue of contested property rights claims which was sometimes crucial historically has been insulated as a visible issue from mainstream political debate. Property claims remain implicitly important in housing politics, but few UK social policy writers today put property rights struggles at the centre of their analysis, although in past centuries the battle over rights in land was a central welfare issue.

Interestingly, the principle of conditionality in welfare (touched on earlier) has been to some degree reversed. Whereas large possessions once implied duty, underpinned by fear of a challenge from the grass roots over their distribution, the poor have increasingly become the central group expected to have obligations. This is not a new idea but has been given revived impetus recently in the context of New Labour's thinking, and relates in housing to debates about anti-social behaviour in particular. Portrayal of welfare assistance as a gift paid for by others (rather than a right or share of wealth) facilitates such a morality, as well as legitimating poor quality provision (see Lund, 1996, p 49, for a good housing example of the political language of the gift). We do not have space to explore this further or consider qualifications to our line of argument, but many factors have contributed (including agency in terms of inter- and intra-class divides, and the demands for surrogate systems for securing social order in the absence of full employment). Current discourses about conditionality affecting social renting have a background in specific historical trends. Today's supposedly 'moral' debates need locating firmly in the context of recent structure/agency interactions.

The differentiation of citizenship

We can supplement our discussions of institutional and ideological factors by considering how citizenship connects to social regulation. First, struggles around citizenship rights and claims help shape regulatory practices. In a sense, citizenship is one of the focuses through which agency and constraints come together (cf Lister, 1997a). Dean with Melrose indicate that social citizenship may be a "strategic resource" which can advance different kinds of struggles; for social redistribution and for cultural freedoms (Dean with Melrose, 1999, p 171). Although there is no universally accepted model of citizenship, there is a degree of universality implicit in the notion, so that citizenship rights can be fought for as aspects of equality, although enforceable rights may be to a degree context-specific. Being about rights, citizenship claims also point away from relationships of gifts and towards non-stigmatised entitlements (albeit sometimes tied in with obligations as well). Consequently citizenship arrangements may have distinctive features within the ensemble of modes of regulation which we have discussed above.

Among social democrats citizenship can be held to include rights focused around social welfare. From this perspective – emphasising social rights – access to decent housing could be both a measure of, and a contributor to, the citizenship status of a household. Even when such rights are acknowledged, however, they may not be conceded unconditionally, and one of the features of the present period is that, alongside struggles to extend rights, are pressures (partly from government itself) to make them more conditional. Citizenship rights and practices may be seen as linked with processes of "constant struggle and negotiation" (cf Kennett, 1998, pp 31-2). As part of the politics here, universalistic arrangements or assumptions can be challenged, renegotiated and redefined over time, difference being accommodated to varying degrees. Dean with Melrose are interested in the possibility of a citizenship strategy which combines concerns for equality with concerns about difference (Dean with Melrose, 1999, p xii). (See also our discussion in Chapter

Eight.) This accommodation can be in less formalised processes or within formal rules, and may involve compromise (see Poulter, 1986, for a discussion of English law and minority customs).

There is a specific point to add about rights struggles. Citizenship's social rights (if this is accepted as a concept) need not be confined to provision outside the realms of markets and private property. It might be suggested that something must be de-coupled from private property, and in effect 'decommodified' in order to be a social or welfare right. For example, Cole and Furbey refer to the dominant definition of housing as "a commodity rather than a social right" (Cole and Furbey, 1994, p 3). Perhaps an implication of this might be that private property rights are not compatible with Marshallian concepts of social welfare (consider Marshall, in Marshall and Bottomore, 1992). Historically, however, social rights have often been seen by ordinary people as including certain kinds of property rights, and it would not be too difficult to interpret owner-occupation as offering important forms of social rights. Thus decommodification needs very carefully specifying before it can be taken as an adequate guide to availability of welfare rights, to comparative performance of welfare state 'regimes', or to the meaning of 'welfare state' itself; and we need not always contrast rights and commodities (although sometimes we should). (For important ideas here see Esping-Andersen, 1990; see also Bonoli, 1997; Lister, 1997a, pp 173-5; Duncan and Edwards, 1999, pp 216-52; Veit-Wilson, 2000, p 16). When we do draw such a contrast we should be aware of the danger of social welfare rights becoming a set of residual provisions for poor people outside the market mainstream.

A second way of relating citizenship to regulation is to perceive varied experiences of being a citizen as parts of wider patterns of division in which people may be constituted differently from one another as far as the practices of institutions are concerned, and located in differentiated ways in terms of human relationships and social expectations. Citizenship rules and practices are important parts of regulatory processes. Historically, the citizenship idea often had different implications for differing groups; the classic instance was the gendered and age-linked requirement that certain men should serve in military activities for the state, and that – in a sense – the state was entitled to demand their lives. Today some individuals are formally less complete citizens than others, and national policy may draw and redraw boundaries for this over time. Substantial numbers of migrants and refugees, for example, may be excluded from full citizen status, and therefore may not be seen as having the same housing entitlements as longstanding British nationals (Shaw, Lambert and Clapham, 1998, pp 12-13). There is also variation in citizenship status over the life course. Some politicians feel that young people should not have full status, and are therefore not entitled to certain financial support when in difficulty; restrictions on young people in respect of welfare benefits in the 1990s had housing effects (see JRF, 1998e; Stewart, 1998, p 50; Clapham and Dix with Griffiths, 1996, pp 40-1). Such approaches prolong young people's dependence, deferring full citizenship and discouraging attempts to establish independent lives. Many households may experience limitations on their status at particular periods. In practical terms, for instance, not having a fixed address may reduce a person's standing in relation to obtaining universalistic national health services, and homelessness can reduce a household's effective social rights (Edwards, 1995; M. Shaw, N. Brimblecombe and D. Dorling, *Housing Today*, 5 February 1998).

There is a difference between formal citizenship boundaries based on firm rules or codes and the more complex processes of socioeconomic differentiation to which we have referred earlier. Effective citizenship status may be considered in relation to the latter as well as the former. Perhaps citizenship can be approached in terms of a group of rights or obligations which shades into a larger set of widespread practices confirming status or facilitating voice. Thus an extensive range of rights and practices can be analysed for a discussion of the experiences of citizenship, and may also be viewed normatively in terms of an agenda for asserting particular claims in the political arena. Day-to-day practices are crucial to the experiences that households have, and can be seen in terms of relative incorporation into the status of being a citizen; often to differing degrees according to variables such as ethnicity, gender, impairment, age and so forth. Obligations attached to citizenship are also very much a matter of day-to-day practices as well as of law. As far as normative analysis is concerned, this can be given an interesting housing dimension, as demonstrated by Clapham and Dix with Griffiths. These authors suggest that citizenship can offer a framework for drawing together some apparently separate ideas and placing them "at the heart of a housing provider's fundamental mission" (Clapham and Dix with Griffiths, 1996). Their study examines specific projects, and uses three categories to discuss citizenship: rights, respect and recognition; skills and abilities needed to exercise rights; and willingness and intention to be an active and responsible citizen (Clapham and Dix with Griffiths, 1996, pp 7-8). They point out that housing organisations are already grappling with citizenship issues "under other names". So as well as being a useful way of looking at aspects of social regulation, and a focus for challenges to unfair practices, citizenship might be a valuable standpoint or philosophy from which housing organisations might approach many practical problems about the rights of tenants, accommodation of disabled people, approaches to youth, and so forth.

In conclusion, we suggest that *the development and organisation of citizenship constitute significant parts of the processes and practices of social regulation* (or alternatively can be analysed as *measures of the effects and character of the regulatory ensemble*). Rights and customs of inclusion, respect, or status are important aspects, fought for from the grass roots, and modifying social control. The agenda is complex, since rights may clash, can be collective as well as individual, can focus on varying facets of a person's needs (including entitlements, protection, or representation), and can involve interdependencies. Alongside rights may be duties, and a right for one person may create an obligation for someone else (as with a parent's duties to a child). The capacity to exercise rights can be crucial, and may depend on money or other resources. At the same time the practices of citizenship are contested and shifting.

Conclusions

There are various modes or forms of social regulation in the welfare state, and we must consider grass roots activities as well as institutions and rules when reviewing them. We can think in terms of an ensemble of interlocking regulatory practices, some discordant and most shifting over time. The ensemble is strongly affected by structural factors, which (although rarely static or independent of changes at the grass roots) help create the constraints and opportunities that people encounter when seeking resources and services,when forming preferences and strategies, and when acting individually or collectively. *People and groups are active agents, and negotiate and plan their ways forward, but in contexts which privilege some and disadvantage others in regular and patterned ways.* Households bring into specific situations resources that vary greatly, and that are influenced by class, disability, ethnicity, gender and age. There is thus an impact from "external systemic and social properties", as Archer calls them, with people being "enmeshed in broader socio-cultural relations which they carry with them" (Archer, 1995, p 11). Interactions between difference and regulation are not neutral, and may involve practices and discourses of "inferiorisation and inequality" (cf Anthias, 1999, p 160). In a general sense, "patterns of social difference" are "socially constructed" (J. Clarke, preface to Saraga, 1998, p vii), but with very tangible material connections and implications. Within the broad patterns of divisions there is further differentiation around self-defined and externally-influenced distinctions and categories: difference *within* difference.

One theme in this chapter has been that caution is required in discussing oppressions or social control. Social policies facilitate as well as constrain, and the welfare state has beneficiaries and participants who may influence outcomes in their own favour. This is why the idea of differential incorporation can prove helpful when thinking about welfare and processes of social regulation. Across the welfare state a range of mechanisms contributes to the management of aspects of welfare and consumption beyond the sphere of direct wages, bringing benefits to households and sometimes confirming privileged positions of the more affluent. *The fundamental component of social regulation is not repression, but incorporation; without incorporation there is no exclusion.* Denying that many people are successfully – albeit differentially – incorporated amounts to a denial of agency for households and politicians. Recognising incorporation goes along with acknowledging the importance of political representation of visible and less visible constituencies and interests. At the same time we should not overlook the ongoing impact of notions of citizenship and of developments in rights.

FOUR

Social regulation in housing

Housing consumers experience various forms of regulation in the sense that we have been using the term. They encounter 'gatekeepers' influencing access to accommodation and are subject to expectations about family and culture. Home-buyers have to meet specific criteria of incomes and health to obtain mortgage finance on reasonable terms. Applicants for renting or for supported or emergency accommodation may come up against rules and officials. A difference between households as perceived by a providing organisation may be a basis for negative or positive discrimination, deterrence or assistance. In effect housing practices help sort people, contributing to differentiation of citizenship as a lived experience. Many activities here – supportive or restrictive – have deep historical foundations, and connect with structural forces, but there are numerous challenges from the grass roots too, sometimes offering alternative discourses about housing rights, needs or citizenship. *To understand housing experiences of disabled people, minority ethnic households or women, it is desirable to consider the broad frameworks within which most households are placed.* Governmental policies and institutions confirm the status and resources of households, help position them in terms of access to accommodation, designate or classify them, and influence pathways during their housing 'careers'. Options for individual households are influenced by public policies across all tenures, these policies in turn being linked with particular discourses about property, health, environment, merit, rewards, risk, conditionality, needs and so on.

To explore some of these matters, this chapter reviews practices and their effects. We begin with markets, and then look at 'non-market' housing, considering social renting and some competing or complementary concerns of contemporary policy. 'Private' housing markets are covered fairly swiftly, since many of their differentiating effects for groups of households are relatively straightforward and predictable, despite the distinctiveness of UK public policies affecting ownership and private renting. A somewhat more elaborate account is needed to explore social rented housing, because the motivations and potential effects of policies and services here have been complex, and perhaps sometimes even contradictory. We draw attention especially to *practices and discourses related to social support and needs, to social control and the regulation of tensions, and to participation and citizenship.* Brief conclusions consider how the structural penetrates into everyday housing activity (contributing to relatively ordered environments of constraints and options), how processes of relative incorporation and exclusion may mean boundaries being developed or managed around difference, and how there has been scope for challenge under the banners of empowerment and citizenship rights. Throughout the chapter we keep in mind the dual forces of institutions and ideas which were referred to earlier, and the specific manifestations of human agency mentioned in Chapter Two. It should be noted that although we divide market from non-market below, the two sometimes overlap for consumers (for example an occupier may own part of the equity while paying rent to a social landlord under a shared ownership arrangement).

Markets, money and social regulation

Market arrangements and private property rights systems dominate social regulation in housing in two ways. First, in direct effects on consumers from the operation of the owner-occupation and private renting sectors, both in terms of particular practices affecting households' opportunities and strategies and through the permeation of ideas and expectations. Rationing (and social and spatial segregation) is largely through the price mechanism, with people sifted by ability to pay, modified by lenders' concerns about minimising risk, and sometimes by discriminatory approaches not related directly to money. Although in principle money can be superior to bureaucracy in that it makes no distinction of gender or ethnicity, various 'gatekeepers' stand on routes into private housing, opening or closing doors to dwellings or finance. At the same time markets revolve around commercial or exchange value rather than the 'use value' of property (Hunter and Nixon, 1998, p 94), a factor affecting perceptions. No one expects an owner to sacrifice economic interests for someone else's benefit. Thus rented property can be kept empty if its owner gains thereby, although its potential use value suggests it could be housing homeless people in urgent need. Dominance of markets, furthermore, encourages familiarity with particular notions of private property rights, while assumptions about people carrying their own risks in 'free' markets may legitimate governmental reluctance to plan comprehensively for protecting consumers here. Second, there are effects via non-market sectors as a result of the dominance of owner-occupation, with assumptions that many people catered for outside markets are therefore dependent clients receiving state gifts. Despite the political strength of private market systems, their practices have been challenged frequently by those seeking to enlarge consumer rights, and have been amended and supervised by governments (we briefly noted in Chapter Two the case of the pre-war mortgage strikes).

Private renting

Although private renting plays a less extensive role today than owner-occupation or social renting, private landlords have some power. They may make a choice of tenant to minimise financial and other risks, and may require a bond (money paid down in advance and held by the landlord during the tenancy) to cover potential costs incurred. Risk-minimising or profit-taking may also mean asking tenants to pay a holding deposit while references and credit rating are checked, an administrative fee and charge for the credit check if the tenant is accepted, or even an 'inventory check' fee. Rules may exclude pets, smoking, or children. When demand is strong, landlords are potentially freer to ration by non-financial criteria, and to impose behavioural or financial demands. There have long been racist discriminatory practices in the sector, and some landlords will not house those who are homeless or in receipt of housing benefit (see Marsh and Riseborough, 1998, p 115). Profitability issues or prejudices may make landlords reluctant to adapt housing for disabled people or elders (making it harder to 'stay put' as people age). Marsh and Riseborough comment that for many poorer tenants the private rented sector is a 'residual' tenure in which they reside because they have little alternative, "including a lack of access to social housing" (Marsh and Riseborough, 1998, p 115). On the other hand there are wealthier tenants receiving higher quality provision. Writing in the 1980s, Daunton pointed to a polarisation of groups, some marginalised and some not, suggesting that the "experience of the tenure does not emerge from the tenure itself", so much as "from the tenants' income level and social status which define the way the tenure is experienced" (Daunton, 1987, p 90).

Of course the sector is not a 'free market', being affected by laws, and by governmental policies on landlord/tenant relationships, environmental health, finance, and rent levels. After 1979 Conservative efforts at reviving private renting were underpinned by reductions in the rights of many tenants, despite heavy commitment of public funds through assistance to households (effectively providing landlord profits through tenant subsidies). Carr notes that by the time the 1996 Housing Act came into force, "the accumulation of 16 years of legislation had resulted in the drastic reduction of succession rights, security of tenure and rent control" (Carr, 1998, p 111). In 1996 the government modified housing benefit rules so that single people under 25 could only claim benefit on non-self-contained accommodation (for earlier changes affecting young people, and implications for street homelessness see Anderson, 1993). As Marsh and Riseborough explain, if such households rely on housing benefit in order to secure accommodation, "then they are being filtered towards houses in multiple occupation" (Marsh and Riseborough, 1998, p 113). Here there are problems of quality, security and safety. During the Conservative period, despite tragic deaths in multiply-occupied dwellings, movement towards stronger controls was limited. (Smith, 1998, provides a good account.) There are now evident pressures for change (DETR and DSS, 2000, chapter 5). Carr comments interestingly on the potential for residential occupation being protected through the operation of consumer standards in contracts, suggesting that in future the occupier identified as a consumer might be more successfully protected than the occupier identified as a tenant (Carr, 1998, pp 121-3).

The relative income disadvantage of many disabled people, minority ethnic households and women (especially those without a male partner) puts them in weak positions in relation to private renting, although this may be modified by availability of means-tested support for rents. Their situations may be worsened if they are perceived as deviant or risky, or have 'special' needs, such as for adaptations, or accommodation for children (!).

The dominant system

Owner-occupation is the central motor for UK housing. Change in the housing system is driven by the regular addition of higher quality owner-occupied dwellings to the stock, and by improvement and enlargement activity here. The new dwellings are occupied primarily (although not always) by better-off households, absorbing substantial resources of materials, labour and environment. There are potentially 'trickle down' benefits for poorer households from this, but market systems of the UK type depend for buoyancy on a ranking of houses in terms of status and quality as well as a degree of social and geographical segregation. People lower down in the system can never 'catch up' with the best-placed owner-occupiers, unless there is an unexpected national lottery win! Enjoyment of owner-occupation is governed by particular forms of conditionality. For most aspiring owner-occupiers, demonstrable ability to service a loan is central, but stands alongside other factors such as any risk that the household seems to represent. A normal market response to higher risk is to charge more for loans, or to require more security. In housing this has sometimes meant the poor paying relatively more (in insurance or interest charges) or obtaining smaller conventional loans than other people.

Households' particular social, physical and economic circumstances lead to relatively good or bad housing. Ill-health, for instance, may influence an individual's credit rating and ability to earn enough to purchase decent accommodation. (In turn, of course, low income may affect health, through associated stress, diet, residential environment, or difficulties in access to health care.) The primary conditions to be met by households concern capacity to pay, while economic failure – with debts – can lead to losing the home. Economic status has been modified by prejudice, stereotyping and discrimination, affecting minority ethnic households and other disadvantaged groups. For example, racist practices by estate agents sometimes aimed at 'steering' black minority ethnic households away from properties in certain white-occupied localities (for fine North American work on this and allied issues see Yinger, 1995).

Owner-occupiers have received considerable indirect financial support from governments. The Conservative years confirmed supremacy of the sector, although it probably became more segmented and stratified, and more subject to risks and difficulties (Murie, 1998). Maclennan notes, however, that housing policy support has, since 1990, "moved sharply against owner occupation", making progress more difficult for purchasers (Maclennan, 1997, pp 46-7). Failure of the Conservatives to intervene in favour of marginal buyers when times became difficult may have been resented and have had significant political effects (see discussion in Hamnett, 1999, pp 68-72). As for the right-to-buy for sitting council tenants, in a sense a benefit – owner-occupation at a low price – was held out to the same group that had previously been the best-placed beneficiaries of council renting, the better-off tenants living in the best houses (see Malpass and Murie 1999; 89, 124-5; Lund, 1996, p 125). Specific local circumstances may have determined how far the new owners were incorporated into the owner-occupation mainstream. Perhaps council house sales policies could be interpreted sometimes as filling gaps in available ranges of choice (for a view on Scotland see Begg, 1996, pp 169-77), and minority ethnic households certainly have taken advantage of the right to buy. As created in 1980, however, this right excluded certain categories of dwellings appropriate for elders or disabled people. Although this presumably reflected acknowledgement of the shortage of such accommodation, the policy could be construed as discriminatory in denying certain people rights allowed for others (for details see Smith, 1989, pp 72-5, 359-60).

Differentiation within and in entry to owner-occupation has been patterned. Many disabled people, minority ethnic households and women have been poorly placed, reflecting labour market status. Hamnett indicates that the skilled working class have been entering home ownership in large numbers, joining the "growing ranks of the middle classes" (Hamnett, 1999, p 57), and that the tenure is quite diverse. Expansion of owner-occupation has been accompanied by increased numbers of households experiencing high risks at the margins of the tenure with little state support (for relevant contributions see Williams, 1997; also Wilcox, 1997, pp 126-9). Wilcox and Ford observe that home-buyers now make up two fifths of all households in the lower half of the bottom income decile (Wilcox and Ford, 1997, pp 24-5), with a significant proportion self-employed. As they put it, "self-employment is volatile", and such mortgagors have an above average risk of mortgage arrears. More home-buying households than in the 1980s do not have household heads in full-time employment. Although government helps some older owner-occupiers by supporting improvement agency services (Harrison and Means, 1990, p 8), there is little in public policy to safeguard owners at the margins or facilitate sustainability of low-income owner-occupation. This omission may be particularly important for minority ethnic households. (For discussion of regulation of lenders, and treatment of owner-occupiers in difficulties, see Whitehouse, 1998; Hunter and Nixon, 1998.)

Apart from affecting individuals, markets can work against localities. This is not just a matter of the 'north/south divide'. The assessment of risk plays a role. This was evident in so-called 'red-lining' in inner urban areas in earlier decades (see discussion in Harrison and Stevens, 1981). In deciding that some inner city areas represented poor security (and in effect drawing boundaries around such areas), some building societies made assumptions about risks represented by particular markets in which black minority ethnic households were numerous. Racist stereotyping was linked with unsubstantiated guesses about the negative impact that ethnic difference might have on future property values. Negative assumptions, once made, became self-fulfilling prophecies, likely to depress ability to raise loans in specific places, encourage private landlordism, raise borrowing costs, reduce monies available for repair, and affect marketability (or price).

As far as gender is concerned, the percentage among women heads of household in Britain in owner-occupation rose over the Conservative period from 38% in 1980 to 51% in 1995, although the figure for men remained much higher at 74% (see Wilcox, 1997, p 107). Figures for owner-occupation have varied between minority ethnic categories; for instance being 84% for the Indian but only 41% for the 'Black' category in the 1993-95 period (see Wilcox, 1997, p 109). Racist and sexist practices in private markets remain difficult to research. Hamnett explains, though, that the gender and ethnic composition of home ownership has changed considerably. Traditionally, home ownership was "strongly dominated by male-headed households", although widows were "prominent among outright owners" (Hamnett, 1999, p 64). He indicates that building society reactions to women have changed, partly because profits "triumphed over prejudice". Nonetheless, female-headed households are still less likely than male-headed ones to be buying on a mortgage, although far more women participate as joint owners with men than once was the case (see Wasoff, 1998).

Housing market responses to impairment are under-researched, although Easterlow, Smith and Mallinson (2000) provide an excellent commentary on health and the market, while Crow notes the concern that predisposition to impairment will be used as a basis for discrimination in financial and medical services (Crow, 1996, p 219; note also JRF, 1995, p 3). Kestenbaum summarises findings from earlier studies (including work of the Disablement Income Group), pointing to various barriers (Kestenbaum, 1996, p 8). A recent small-scale exploration by D. Naylor highlights problems (unpublished BA dissertation, Leeds University). Using case studies to test property availability and lender responses in 1999, Naylor explored prospects for disabled people. The number of suitable older properties available in the parts of the Leeds market selected was low, and this was matched by a poor situation for new dwellings, where none were yet being built incorporating proposed changes to Part M of the Building Regulations (which would change accessibility of dwellings). Lenders were approached with particular cases, to see their reactions. There seemed to be some belief that adaptations would not increase values. Mainstream lenders showed unwillingness to arrange finance in certain cases put to them, in one instance despite very good security in terms of owner-occupied property. Drawing on sources from within the financial sector Naylor also reported that only 5 out of 122

Council of Mortgage Lenders members apparently were prepared to consider accepting benefits in assessing loan applications. Our interpretation is that owner-occupier markets are conditioned not only by requirements about households having access to capital and steady income, but by evaluations of risk in which impairment or ill-health play a part alongside the obstacles, uncertainties or stigma of the housing benefits system.

At the heart of social regulation via markets are the positions households occupy in relation to the world of paid work and inherited wealth, and in relation to concepts of risk. Those meeting the necessary criteria have sometimes been greatly empowered by owner–occupation (cf Harrison, 1995, pp 23-5). The primacy of markets, money, and specific forms and distributions of property rights in housing is crucial. Additionally, dominance of owner-occupation legitimates a highly selectivist approach to many forms of non-market provision, placing those who are outside the market as different. In a sense, *owner-occupation casts a powerful shadow across other tenure forms.* Many selectivist strategies embrace efforts to contain tightly the costs of poverty for the public purse, whereas market institutions constantly seek to expand consumption by households.

'Non-market' housing provision

The central channel for non-market provision in the UK has been council (municipal) housing, supplemented by housing association dwellings, and specialised accommodation targeted at specific client groups (such as frail elders). Although in its history council housing has accommodated better off members of the working class, it has potentially been an effective means of reducing connections between poverty and poor quality dwellings, and thus between labour market status and quality of life (for the sector's advantages see Murie, 1997). This effect has frequently been modified by restrictions on access and by differentiation within the sector, but in recent years the housing has primarily served relatively disadvantaged households (Malpass and Murie, 1999, pp 123-7). Before reviewing aspects of practice and discourse, we briefly sketch some background on the provider organisations. The housing management, development and services literature is informative, but space requires us to be selective (useful texts include Cope, 1999; Harriott and Matthews with Grainger, 1998; and Pearl, 1997).

Changes since 1979 between and within housing agencies have affected ownership of assets, staff, client households, relationships with other organisations or departments, and links with wider local communities (see contributions in Marsh and Mullins, 1998). Key trends have involved de-municipalisation, competition, and managerialism. Walker notes growth of a strong performance measurement culture, business planning, "strategic management and change management techniques", enhanced "customer power" and innovative methods of service delivery (Walker, 1998, p 78). A policy shift away from relying on local authorities providing council housing was paralleled by encouragement for growth in the housing association sector, under a financial regime which brought a mix of private with public funding, and brought association tenancies closer to the private market (see Randolph, 1993; Mullins, 1998). Housing associations have moved "from the margins to the mainstream" (Best, 1997, p 103), but now carry more of the financial risks associated with development. Potential involvement of new types of organisations in social renting was recognised by the term 'Registered Social Landlord' (RSL), denoting the enlarged range that might receive recognition from governmental agencies and funders (see Walker, 1998, p 76). Local authority services changed under the impetus of tighter financial regimes, pressures to reduce the directly-managed stock, urban renewal policy, and increased tenant rights. The reduced roles of councils as direct providers, and their ongoing involvements with overall strategy, have pointed to more emphasis on inter-organisational networks, and on mechanisms such as common applicants' registers for potential tenants in need (see Goodlad, 1993, p 109).

The indebtedness of housing associations to private financiers alters the nature of accountability. As Mullins explains (discussing stock transfers), funders have "latent power", and have required "regular monitoring of performance against the business plan" and covenant agreements on such matters as rent collection and keeping properties occupied (Mullins, 1998, p 143; cf Malpass, 1997, p 84). The applicability of a market-like model to associations, however, may be offset by the weight of their charitable commitments, local partnerships, and relationships with councils. There is still public investment, and ongoing governmental organisational and financial regulation (see Malpass, 1997; and Mullins, 1997). Associations may also try "to balance the pressures of becoming or remaining financially strong and viable" with the concern "to stay close to the community and the customer" (Williams, 1997a, p 127).

Inter-organisational contact for housing providers ranges from joint working on broader strategy to cooperation in meeting specialised needs, or developing 'housing plus' work beyond basic property services. Policy implementation is "increasingly dependent upon securing the collaboration and cooperation of, and between, groups of diverse service-providing organisations", many of which are 'independent' in the sense that they are outside direct statutory control, although they are nonetheless "a necessary feature of the policy implementation process" (Reid, 1995, p 133). Terms like 'partnerships', 'alliances' and participating 'stakeholders' have become commonplace. Smith and Mallinson refer to the language of welfare restructuring being "peppered with" the term "alliance", important because it carries the idea that gaps in provision can be "plugged by a process of inter-agency collaboration" (Smith and Mallinson, 1997, p 174). Problems may include potential contradictions between the competitive environment and calls for collaboration, or differences in organisational and professional cultures and legal responsibilities (for housing and social care see Oldman, 1998; also Means and Smith, 1996). Arblaster, Conway, Foreman and Hawtin note that the "widespread lack of resources for social housing, health and social care threatens the willingness of agencies to work together", and indicate that the introduction of markets into social care has resulted in a "proliferation of agencies which compete amongst themselves for contracts" (Arblaster et al, 1996, p x). Power relationships may arise or be expressed in inter-organisational contacts, as organisations bring into inter-organisational relationships "distinctly unequal powers and liabilities" (Reid, 1997, p 127). This can be important where small organisations attempt to represent disabled people, minority ethnic communities or women's interests.

'Gatekeepers'

One way of inserting agency into an account of how the structural becomes the local is to consider the roles of officials as 'gatekeepers', and their interactions with consumers. Housing staff (or 'officers') have dealt with tenancy allocations and management and, historically, elected councillors have also sometimes taken part (see Cole and Furbey, 1994, pp 122-5). Gatekeepers usually make decisions or offer guidance on the basis of rules, values or expectations. The practices of organisations and behaviour of their staff have constrained households' choices. Excluding people from tenancies, or directing them into particular dwellings, has been a means of controlling access into (and transfers within) the stock, and sometimes of disciplining 'problem families' or rewarding 'respectables'. Some groups lost out regularly (see Short, 1982; Mullins and Niner, 1998). Adverse experiences for minority ethnic and female-headed households were parts of a broader pattern in allocation practices linked to 'respectability' and status hierarchies. Both gay and lesbian couples could experience hostilities or be overlooked by public providers (see Smailes, 1994).

It might seem that officers wield considerable power, and there is certainly scope for judgemental and moralistic elements in decision-making processes (for homelessness assessments see Cowan and Gilroy, 1999, especially p 178). Looking at this differently, it can be argued that the exercise of discretion is 'an operational requirement' in needs assessment and dwelling allocations procedures, and is not necessarily problematic where accountability is adequate (see Smith and Mallinson, 1996, p 353). What happens in housing allocation and management, however, is not unrestrained 'agency', or autonomous action. Households play active parts, drawing on resources such as the ability to wait, which has conferred the power to refuse a tenancy offered in a 'bad area' (cf Spicker, 1987, p 24). This may mean people in less severe circumstances or on higher incomes gaining access to better properties, time confirming the effect of existing socioeconomic distinctions (for valuable comments see Clapham and Kintrea, 1986). Even homeless people, however, may have some capacity to resist their exclusion, or to pursue their own strategies (cf Neale, 1997, p 47).

As well as interactions with households' preferences, formal and informal policies of housing organisations influence officers' actions. We could expect to find professional ideologies important, yet heavily contingent on organisational, political and financial contexts. While the recruiting patterns and occupational culture of a work-force can be important (see for example Macpherson, 1999, p 25, on police service culture), there are many other factors operating as well. Local authority housing managers may allocate on the basis of values and assumptions linked with the resource limitations and operational environments in which they work (see Spicker, 1987). Limits in responding to specific groups are set by factors such as the availability of stock, while ongoing effects of patterns of investment might 'sideline' certain types of needs (see Brownill and Darke, 1998). Perhaps social housing practitioners have not had a very high degree of autonomy (although see Franklin, 1998a, p 214), being subject to control, influence or pressure from a variety of other 'actors' within and outside their organisations (and sometimes including tenants' representatives). Specific legal or administrative codes and guidelines now affect them on such matters as 'race' relations, equal opportunities and tenant consultation. In some instances – notably with homelessness from the late 1970s –

central government has set very specific rules about access for priority groups, albeit providing "a shroud" which legitimated "the exclusion of substantial numbers from housing" (Cowan and Gilroy, 1999, p 161). Official guidelines and legal frameworks are important, with varying implications for how differing people are dealt with (see for example Garside, 1993). Practices of deterrence or discrimination may develop, but framed by expectations. Generally, the allocation process "hardly occurs on terms of housing managers' own choosing" (Cole and Furbey, 1994, p 141). Unsurprisingly, different considerations may apply in gatekeeping access to 'difficult-to-let housing' as against dwellings in short supply (Mullins and Niner, 1998, p 179).

For social rented housing managers, different strands of professional thinking have co-existed over time (relevant studies include Kemp and Williams, 1991; Cairncross, Clapham and Goodlad, 1997; Franklin and Clapham, 1997; Franklin, 1998a; Haworth and Manzi, 1999). Staff roles also reflect diversity between employers in organisation and priorities, and arrangements for any services outside routine housing tasks. Discourses about tenants and managers have sometimes been used to justify the latter's authority in managing stock with only limited reference to the former (cf Cairncross, Clapham and Goodlad, 1997, p 52). As with many professions, such an approach to those categorised as 'clients' can be associated with broader claims to knowledge about needs. At a general level the shadow cast by owner-occupation affects the character of the housing service, creating environments where management of social 'problems' is a heightened component of political discourse and professional work. Nonetheless, several specific sets of goals and practices affect interactions with consumers in social rented housing and allied provision (such as specialised accommodation for vulnerable households). Leaving aside managerial trends and issues touched on above (see also Jacobs and Manzi, 2000; Walker, 2000), we concentrate now on three overlapping policy strands, each with accompanying practices and discourses (cf Spink, 1998; Haworth and Manzi, 1999; Pearl, 1997, chapter 2).

Social support and needs

Non-market or 'social' housing is generally assumed to be meeting needs inadequately met by markets. We can note three features. First, there is an honourable tradition of supporting and sheltering vulnerable people, and catering for households with children, within housing and allied services (although permeated with a degree of paternalism and notions of dependency). Second, council housing has become more responsive to certain low income households (such as single parents), but its status has fallen, perhaps with an accompanying shift from expectations about shared values of 'respectable' life to more concern for intensive management, and recognition of diversity. Third, defining 'need' is complex and potentially contested.

Housing management has long had explicit or latent 'caring' roles (cf Smith and Mallinson, 1997, p 177), these being evident in the notion of allocating according to need and in specialised provision. Confirmation of council housing's social welfare functions is found in specific legal obligations such as those under homelessness legislation. Housing management's welfare commitment is illustrated by Franklin and Clapham's comment on specialist housing workers who prided themselves on their personal knowledge of their tenants and showed a willingness to be supportive, referring to a "wee bit of tender loving care" (Franklin and Clapham, 1997, p 17). Oldman notes the record of joint working between social services departments and housing organisations, although generally at individual case level (Oldman, 1998, p 63), and some housing associations are well known for their specialised provision (see Cope, 1999, p 257). How best to combine housing and support services for specific vulnerable groups has been an important matter of debate in industrialised countries (Means, 1996, p 207), key UK themes being the shift away from 'traditional' socio-medical institutional provision towards 'care in the community', and increasing emphasis on user involvement and person–centred approaches (see Chapter Five). Apart from being involved with community care, landlords may also go beyond basic property management by offering 'housing plus' activities ranging from advocacy and welfare rights work to community capacity building and employment initiatives.

Mainstream council housing for many years offered reputable locations for traditional working class households with members in full-time employment. The fact that its allocation often excluded or down-graded claims of certain groups – including minority ethnic and single parent applicants – was evidence of council housing's established status with the 'respectable' white working class (cf Malpass and Murie, 1999, p 65). In recent decades, however, the service has been housing more disadvantaged people while the relative quality and status of its environments and dwellings seem to have been declining. The term 'residualisation' has been widely used, referring to the changing composition of populations in council housing, the assumption that the sector now plays a secondary role with inferior status to that of owner-occupation, and deterioration of physical conditions. As an extensive literature explains the trends, there is no need to review detailed debates here (see for example Malpass, 1990; Malpass and Murie, 1999, pp 123-30; Pearl, 1997). Council housing has changed, with good properties sold through the right-to-buy, and few new dwellings built, increasing its image as the tenure of discredited high rise blocks, disrepair, and 'sink estates' (although residualisation processes are not geographically uniform, and Scotland may have differed from England or Wales). There are demand variations, with 'surpluses' in some locations (see Cole, Kane and Robinson, 1999), and an age shift, whereby council estates contain young and old, but fewer from middle years (Malpass and Murie refer to a "hollowing out of the middle"; 1999, p 124). Cole and Furbey suggest that growing "levels of disenchantment with state housing" have emerged from the actual experience of living on council estates (Cole and Furbey, 1994, p 5), but certain dwellings are still sought after and we could expect satisfaction to depend strongly on available resources, dwelling quality and so forth. Some parallel changes have affected housing associations, where (similarly) 'difficult-to-let' housing has emerged (Pawson and Kearns, 1998), although the sector has most of the newest units of social rented stock.

The right-to-buy "speeded up the process through which the reputation and attractiveness of council housing has been damaged" (Jones and Murie, 1999, p 12). Numerous 'traditional' council tenants have gone into owner-occupation, with councils increasingly providing for those without "the economic power to move into home ownership", especially "poor, elderly and unemployed" households (Cole and Furbey, 1994, p 5; cf Wilcox, 1997, p 45), or those who have lost owner-occupied homes (Ford, 1999, pp 172-3). Housing difficulties elsewhere contribute to female-headed households being heavily represented in council housing (Wasoff, 1998, p 131). Increasing proportions of tenants are dependent upon benefits, the value of state pensions and benefits has "not kept pace with inflation or earnings growth", and there is a poverty trap from which it can be difficult to take a job without being out of pocket (because of loss of benefit to cover rents) (Lee, 1998, pp 62, 69; McCrone and Stephens, 1995, pp 172-3). Whereas there have previously often been so-called 'problem estates', difficulties now seem more pervasive across the stock. Borrowing phrases from Murie, we can say that rather than breaking the link between low income and poor housing, council housing now might have become part of that link (Murie, 1987, p 30). The pattern of a particularly disadvantaged section of the working class population channelled into council estates may be more striking for the white population, however, than for minority ethnic households (see Lee 1998, pp 64-5).

'Housing need' concepts legitimate strategies to improve supply, affordability or quality, and to prioritise categories of people as recipients for assistance. Need analyses become mechanisms for defining, classifying, and measuring shortfalls, circumstances, or relative vulnerability. For instance, disabled people's needs for housing adaptations may be evaluated by a local authority, with consultations between departments, and involvement of an occupational therapy service (see Bull, 1998; Bradford, 1998). (Perhaps need can become translated through this type of practice into a guide to remedying selected individuals' problems rather than reducing physical barriers for all.) More generally, for practitioners, judgements of needs become essential for rationing resources between organisations, localities, or individual households. Especially where a service is not seen as a 'right', but more as a 'gift' or form of paternalistic 'care', decisions must be made about which households most 'deserve' the gift, and about the relative urgency of their needs. With selectivity in service provision, need may become part of the apparatus of practitioner authority, albeit potentially contested by politicians or users and complicated by inter-organisational working. Although professional 'standards' or 'benchmarks' may appear objective, practitioners' values can be important. In the 1980s Spicker analysed the defining of needs in the process of council house allocation, and referred to an "ideology of need" (see Spicker, 1987 and 1989).

As already indicated in our discussion of gatekeepers, however, professionals' decisions reflect organisational and resource constraints. 'Needs' are conceptualised and reconceptualised in specific and changing environments. Clients – such as older people – may not always be encouraged to articulate needs and wishes that cannot be readily met (see Shaw, Lambert and Clapham, 1998, p 10). Defining needs is to a degree political, and the 'micro-politics' of needs-definition has changed with increased involvement of service users and communities. There have been specific studies on minority ethnic housing needs, and some discussion in practitioner settings is sophisticated on questions of ethnic diversity and cultural sensitivity (for example see London Research Centre and Lemos and Crane, 1998). Furthermore, following the Stephen Lawrence Inquiry, the countering of indirect and institutionalised forms of racist practice has had more prominence in public debate, and some practitioners may have become more alert to the dangers of "collective failure of an organisation to provide an appropriate and professional service to people because of their colour, culture or ethnic origin" (Macpherson, 1999, p 28). This has significance for approaches to need. There has also been more recognition that needs assessment might take account of a widened range of difficult household circumstances. Nonetheless, we should note that concern with needs overlaps with social control and 'social engineering' (for some parallels in analysis of the discourse of 'care', see Priestley, 1999). Helping vulnerable young people, for example, might shade into persuading them into settled housing ways or training. The term 'care' itself can have custodial or surveillance overtones. As far as assisting women is concerned, in the past the desire to help and the measuring of need may have been overlaid with moral judgements aligned to beliefs about prioritising traditional or 'proper' families. Even today, when practitioners are supposedly more ready to respond sympathetically on issues such as domestic violence, judgemental thinking may persist (see Chapter Seven).

Social control and the regulation of tensions

Social order issues are currently prominent within housing debates, but social control practices are not new, as our discussion of gatekeepers indicated (cf Haworth and Manzi, 1999, p 155). Cole and Furbey suggest that, historically, Labour failed to secure a radical departure in council housing from traditional landlord-tenant relations (Cole and Furbey, 1994, pp 125-6). Although much was positive in being a council tenant, management was paternalistic, and supervision, segregation and even humiliation of tenants were significant in council housing history (see for instance Tucker, 1966; Damer, 1974; Ward, 1974; Henderson and Karn, 1987). Officials sometimes explicitly 'graded' tenants or prospective tenants, while "unmarried mothers", cohabitees, "dirty" families, and "transients" tended to be grouped together as "undesirable" (see Central Housing Advisory Committee, 1969, pp 30-3). Punitive practices were sometimes applied to households in difficulties (for instance, evicting people or dividing homeless families and taking the children into care; for an example see the same report, p 22). Control and order issues arise in all housing sectors, but in owner-occupation tend to be handled via mechanisms such as restrictive covenants or traditional legal remedies (although government can make rules, as it is doing in relation to neighbour disputes caused by excessive growth of conifers). In social renting, however, issues of order have long been integrated to some degree into management discourses.

Nonetheless, recent changes have been important. The Conservatives encouraged councils to exercise more control over tenants and 'anti-social behaviour', extended grounds for possession, and allowed 'introductory' (probationary) tenancies (see JRF, 2000d, p 3). Brown says that provisions in the 1996 Housing Act sought to "legitimise opposition to a range of previously acceptable behaviours", and introduced new ways of controlling public sector tenants. As he indicates, powers of injunction, arrest and eviction, relating to activities by visitors as well as tenants, represented a radical change (Brown, 1999, pp 75-6). Labour has added the idea of partnerships to develop a strategy for tackling crime and disorder locally and maintaining community safety, and powers for parenting orders, child curfews and anti-social behaviour orders. Housing strategy fits within government's larger programme (for comments on the 1998 Crime and Disorder Act see Charman and Savage, 1999, p 201; also Muncie, 1999). Labour seems to be increasing the roles of councils in the control of crime (see Papps, 1998, pp 652-3), and there are pressures for a stronger quasi-policing function in housing management. Multi-agency working is being emphasised, bringing closer contact with police services, with councils now expected to consider crime and disorder reduction while exercising other duties (see for example joint briefing, *Crime and disorder*, by the National Housing Federation and the Local Government Association, nd). Labour's message is that "anti-social behaviour mostly affects those communities that can least afford to pay for its consequences", and that government is "determined to root it out" (Raynsford, 2000, p 14).

We should not understate a possible fit with feelings among tenants, albeit not necessarily on detail or ways forward (cf Dwyer, 1998, pp 509-10). A disappointing landlord response to a cry for help can exacerbate stress caused by abuse or violence. Harassment may be experienced by gay men, lesbians, minority ethnic households or disabled people who (in the era of 'community care') may be living in low-status estates and have little choice about it (see Chapter Five). Housing staff themselves may be at risk of violence, while potential complainants and witnesses may face intimidation. There is certainly concern among residents as well as managers (for instance see the stance of a Tenant Management Organisation described in *Nuisance*, the newsletter of the Social Landlords Crime and Nuisance Group, March, 2000, p 13). A National Housing Federation statement points to the high risks of some crimes for residents in social rented housing estates, and to the problems generated by fear of crime (NHF, *Housing and crime: safe as houses*, 1999; cf Policy Action Team 8, 2000, pp 7, 21). Legislation can be legitimated as being about protecting people. For example, government claims a wish to put "action to combat racism at the centre of anti-social behaviour strategies" (C. Clarke, foreword to Policy Action Team 8, 2000).

The government's approaches to social order, however, have not been applauded universally. Brown argues that there is insufficient evidence of growth in anti-social behaviour, while lack of agreed definition allows inclusion of a range of activities that can "appeal to the majority as requiring action and legislation" (Brown 1999, p 77; cf Nixon and Hunter, 2000, for the range of behaviours; also Scott and Parkey, 1998, for a useful overview). Papps suggests that the emphasis is on legal remedies rather than mediation or conciliation, and on responses which have individualised the treatment of anti-social behaviour, "rather than attempting a more holistic approach by addressing the much wider issues of poor educational opportunities, high rates of unemployment and high levels of substance misuse, for example" (Papps, 1998, p 653). Actions may have perverse consequences, with eviction of disruptive tenants having negative effects elsewhere, displacing problems to the private sector (see Papps, 1998, p 651; also JRF, 2000d). Developing multi-organisational responses enlarges access to personal records and the recording and exchange of information across service boundaries. There are implications for civil liberties, while landlord/tenant relationships may be an undesirable basis for supervision, especially when there is no comparable surveillance in other tenures. Reports suggest concern about the relationship between anti-social behaviour orders and new human rights law (see *Housing Today*, 11 May 2000; *Nuisance*, December 1999, pp 14-15). It is also questionable how far overdue measures like stronger anti-racist arrangements need be focused through tenure. More generally, although prevention is acknowledged at central government level as crucial (see Policy Action Team 8, 2000, p 11), resources may not be available for a meaningful strategy (especially where this requires more housing staff 'on the ground'); and preventative tactics can be oppressive as well as supportive.

The issue of behaviour is being highlighted forcefully by some landlords. For example, a new newsletter for tenants produced by Leeds City Council's housing services department in conjunction with the tenant involvement committee carried the front page headline 'Leeds gets tough on Anti-Social Tenants' (*Housing Leeds*, 1, October 1996). The council explained changes in its tenancy agreement making it easier to take action against "the small but troublesome minority" who cause nuisance through unacceptable anti-social behaviour. Unacceptable behaviour would here include harassment, abuse, using premises for illegal or immoral purposes, engaging in unlawful activities, engaging in drug dealing or permitting others to consume or possess illegal substances, carrying out vehicle repairs, parking unroadworthy vehicles within the curtilage of dwellings, or using the premises as a scrap yard. We cannot say how typical this approach is, but there are certainly many local initiatives to address crime, conflict and behavioural issues in housing contexts, as well as to bring extra support to vulnerable residents. Examples have included a council 'gang busting team', use of injunctions excluding drug-dealers for anti-social behaviour, possession proceedings, and mediation services (see *Nuisance*, March 2000; Pearl, 1997, pp 71-5). Another idea is an estate ranger service paid for through a small addition to rents; similar developments include patrols by private police, and neighbourhood warden schemes (fifty of which are being supported by central government; see *Housing Today*, 21 September 2000). To combat crime, tenancy enforcement assistants may work as professional witnesses, enabling surveillance and monitoring of situations and estates to be planned in advance, and gathering evidence in cases which might involve serious neighbour nuisance, harassment and/or criminal activity (*Housing Today*, 11 June 1998, p 22). Meanwhile, one housing association is reported as piloting a system offering two standards of service, with 'gold service' for its 'best' tenants, including a rent discount and faster repairs for those who have had a clear rent account for six weeks and have not breached their tenancy agreement (Cooper and Hawtin, 1998, pp 72-4; *Housing Today*, 26 March 1998; see 4 May 2000 for the possibility of this system being used elsewhere).

Lettings practices can be affected by social order concerns, and pre-tenancy checks may mean liaising with organisations such as the police, and excluding offenders. It is unclear whether councils and housing associations have converged here (for implications of common housing registers see Mullins and Niner, 1998, pp 189-92). Ideas can be illustrated, however, from a 1998 letter and checklist used by an association in northern England when consulting previous landlords about prospective tenants. The association says that investigations are carried out "in response to requests from existing residents who want us to improve the quality of life on the scheme" by "tackling the issue of anti social behaviour". Questions asked include whether the applicant has been evicted and (if so) on what grounds, and if the applicant has been subject to an injunction or court order preventing them or a member of their household from causing noise nuisance or harassment to their neighbours. Other questions cover possession notices, complaints of noise nuisance, violence or threatened violence to staff, drug-related problems manifested in anti-social or illegal behaviour, damage to the dwelling, outstanding repairs bills, rent arrears, and court orders. Perhaps supply and demand changes have had paradoxical effects for landlords. On the one hand rationing processes have changed as need has been prioritised, as some overtly discriminatory practices have been discarded, and as a significant 'surplus' has emerged for some localities. One 1999 housing press report, for example, refers to "increasing competition for tenants" in some places, and is supplemented by reference to proposed demolition of a brand new estate in Newcastle "because of lack of demand" (*Housing Today*, 11 February 1999). On the other hand there is the desire to retain respectable and deserving tenants through protecting their social and physical environments, and if necessary excluding 'undesirables'. Allocation still selects and rations, even though reflecting a variety of goals (Goodwin, 1998; Bayley, 1999). Although demand in some places is falling for dwellings, demands on tenants are increasing.

Social control strategies may form parts of packages aimed at regenerating or 'turning around' difficult or unpopular estates. Cole, Kane and Robinson classify measures introduced by landlords responding to low demand, and include policing and security alongside lettings policy, stock developments, community involvement, mixed tenure initiatives, 'housing plus', marketing, management initiatives, and environmental improvements. Landlords were found "to be typically introducing packages of measures, rather than single initiatives" (Cole, Kane and Robinson, 1999, p 37). Under policing and security were sponsored police activity (for instance where landlords fund community police officers), security patrols, improved building security, anti-social behaviour response teams, neighbour dispute resolution, high profile evictions, and 'lettings checks' (Cole, Kane and Robinson, pp 41, 44).

We may add that political dissatisfactions over the composition and lifestyles of the populations of estates, allied with worries about falling demand, may lie behind interest in changing patterns of entry to create more 'mixed' estates and 'sustainable communities' (see DETR and DSS, 2000, s 9.30; Cowans, 1999; for an authoritative intervention see Murie, 2000). One practical issue in a locality studied by Cattell and Evans was the "exodus of men". A respondent remarked on how in his block he was the only one going to work, the rest being mostly single parents. In the event of problems (for example with drunks) "they all wait for me to do something about it", whereas in the past, when there were lots of men, "they'd all come out to sort out any trouble" (Cattell and Evans, 1999, p 26). The composition of estates clearly is important, yet the merits of social engineering strategies may be doubtful. Turning estates successfully into so-called 'mixed communities' (through mixed tenure, or lettings to people with less problems), might require significant 'gentrification' of an area and its facilities, and sifting of remaining low income households. In areas of housing shortage the strategy might exclude some of those in most need.

Some councils or practitioners may not wish to deploy particular new powers or procedures. For instance they may view eviction as a last resort reached only if other methods fail. Cole, Kane and Robinson provide an example where a local area manager cited youth work on a small scale as an alternative to repossession action in the courts (Cole, Kane and Robinson, 1999, p 40). Perpetrators in serious anti-social behaviour cases may themselves have multiple problems, sometimes having "particular vulnerabilities or special needs such as mental health problems or other disadvantages"and high levels of poverty (JRF, 2000d, p 3; see also the victim's and accused's stories, accompanying Nixon and Hunter, 2000). There has nonetheless been a "significant increase in landlords' use of legal remedies, with more notices seeking possession served and substantially more possession actions taken on the grounds of anti-social behaviour" (Nixon and Hunter, 2000, p 32; cf *Housing Today*, 26 October 2000). In earlier writing, Hunter and Nixon indicate that, given the focus on providing for those in greatest need, social landlords had not traditionally been so ready as mortgage lenders to commence legal action for non-payment; eviction may not lead to recovery of rent arrears (Hunter and Nixon, 1998, p 93). There may be a concern for sustaining tenancies, with implications for family welfare and children. The perceived need therefore might be for a range of support services coupled with improved management, and perhaps specialist nuisance teams or officers (JRF, 2000d). Although support shades into supervision, its goals can also be in tension with control.

The control of behaviour through landlord power illustrates four particular points about regulatory practices in housing. First, *different tenure arrangements imply differing degrees and forms of supervision*, even if neighbour nuisance is actually more tenure neutral than recent rhetoric might suggest (the differentiation connects to the social division of welfare discussed in Chapter Three). The recipient of a supposed 'gift' – especially the council tenant – may be treated differently from the person who has access through the market. The tenant is expected to behave in specific ways in return for the tenancy; this can go beyond prohibitions and even be about a compact on supporting estate life through mutual aid (M. Young, *The Guardian*, 18 September 1996; Dwyer, 1998). Papps indicates that when landlords respond to behaviour on mixed tenure estates (where sanctions available against perpetrators in privately owned properties are weaker), council tenants potentially face more punitive treatment (Papps, 1998, p 651). Conditionality is increasingly a feature of being a council tenant. Haworth and Manzi refer to "managing the underclass", citing duties that tenants have, stringent conditions in tenancy agreements, control of "unneighbourly behaviour" and use of introductory tenancies. Tenants are having to "earn their security" of tenure, proving that they deserve a settled home (Haworth and Manzi, 1999, p 161). Raynsford (Labour's Housing Minister) has indicated recently that measures government is interested in include neighbourhood agreements setting out the standard of behaviour residents are expected to maintain alongside the kind of support and services they can expect (Raynsford, 2000, p 14; cf Harriott, 1998, on 'zero tolerance in housing'). So there seems to be a notion of achievable general standards paralleling the interest in more intense regulation of selected perpetrators through surveillance, 'resettlement' and packages of services (see Policy Action Team 8, 2000, p 12). Given governmental interest in behaviour in private renting (see DETR and DSS, 2000, pp 50-2) perhaps we should not interpret changes in tenure terms alone, but should link them to wider patterns of conditionalities imposed on people receiving financial assistance from the state. Although government may not follow through on this aspect of its Green Paper, there has clearly been some wish to encourage "responsible behaviour amongst all those who receive help with their housing costs" (2000, p 52). The recent Policy Action Team report suggests an interest in more control within owner–occupation too, but the same levers are not at present available (Policy Action Team 8, 2000, see especially p 13).

A second point is that sometimes there *may be a choice between stressing the treatment of individualised deviance, threat, failure or vulnerability as against attempting a more holistic approach* addressing wider difficulties of education, unemployment, substance misuse, and low incomes. Third, there are *tensions between supportive traditions and the wish to control disruption or contain the risks to others that some people represent.* Certain individuals are dangerous, and management of high risk situations can be complex and difficult (this may be so with some instances of mental disturbance; or with abuse of partners or children). As recent events have shown, difficult questions surround the housing of sex offenders, the involvement of housing officers in processes of risk assessment and management, and the relationship which ideas about risk have with concepts of need, rehabilitation and 'care' (for insights see Cowan and Gilroy, 1999; also JRF, 1999a). It may be that anticipation of particular behaviours forms the basis of restriction (as with a curfew or a refusal to grant a tenancy), or that a label becomes applied to an individual in the interests of 'community' safety. People may be perceived as undeserving of the service, support or housing that they might expect (on the basis of their vulnerability), because of moral or risk-minimising imperatives. On the other hand, where support and supervision are inadequate because of resource shortages, some tenants with behavioural problems may indeed become intimidating and damaging neighbours (for example see N. Arksey, in *The Guardian*, 30 August 2000). Reconciling support and control requires substantial funding.

Fourth, *social order concerns will be shared with many tenants*, and intermixed with assumptions about respectability and behaviour grounded partly in material intra-class divisions and in opposition to deviant groups. The social construction of these groups may have shifted as certain types of difference have become more accepted, but there are always people seen as undesirable. As Cairncross, Clapham and Goodlad indicate, tenants may not perceive themselves as a homogeneous group (Cairncross, Clapham and Goodlad, 1997, p 107), and fragmentation within council tenure is certainly not new. There have long been differences in status between estates and tenants within estates, and we can see mutual reinforcement of 'agency' on the one hand here (reflecting household aspirations, identities, perceptions and lifestyles), and institutional factors (labelling, allocation, pricing and policing) on the other. Today, grass roots agency plays a role through resistance by tenants to their estates being seen as residual, and against inclusion of people who represent threats, such as drug dealers or abusers of children. Perhaps demands for surveillance and control may be in tension with discourses of individual tenant empowerment, but tenants themselves are disempowered by violent, racist or criminal neighbours, and control is not solely about authoritarian landlordism. Involving tenants in management might bring tensions into focus; for instance where professionals wished to maintain confidentiality about particular medical or criminal histories (such as for sex offenders). A 'respectable' tenant might seek access to information and protection on the ground that tenants have less freedom than owners to move away if their situation becomes threatened. Yet practitioners might be anxious to avoid offenders being known and thus driven into hiding, away from supervision or treatment (for issues see T. Bell and R. Forshaw, in *Housing Today*, 17 August 2000). It is worth adding that the case of sex offenders is a reminder that by no means all forms of 'difference' are entitled to equal consideration, and that certain 'cultures' are extremely dangerous to other people.

Participation and citizenship

The last twenty years have seen "dramatic changes in the rights of both local authority and housing association tenants", these rights including collective as well as individual ones (see Hood, 1997, p 96; although see also 1999). To some degree tenant participation, capacity building, user control and empowerment have become part of the rhetoric of governmental housing activity, and of the repertoires of local professional and political practice. During the Conservatives' period, stress on consumerism influenced expectations about landlord accountability, councils needed to enhance their images as providers, and difficulties posed by economic constraints, stock quality problems and neighbourhood decline seemed to require cooperation with residents. Meanwhile, grass roots pressures made inroads against paternalism. Gilroy (1998) summarises key steps, noting opportunities for tenants collectively to take over estate management through management co-ops, training and development grants for groups, and the 'right to manage'. Labour has carried developments further, requiring participation compacts to be established between councils and their tenants. The compacts are agreements between local councils and tenants setting out how tenants can get involved collectively in decisions, what councils and tenants want to achieve through compacts, and how the compact will be implemented and checked. The tenant is told that "it will give you more say in how the council manages your home" (DETR, *Tenant participation compacts: a guide for tenants*, 1999).

Writers analysing participation have focused especially on council housing estates and on areas undergoing regeneration, against a backcloth of an increase in central government interest in customer rights, charters, and so forth (for example see Gilroy, 1998; Stewart and Taylor, 1995; Niner, 1998). Although Hood (1997) provides some comparison between the two sectors, the local authority scene has generally received more coverage than housing associations in the literature (but see Ward and Lupton, 1998). Ideas have sometimes been deployed about a ladder, continuum or scale along which varying degrees of involvement can be placed, ranging from therapeutic exercises through consultative ones to actual transfers of control (see Riseborough, 1998). There have been wide-ranging, theoretically-orientated or comparative analyses of participation and empowerment (for instance Somerville, 1998; Cooper and Hawtin, 1997, 1997a, 1997b, 1998; Bengtsson and Clapham, 1997). There is also good historical material (notably Grayson, 1997), indicating the significance and character of tenants' collective action in its specific public sector housing contexts (see Hawtin and Lowe, 1998).

Distinctions may be drawn between different management approaches to participation. For example, Cairncross, Clapham and Goodlad (1997) refer to 'citizenship' and 'consumerist' approaches, the former fitting well with community development and collective empowerment through shared voice and co-operation, the latter focused on 'customer' concerns. Local provider strategies have moved in some places towards decentralisation of management and implementation, and a neighbourhood emphasis, opening the way to fuller partnership with local people (for neighbourhood management issues today, see Benjamin, Roberts and Dwelly, 2000; JRF, 2000). Individualistic and collectivist orientations may coexist among tenants, who may have an instrumentalist view towards methods of involvement (see Cairncross, Clapham and Goodlad, 1997, pp 127, 178; although also Cooper and Hawtin, 1998, p 71). What matters to councils and tenants may revolve around what appears productive in practical housing services terms. Some landlords have been less interested than others, and central government has been crucial; Riseborough observes that evidence suggests that social landlords have been directed and pressured to "do tenant involvement" as a result of central control through regulation and funding (Riseborough, 1998, p 239). In any event, there might be many circumstances where – as Cairncross, Clapham and Goodlad indicated for housing associations in 1997 – "downward accountability" remained weak (Cairncross, Clapham and Goodlad, 1997, p 14). A recent 'stocktake' of local authority activity in England (Cole et al, 2000) reveals that few authorities had a fully comprehensive approach, and notes variations between types of authorities and regions. What appears most surprising is limited penetration of some participatory practices, but the authors note that councils are drawing on an increasingly varied repertoire of methods to consult with and involve tenants. Perhaps, as Gilroy puts it, "everywhere the tenor has been shifting from viewing tenants as passive recipients of landlord bounty to customers or partners", a movement including housing associations alongside local authorities (Gilroy, 1998, p 22).

Participation in urban regeneration raises some particular issues, given the community-orientated or holistic nature of some regeneration thinking, and concerns for sustainability (see for instance Gilroy, 1998, pp 30-5). The need to gain support for community and neighbourhood regeneration exercises (and thereby to make them look convincing in bids for funds) may have hastened developments in participation. Like regeneration, services on the housing/community care boundary also raise specific issues (see Chapter Five). Within housing associations that specialise in provision for people with learning difficulties, for older people with dementia, and other vulnerable households, there has been some attention given to finding ways of involving tenants more (see Ward and Lupton, 1998, pp 188-9; although also cf JRF 1996b; for sheltered housing see Davies and Gidley, 1998, p 218).

Participation is not unproblematic. It might be interpreted as a regulatory mechanism developed to compensate the excluded, to incorporate them, or to help them play larger parts in managing their problems. Some people may not be able or wish to devote the time needed for it. Attending committees of some voluntary sector organisations, such as established housing associations, may well be difficult for women with children, as it may be for people with impaired mobility, unless provision is made to reduce barriers in terms of meeting places, times, and lack of supporting services. Although some tenants may have been "renamed as stakeholders and have been called upon to become decision makers alongside local authority officers and business people" (Gilroy, 1998, p 22), there can be an imbalance between partners. Some official exercises in participation merely target implementation rather than strategy. There may be potential conflicts within and between residents' groups, quite apart from those with professionals or councillors. Power struggles and factionalism may occur (in examining contracting for housing management services, Vincent-Jones and Harries encountered the term 'mafia'; 1998, p 61). Some observers imply that mainstream debate on community participation has neglected or marginalised 'race', class, gender, disability, age and sexuality (cf Cooper and Hawtin, 1997a). Organisations run by consumers can be as partisan and prejudiced as professionals. Occasionally, as Birchall puts it, the "motivations for forming an association are explicitly racist or elitist" (Birchall, 1997, p 184). A CRE report on tenants' associations observed that people from minority ethnic groups have been council or housing association tenants for many years, yet few "are involved in local tenants' associations, even on estates where they form a clear majority of the residents" (CRE, 1993, p 5). It notes that some tenants' associations have instigated racist activities to discourage minority ethnic families from moving into estates, or have tried to stop them from using community facilities.

Alongside the rise of participation have come increased equal opportunities expectations and rules, helping empower some households, and potentially dampening differentiation of housing citizenship experiences. Change has been stimulated by challenges from within previously excluded groups, and by laws on equal opportunities and 'race' relations, although there may be differences between UK countries as far as responses to diversity are concerned here (see MacEwen and Third, 1998, on Scotland). Monitoring and targeting within housing organisations have developed to help towards equal opportunities goals, although underdeveloped areas remain in law and practice (see for instance Smailes, 1994, pp 170-1). There have been changing preoccupations for central government and its agencies, and more official acknowledgement recently of institutionalised racisms (Macpherson, 1999; see comments in Thomas, 2000, pp 62, 108). For housing associations, as one recent report notes, Housing Corporation performance standards "emphasise the need for effective equal opportunities policies", the importance of letting homes to people in greatest housing need, and the need to provide "a responsive service to vulnerable individuals and communities". Appropriate responses to ethnic and cultural diversity may be seen as "essential to the development of Best Value" (London Research Centre and Lemos and Crane, 1998, p 1). Furthermore, there is some acceptance of forms of provision in which specific groups may play key managerial roles (notably black and minority ethnic housing associations and women's refuges), or in which self-management is emphasised (as it can be with disabled people's provision). Difference has begun to become an explicit part of professional discourse; as an aspect of needs-definition, and as a component of a more flexible notion of housing rights.

Discourses within housing organisations about household empowerment could go further in the direction of collective and individual rights. There is also considerable potential for innovation on participation (see for example Davies and Gidley, 1998, p 215, on multi-landlord based structures). Perhaps fashioning a fuller housing citizenship discourse might help in developing a more empowering housing practice (see discussion of Clapham and Dix with Griffiths, in Chapter Three). A bearer of rights is often better positioned than someone seen as a client, and there is a difference between collective involvement through participating in managing a council estate, and actually acquiring management rights on the basis of a change of ownership. Lusk indicates that the Conservatives showed consistent support for tenant-controlled organisations to manage, but not to own, their estates; Conservative support for the ownership option was shorter-lived, although he suggests that Labour will give this revived encouragement (Lusk, 1997, p 67). (For forms of collective ownership note Smith, 1997, pp 179-80.) This relates to a larger set of issues and histories to do with state neglect of options involving tenant self-management and ownership through co-ops and similar forms (for co-ops see Clapham and Kintrea, 1992). There are also questions about possibilities for other community-owned assets, such as workspaces, leisure facilities, or contracts to provide services (JRF, 2000).

Conclusions

Social regulation in UK housing is sometimes fragmented and ambiguous, especially in its non-market aspects, yet has clear effects, maintaining relatively ordered environments of constraints and options. Housing responses to difference are structured to an extent by three general factors dominating operation of the regulatory ensemble.

The first is the priority of profits, markets, social stratification, and status related to wealth and earnings. Money and markets penetrate deeply into almost all spheres of housing policy and practice, directly or indirectly, and condition, underpin or validate dominant ideologies and discourses as well as actions. The *primacy of markets, money and specific forms and distributions of property rights in UK housing provision and access is crucial.* The continuity of social divisions in housing is itself evidence of the significance of structural factors, captured in simplified form in the thought that the poor are 'always with us', and frequently homeless or living in the worst dwellings. Whatever may be the distinctions between small groups or among individual households, there is a persisting broader set of patterns of difference (thus *difference within difference*). Ideologies of economic liberalism and individualism legitimate heavily-policed selectivist approaches to many forms of provision outside the market, and continuing efforts to contain the costs of poverty for housing providers and government. Management ideas associated with private markets and commerce have penetrated increasingly into non-market spheres (for managerialism in social welfare see Newman, 1998).

The primacy of markets means that support received by poor people tends to be seen as a gift rather than a right, while non-owning or non-earning households can sometimes be cast as inferiors. This legitimates low environmental standards for council estates, and potential characterisations of elders, youth, single parents and many disabled people as less than full housing citizens. The supposedly 'non-productive' (unless they possess wealth) may become objects of therapy, conditionality and sometimes stigma, as well as support. The patterns here connect closely with labour market trends, differentials and characteristics. The 'classic' groups marginalised through labour markets have been low-paid women workers, black minority ethnic households, disabled people, low paid, unwaged or unemployed households more generally, and retired people without access to occupational pensions (including many women). Consequences are felt in restrictions on their housing choice.

Limits are also set on how far private sector actors are expected to bend their activities to cater for diversity, varying needs and risks among consumer households. *Economic liberalism inhibits chances for a regulatory ensemble building a notion of shared citizenship rights in the consumption arena across market and non-market realms.* The notion of the consumer citizen narrows to little more than a market customer. There is sometimes an assumption that while 'special' or residual needs may be met through professional or political interventions, most 'normal' needs are satisfied readily through the 'natural' means of the private market. Furthermore, if the majority require regular earnings to secure their accommodation, and carry their own risks, this maintains work incentives. Thus the creation of selective safety-net services occurs in an artificially separated realm, providing legitimacy for giving consumers in private markets inadequate attention or support. Ludicrously, private sector 'needs' may simply be translated into crude figures for developers' land supply requirements. Of course, despite the dominance of economic liberalism, market operations and outcomes are contested frequently in the political arena. This has led to governments creating controls and modifications, ranging from health and environmental standards (affecting construction), to policies designed to assist low-income purchasers (such as shared equity arrangements permitting part-purchase). Such measures, however, have not changed the broad character of market effects.

The *second factor* is *differential incorporation within welfare systems*, which was outlined in Chapter Three. The welfare ensemble through which aspects of consumption are managed has helped confirm the differentiated citizenship status of households, incorporating some established groups more satisfactorily than those of lower standing, albeit bringing much-needed support to many on low incomes. The social division of welfare has contributed to the "spatial division of welfare" (Harrison, 1995), and to social segregation. The fragmentation of forms of housing assistance – ranging from means-tested support to tax reliefs – has had the effect of reinforcing political and socioeconomic divisions. Channels of welfare designed for 'residual problems' or 'special needs' may take centre stage in political debate, thereby legitimating lack of attention for the larger picture, and helping conceal the limited nature of the blunting of market effects that has occurred through the overall welfare system. There are many political results from the ongoing welfare ensemble. For example, Clapham and Smith indicate that 'special needs' provision played a crucial role in "legitimising neo-liberal housing policy during the 1980s" (Clapham and Smith, 1990, p 204). Provided that processes of relative incorporation satisfy enough middle class and better-off working class constituents, housing problems can be portrayed politically as discrete and technical, open to solution through highly selective targeting rather than through more general attempts to improve overall conditions of supply, quality and costs. Yet selectivity has failed to solve persistent problems of poor housing, homelessness and affordability. Historically, among the relative losers were many minority ethnic households, disabled people and single parents. Private markets are often crucial in welfare system ensembles, and it would be foolish to focus on the 'decommodified' or non-market side of welfare as if it constituted the sole feature by which to examine and distinguish a social welfare system or 'regime' (see Chapter Eight). In Britain owner-occupation is no longer a secure haven, and funding and consumer rights here are important for housing welfare.

The *third factor* reinforces and overlaps with aspects of the other two. It is a *cluster of entrenched practices and ideas* through which there is *pressure for forms of social integration* to ensure order, while *certain kinds of difference are managed by institutions as 'otherness' or failure*. People may be seen as different from some assumed norm. Thus, for example, given the primacy of paid employment, we find the non-earner or low earner the subject of policies to meet or manage 'need'. Some disabled people may be seen as appropriate targets for various 'interventions' in their lives. For a range of low-income groups surrogate systems develop, not only to sustain life (albeit paying regard to a moral ranking of the deserving), but also to influence behaviour and ration resources among those for whom labour market disciplines and incentives cannot be relied upon (especially in periods of increased social polarisation). Boundaries of nation and membership are drawn to downgrade claims of 'outsiders'. Although certain types of assistance are 'life-lines' for disadvantaged people, policies may respond to wishes of the better-placed to maintain their socioeconomic distance (or to desires for a social order and forms of assistance that can mute disruptions), as well as to effective resistance and challenge from grass roots interests among marginalised people themselves.

As housing demonstrates, established discourses cast need in particular forms, confirm the special status of certain groups (positively or negatively), and create deep ambiguities in some welfare systems, highlighting discipline, conditionality and paternalism along with assistance and support. Selectivist systems targeted on the poor are a crucial part of this, frequently vulnerable to meanness, stigmatisation, and dependency on professional power. They are also subject to new managerialist devices increasingly permeating practice, sometimes substituting ideas about competition or organisation of tasks for fuller resources, and deflecting energies away from concerns with welfare. Furthermore, 'otherness' is sometimes treated as something not to celebrate but to control, oppose, integrate in a subordinated way or separate off. Integrationist perspectives in service delivery may disregard some of people's central experiences (such as disablist or racist treatment), and undermine knowledge, skills and solidarities that groups have (cf Penketh and Ali, 1997, pp 110-11). Conversely, where difference is acknowledged it may sometimes become a focus for managerialist strategies diverting attention from wider inequalities.

Agency, challenge and change

As we have indicated previously, structure is not merely about oppressions, so that environments for housing 'careers' and strategies can be enabling and supportive as well as restrictive and oppressive. Furthermore, despite the powerful influence of structural factors, the practices of institutions in the housing field are open to modification, while interpretations and applications of public policies are affected by numerous ongoing interactions between people. As this chapter has confirmed, although constraints and opportunities are highly ordered, the landscape for consumers is very complicated, not least in the non-market sectors. One of the reasons for complexity within regulatory outcomes is the multi-dimensional and multi-directional nature of human agency and its effects. There are many ways in which agency influences how the structural becomes the specific and detailed. Struggles take place not merely against institutions but within, for, or between them and (overtly or less so) between different interests among consumers. Mobilisation of bias and agenda-setting processes frequently benefit better-off households, and difference remains highly regulated partly because of demands for particular kinds of order, and competing expectations about status and rewards. On the other hand, boundaries developed or managed around difference may be challenged through collective action under the banners of empowerment or citizenship. Social welfare movements (such as the black voluntary housing movement, or tenants' movements) may operate or take shape in the distinctive social, political and administrative environments of social regulation (see Harrison, 1995; cf Hawtin and Lowe, 1998, p 27). As we shall see in the next chapter, ideas related to rights and citizenship can have considerable potential relevance for grass roots challenges.

FIVE

Disability and housing

This chapter comments on housing circumstances for disabled people, considers market and non-market provision, discusses universal and inclusive standards, and concludes with observations about change, citizenship and self-management. First, however, we position ourselves in relation to general debates about disabling environments, and emphasise the importance of disabled people's ideas and campaigns.

Disability is understood below as something resulting from persistent devaluing of people with impairments, their exclusion from good incomes and jobs, and lack of concern for their needs in the arrangement of physical spaces and social networks. This perspective derives primarily from advocates of the social model of disability who challenged earlier formulations within medicalised or individualised accounts in which disability was presented as an attribute of particular people deviating from a supposed physical norm (see Barnes, 1994, p ix; Oliver and Barnes, 1998). In very immediate senses individuals feel limitations from an impairment, and physical or sensory impairment may trigger disadvantage in labour markets or in access to aspects of social life. Yet societal responses are also crucial, and varied over time and place, for disability is "culturally produced and socially structured" (Oliver, 1990, p 22). We do not think of disability as located in the individual, as a characteristic defined by a medical condition or functional limitations. Rather, we see it as a product of social and environmental processes which constitute people as disabled.

This is not to deny the importance of impairment or illness, or the diversity of individual feelings about these. Chronic illness may influence daily living, social relationships, and people's sense of who they are. Impairment may bring pain, fatigue, and depression, but also positive attributes, while an individual's sense of difference related to this may be an important part of identity (see discussion in Crow, 1996; Morris, 1991, pp 17-18; cf Allen, 1998, pp 96, 102). We also accept that some people experiencing mental distress or behavioural difficulties might be a worry to others, to a degree independent of societal structures (or the social construction of mental health). In tandem with the social model's use of 'disability', therefore, 'specific impairments' refers to people's distinctive physical, mental, health or socio-medical attributes, often generating particular preferences or needs, and lying along a continuum on which everyone has a place. The word 'impairment' is not entirely satisfactory, sometimes taking on a judgemental tone, while norms about specific human functions are to a degree socially constructed (so that impairment is not just a physical matter). Nonetheless, we intend as neutral a meaning as possible below. Impairments of faculties or functions are relative, of varied severity, changing, sometimes temporary, and diverse. Yet some impairments do not become disabling or may remain unseen, and reactions to them are crucial. For example, in Western societies it may be more socially accepted today that some people do not have children, and infertility as an impairment is less stigmatised than in the past (although it can still bring pain akin to the sense of loss brought about by bereavement). Traditional attitudes to family bear less heavily on the childless now, and are thus less disabling. Meanwhile, social attitudes to ageing can sometimes magnify relatively minor functional limitations, constructing older age generally in such a manner as to assume serious inadequacies in a range of capacities, and affecting responses to elders. Thus older age has a potential in western societies to be made disabling in itself.

In effect we can refer to two dimensions captured in the notion of *difference within difference* introduced in earlier chapters: complex experiential diversity on the one hand, within (on the other) a more longstanding pattern of disadvantage based around societal responses to difference between the supposedly 'able-bodied' and some of the less so. Thus diversity of impairments, experiences and preferences among disabled people does not preclude awareness of broader and longlasting factors in social policy environments that may empower or disempower them (cf Pinder's reference to "the multiple voices which are in our midst", and "the experience of difference-within-difference"; 1997, p 279). Disability is also cross-cut by divisions of ethnicity, gender and sexuality, giving rise in some cases to complex multiply-faceted experiences of disadvantage (for simultaneous oppression see Campbell and Oliver, 1996, chapter 7). In addition, the socioeconomic distribution of ill-health and impairment may itself be related to differential exposure – from before birth and across the lifespan – to risks associated with socioeconomic positions. Impairment is not randomly distributed, but is influenced by economic status (cf Oliver, 1990, pp 13-14). Thus the very personal incidences of illness or impairment may be affected by structural factors, quite apart from the latter's impact in confirming broad patterns in which specific impairment or limitation is subject to disabling practices (and in contributing to the social construction of specific impairments).

At the same time, given our comments in earlier chapters about structure/agency relationships, we perceive agency playing diverse roles in the ongoing development of structure here. Structural factors can confirm barriers both to 'doing' and to 'being' (the latter referring to the realm of ideas and self-identities) (cf Thomas, 1999a, p 60), influencing people's responses to impairment. Yet those individual and collective responses in turn influence the development of factors maintaining, constructing or reshaping disability itself. Furthermore, experiential narratives "offer a route in to understanding the socio-structural" (Thomas, 1999a, p 78), as well as perhaps revealing possibilities for positive strategies and forms of resistance.

The social model of disability referred to above is important politically, clarifying the significance of rights and barriers. Barnes refers to the disabled people's movement as one of the most potentially potent political forces in contemporary British society (foreword to Campbell and Oliver, 1996), and its capacity to transform a "disabling culture and welfare system into a celebratory and liberating one" has been highlighted (Oliver and Barnes, 1998, p 76). The development and articulation of the social model focusing on disabling environments has played a significant part (Campbell and Oliver, 1996, p 20; Barnes, Mercer and Shakespeare, 1999). Rights to independence, social interaction and choice have been crucial issues, with disabled people challenging their segregation and the perceptions of them as individualised subjects for concern or supervision rather than active players.

Housing and disabling environments

Housing is a potential component in disabling or enabling environments, through its physical characteristics, administration and finance. People experiencing chronic illness and impairment encounter restrictions and barriers in physical environments that contribute to conditioning their lifestyles, and may affect possibilities of their interacting with other people. Most housing has not been designed with older age or impairment in mind, and domestic environments often inhibit effective self-management of illnesses or impairments, and may exacerbate a condition. Inconveniences of particular homes burden households and reinforce dependencies, affecting disabled people and their relatives. Furthermore, a dwelling may be poorly-suited as a base for a particular package of support from health or social services. Housing affects lifestyle options, and comforts or difficulties of daily experience. Whereas good environmental design can be inclusive, inviting the widest possible range of users, at its worst the built environment represents almost an 'assault course' that threatens independence and social integration (Barker, Barrick and Wilson, 1995, p 10; cf Imrie, 1996, p 164). Drawing on a valuable study focused on housing experiences of disabled children, Oldman and Beresford suggest that the message of the social model is compelling in the case of housing; for "it is the house, its steps and stairs, its too narrow doorways, its overall standardised design, its lack of space, etc. which creates disability" (Oldman and Beresford, 2000, p 430).

Housing has taken on increasing importance as the relative significance of older age and chronic illness has grown (see discussion in Bury, 1997, pp 112-16, 120-1), shifting the age-distribution of disability and chronic illness within the population as a whole, with the home being a crucial location for managing health in older age. This is not to suggest that housing is the central causative variable; many other determinants also operate, including people's incomes, networks, and available support. These factors interact with disabled people's strategies in general, and their approach to managing their specific impairments. Nonetheless, many disabled people depend greatly upon the home or immediate locality, because of problems of physical accessibility elsewhere, mobility and money, or because of constraints placed on their lifestyles by attitudes of non-disabled people. Inadequate housing facilities, space, siting, security and design are very important, and can give 'home' some negative meanings. This applies for people with a wide range of impairments, sensory, mental or physical.

Disabled people and their housing circumstances

According to the Department for Education and Employment (DfEE, 2000), disabled people account for nearly a fifth of the working-age population in Britain, and for about one eighth of all in employment. As the department puts it, there are over 6.5 million people with a current "long-term disability or health problem" with a substantial adverse impact on their day-to-day activities or limiting "the work they can do". Between 50,000 and 100,000 people in Britain have been "disabled" for more than twenty years (JRF, 1993a). Overall rates of impairment rise with age (see DfEE, 2000), particularly with older age. At the same time young people and those of 'working age' are affected by impairment or illness. For instance, a recent claim is that one in five children suffers 'mental stress', while over 91 million working days are said to be 'lost' to mental ill-health every year (*Fundamental Focus*, the Mental Health Foundation, April, 1999). Although arthritis is often regarded as a condition of old age, over 12,000 children and a million people under the age of forty-five are estimated to be affected by it (for discussion see JRF, 1992). Data on numbers experiencing specific impairments can be problematic, given choices of identification or definition (note Abberley, 1991). The lives of supportive relatives are also relevant, so that numbers influenced by disablement are far greater than estimates of impairment. Nonetheless, figures can be useful even if qualified. Barker, Barrick and Wilson, for example, indicate that "the number of adults who are blind or partially sighted" has been "conservatively estimated at nearly one million", with visual impairment affecting around one in seven of those aged over 75 (Barker, Barrick and Wilson, 1995, pp 8-9).

Disabled people are often poorly housed and the labour market plays a crucial role in this. They are over six times as likely as non-disabled people to be out of work and claiming benefits, although many want to work. When employed, they are more likely to work part-time, be self-employed, or occupy poorly paid jobs (DfEE, 2000; JRF, 1991; Oliver and Barnes, 1998, p 43). Thus many lack purchasing power within private housing markets. A disabled person may also have extra expenses in daily life which do not arise for an able-bodied person (costs of medical contacts and drugs, transport, or maintenance and adaptations of the environment). Furthermore, lower-income families are more likely to include a disabled child than higher-income families (Oldman and Beresford, 1998, p 11). Unsurprisingly, as a group, disabled people tend to be "disproportionately reliant on social housing", although this is also where there are some affordable accessible dwellings (Laurie, 1991, p 24).

Specific groups are very under-supplied with suitable dwellings. For example, it has been reported that large numbers of people with mental health problems are inappropriately housed, with a need for more independent housing, with support, in self-contained accommodation rather than shared housing (see King, 1998). There may be hidden problems of homelessness, with some unable to leave institutions, hospitals, or the parental home. Provision for people with learning difficulties has been described as "among the most threadbare", with supported housing providers setting up their schemes "around the patchy benefits system rather than responding to need" (Weaver, 1998). Fiedler has referred to a 'living options' lottery, since the amount and kind of help a disabled person has received has been "determined less by need than by chance" (Fiedler, 1988, p 5). As far as children are concerned, it is believed that around 150,000 families in Britain include a severely disabled child, substantial numbers live in housing that is cold, damp or in poor repair, limited play space affects many families, and there are sometimes difficulties with stairs, and a lack of room for storing essential equipment (JRF, 1998d, 1998h; Oldman and Beresford, 1998, pp 13-28). Such circumstances may have an impact both on the pressures experienced by parents or siblings and the degree of independence the child can achieve.

Studies tackling minority ethnic housing needs have noted the importance of disability or chronic illness (for example Ratcliffe, 1996; Gidley, Harrison and Robinson, 1999). Begum (in research touching on housing while covering Asian disabled people) points generally to the "dual impact of race and disability", often placing people in a unique, and "particularly disadvantaged position" (Begum, 1992, p 13). Interestingly, 70% of Asian disabled people and carers here were in owner-occupied properties, which we might take as a reminder that tenure variation by ethnicity may be an issue to bear in mind in respect of strategies to assist disabled households. A Rowntree study by Zarb and Oliver (see JRF, 1993a) found that older disabled people from black minority ethnic communities are more likely than their white counterparts to face problems like extreme isolation and very low incomes. A recent report suggests considerable and growing need for sheltered bed-spaces, very sheltered units, aids, adaptations and residential care among Asian elders in London (Sandhu, 1999). For the other end of the age range, Chamba, Ahmad, Hirst, Lawton and Beresford have noted institutionalised racism, lack of consultation with black communities, and stereotypical beliefs about black families as problems previously identified within service provision to black families with a disabled child (Chamba et al, 1999, p 1). In their research these authors point to financial hardship, and to other problems faced by minority ethnic parents with disabled children, including the unsuitability of much of the housing they live in (Chamba et al, 1999, pp 6-8). Contrary to stereotypes about minorities, it may not be feasible to receive support from an extended family (Chamba et al, 1999, p 18). Furthermore, hostilities outside the home may occur just as for a white disabled child. As one respondent is quoted as stating, "My son is beaten up by neighbourhood children, because of the way he is" (Chamba et al, 1999, p 7). Indeed, racisms might add to such problems.

Market and non-market provision

Having provided a brief reminder of the large numbers of people with significant impairments, and of some of the housing difficulties they face, we now consider how institutions and practices respond. It is important to mention private market design and provision. The limited financial impact of disabled people is one reason why private developers have been so uninterested over the years in making owner-occupied housing convenient and accessible (for problems of access to finance see Chapter Four). British governments have been slow to develop legislation and codes to ensure equal treatment or raise environmental standards in market-dominated contexts (although see below for grants, building regulations and anti-discrimination legislation). Private sector organisations have few obligations, and speculative builders may build for general markets rather than specific clients, minimising risks of losses through marketing strategies which are unlikely to focus on impairment except in unusual cases (cf Easterlow, Smith and Mallinson, 2000, p 376). Even a swift glance at estate agents' literature is enough to reveal deficiencies such as difficult steps or narrow doorways (although bungalows cater for certain needs at a price). Many design features are difficult or expensive to change. The picture is often worse for older dwellings, but even in new flats designed especially for wealthier retired elders, limited attention may be given to adaptations or other ways of meeting changing needs. Developers may make adequate arrangements if profitable. Private landlords' and individual owner-occupiers' concerns are also frequently with profits and risk-minimisation. Publicly funded adaptations may be removed prior to sale of a dwelling, their existence being felt to prejudice marketability. Such practices clearly inhibit 'recycling' of adaptations (and might sometimes apply also in social rented housing) (JRF, 1995).

Non-market provision no longer locates disabled people in the parish workhouse as dependent 'others', outside the normality represented by ordinary housing and labour markets (see Timms, 1998, p 69; Oliver, 1990, pp 32-6; Lund, 1996, pp 159-60). Instead, in modern times the term 'special needs' has been used, often identifying distinctive housing issues, and the desirability of relatively intensive forms of housing management or highly specific design requirements, although not without continuing dangers of singling out groups as personally lacking in some way, or segregating them (see Clapham and Smith, 1990; cf Garside, 1993, pp 320-2). Ideas about 'special needs' on the housing/social care interface have been affected by developments in 'community care'. In governmental terms the latter covers services and support for people affected by problems of ageing, mental illness, mental 'handicap', or physical or sensory impairment, to enable them to live as independently as possible in their own homes, or in 'homely' settings in the community. Social housing landlords also rent ordinary housing to disabled people, and provide adapted or purpose-built dwellings catering for particular requirements of specific impairments. There has also been highly institutionalised accommodation tied in with health services, although less favoured by recent governments. Below we discuss selected issues in non-market provision in more detail under three headings.

Local authority duties and social rented tenancies

Local authorities have long had statutory obligations to disabled people, including housing duties under the 1970 Chronically Sick and Disabled Persons Act to "have regard to the special needs of chronically sick or disabled persons" (Ch 44, S.3). (Scotland has had specific legislation.) The 1970 provisions, however, now "sit within the wider scope of the new community care arrangements arising from the NHS and Community Care Act 1990" (Bull and Watts, 1998, p 19). The legislative backcloth to provision for disabled people has been affected by policies on social services' powers and duties, children in need, carers, and improvement grants (Bull and Watts, 1998). Homelessness legislation has also been relevant, although it is unclear how far local policies have taken disabled people's needs into account (for homelessness and mental health see Bhugra, 1996). Government favours giving 'reasonable preference' to (among others) households consisting of or including someone with a particular need for settled accommodation on medical or welfare grounds. 'Settled accommodation' is relevant, for example, for visually impaired people, as it can take upwards of two years to acquire familiarity with their environment and surrounding locality (RNIB, *Housing Service Newsletter*, Spring 1997, p 8, briefing on the Housing Act 1996). Although homelessness arrangements appear to cater for people 'vulnerable' as a result of old age, illness or impairment, councils' restrictive rules nonetheless may have adverse effects. A Shelter report describes one case where a 74-year old man with severe impairment was evicted from his council tenancy as rent arrears had built up, because his 'live-in carer' had failed to pay in the rent taken from him. He applied as homeless and was eventually housed in a hostel unsuitable for his needs. Apparently, although wishing to move into sheltered accommodation he was on the council's exclusions list because of the past arrears (Goodwin, 1998, p 28).

Local authority and housing association general rented housing allocation has been influenced by medically-based assessments. Smith and Mallinson state that the idea of prioritising 'medical' needs in housing access and allocation has "always been popular among local authorities", and the system of medical priority for rehousing is one element in "a suite of housing services available to people with health, mobility and support needs in any given area" (Smith and Mallinson, 1997, p 179). The supply of appropriate accommodation, however, may be outstripped by demand (Smith and Mallinson, 1997, pp 184-5), while unless a disabled person is assessed as having a high medical priority, he or she may not be rehoused, and being disabled and in ill-health are not the same. In some instances an applicant's present housing may be unsuitable because it is restricting rather than because it makes a 'condition' worse, and an emphasis on severity of condition could be misleading. (For discussion see Derbyshire, 1998, pp 61-2.) In any event, availability of affordable and appropriate tenancies remains important. The declining supply of decent council accommodation (see earlier chapters), and local residualisation processes, may mean people with support needs having to be allocated to unsuitable accommodation on run-down, unsafe estates. Such circumstances exacerbate vulnerability, undermining the benefit of any support provided. In one area Arblaster, Conway, Foreman and Hawtin were told that "very vulnerable elderly are constantly being burgled and victimised" (Arblaster et al, 1996, p 11; for children see Oldman and Beresford, 1998, pp 14-15). Hard-to-let properties provide a poor base for people with learning difficulties, mental health problems or physical impairments (cf Watson, 1997). This side-effect of residualisation has not featured much in public debates (for the importance of location see especially Lund and Foord, 1997, pp 36-46).

Output of specialised units has been far more important in relative terms within local authority (and RSL) completions than within market sector production. 'Wheelchair standard' housing has incorporated extra space and design standards required by permanent wheelchair users, while 'mobility standard' has referred to design criteria developed from ordinary standards in the direction of greater convenience and adaptability (see Bull and Watts, 1998, pp 20-1; Dodd, 1998, pp 152-5). Numbers of fully accessible dwellings have been relatively small, with a particular shortage of units with more than one bedroom for disabled people with families, or for single people with personal assistants (JRF, 1991; Oliver and Barnes,

1998, pp 45-6). Lund and Foord note that wheelchair/mobility housing production has declined as council building has diminished (Lund and Foord, 1997, p 25). Housing associations, dominant in newbuild in the last decade, did not set themselves very demanding targets for accessibility (see MacFarlane and Laurie, 1996, p 38), although some specialist providers have strong records. Estimates have been offered of the numbers of 'accessible' dwellings needed (for example Rostron, 1995, pp 35-6), but depend heavily on methodology (see Stewart, Harris and Sapey, 1998).

Provision on the housing/social care/health services interface

The term 'community care' covers varied activities related to a range of 'recipients', while 'social care' implies a still wider range of interventions. The exact meaning of the word 'community' here is potentially contentious (see Goodlad, 1993, p 131), but has connotations to do with locality, home, and close social (family) relationships. Notions of 'care' are also open to question, especially if implying dependency and custodial roles (cf Oliver and Barnes, 1998, p 38). Nonetheless, the favoured idea of people 'remaining' in the community contrasts strongly with life within residential socio-medical institutions, even if the extent to which it should imply wider mobilisations of collective community resources is uncertain. There is a view that community care has been very much about containing costs, with allied criticisms of funding arrangements and marketisation (for interesting interpretations see Allen, 1997, pp 93-6). Furthermore, support in the community can be difficult to provide (cf Spicker, 1989, p 101), and problems have arisen in collaboration across departmental and organisational boundaries (see for example Arblaster et al, 1996; note Shaw, Lambert and Clapham, 1998, p 7). Nonetheless, local social services and housing departments have been expected to work together and in consultation with health authorities, other housing providers and the voluntary sector, to plan community care services, and to make arrangements for assessment of the care needs of individuals and provision of services on the basis of these (see Goodlad, 1993, p 133; Reid, 1995, p 144). Housing requirements should be dealt with as part of needs assessment (Hudson, Watson and Allan, 1996, p 1; JRF, 1998). Housing is clearly an important foundation for assistance, one of the keys to independent living; issues of housing and support are, as Franklin says, "inextricably related" (Franklin, 1998, p 166). This does not mean that housing strategies or services have been effectively or comprehensively integrated with social care, but the desirability of this has been recognised (for analysis see Lund and Foord, 1997). As Smith and Mallinson put it:

> Although housing has been a relatively neglected aspect of the shift to community care, it is increasingly clear that in principle the whole philosophy of deinstitutionalisation is predicated on the availability of adequate, adaptable and affordable accommodation in the community for those with care and support needs. (Smith and Mallinson, 1997, p 178; cf JRF, 2000b)

More negatively, it might perhaps be argued that because housing in 'the community' appeared to offer politicians a vehicle for saving public expenditure on other forms of support, the real potential cost implications of the strategy have never been faced, so that housing's roles have remained under-developed.

The idea of support linked to housing can be interpreted variously. 'Supported housing' might include sheltered housing, hostels, and (planned) shared housing, targeted at groups for whom a range of support services may be offered. Government policy and funding have been important in developing and helping shape this housing, although there have been difficulties over finance (see for example Means and Smith, 1996, pp 13-14). Some accommodation has been offered as part of a package integrating housing and support, as in the case of sheltered housing for older people. An appropriate package for elders today might potentially range from conventional sheltered or 'very sheltered' accommodation, through alternatives such as dispersed accommodation served by community alarm systems, to care and repair schemes and aids and adaptations to help people stay in their own homes. Tinker, Wright and Zeilig note that by the end of the 1980s difficult-to-let sheltered housing was being identified as a problem (Tinker, Wright and Zeilig, 1995, p 1); there may be over-provision of traditional or ordinary sheltered housing, and under-provision of very sheltered housing with extra-care support (DoE, 1994).

When thinking about 'support' in housing contexts, however, it is important not to be mesmerised by the idea of a specific supported housing stock. We can look across a wider range of housing circumstances, including owner-occupation, unadapted council housing, and so forth. As Crawford and Foord warn, the importance of "well designed, suitably located, normal housing", which can be adapted to meet new and changing needs, is "consistently under-emphasised" (Crawford and Foord,

1997, p 98). Ideally, types of supported housing are best thought of as parts of a continuum of available forms including very ordinary dwellings (see for instance Spicker's list of six main kinds of options appropriate for psychiatric patients with differing needs; 1989, p 102). Specific circumstances of an individual can be crucial. Supported accommodation may relate to a variety of clients and needs (see Franklin's summary of the range, 1998, pp 168-9). When accessible accommodation is separated off into purpose-designed schemes, as 'special needs' housing, residents may be unable to choose who they live near, or be grouped on the basis of a medical evaluation of specific impairments (whatever else they might have in common), and may have to accept standardised packages of services and resources. It has been argued that, in the past, organisations run by non-disabled people made faulty strategic decisions, such as targeting provision on residential homes rather than buying houses and letting them to disabled tenants (see Mason, in Campbell and Oliver, 1996, p 43). Macfarlane and Laurie note that separate 'special needs' provision is often geographically distinct from ordinary housing, and "denies disabled people the opportunity and right to participate in remunerative employment and fulfilling personal relationships" (Macfarlane and Laurie, 1996, pp 8, 23). They argue that the 'special needs' approach creates "ghettos of disabled people", and sets up "an expensive hierarchy of buildings, administration and professional specialists" (Macfarlane and Laurie, 1996, p 8). There can certainly be heavy commitment to fixed capital investment.

Social care traditions tend to classify in ways that can sometimes stigmatise people, and even affect their sense of self-identity and dependence. Means notes some classification processes in housing, allocating people to discrete categories of impairment or social situation. One may be expected to define oneself as "an alcohol abuser, a young homeless person or someone with a mental health problem", but one is "not meant to be all three" (Means, 1996, p 217). People cut across categories, but have to present themselves a particular way in order to get help. They may be defined very much by what they are assumed unable to do, rather than being seen as complete actors with their own ideas and attributes. Although many disabled and older people require a combination of housing and support services, or an adapted dwelling, their basic housing needs are similar to other people's. Needs can change over lifetimes, but some requirements may be very much normal attributes of ageing. Focusing on 'special' needs may make it look as if there is a small finite problem involving a group with medical or physical characteristics, for whom an essentially technical housing solution can be designed. Everyone else can then have 'normal' houses. Many older or disabled people, however, have a preference for access to mainstream housing (provided it caters for individual needs and is linked with adequate support) rather than segregated services (Means and Smith, 1996, pp 6-7). People with impairment may also want to be owner-occupiers, although low incomes and other factors limit options (see Chapter Four; also Kestenbaum, 1996, p 8). Using the term 'specialised housing' (as for example in DoE, 1994) may be more reasonable than thinking of special needs accommodation. Almost all dwellings are adapted to their occupiers' requirements, and become specialised; some are just more specialised than others. Isolating 'special needs' cases as a small minority issue may also work against prevention and adequate services. Given more resources, policies might aim at protective, proactive or preventative measures, rather than just targeting clients struggling to stay put or facing imminent crisis (see Harrison and Means for the intensive/extensive debate; 1990, pp x, 30-31; also JRF, 1999). Furthermore, as Watson observes, the "narrow reach" of community care needs assessment leaves many people without access to organised support services, although their requirements may be recognised by practitioners (Watson, 1997, p 4).

Despite the reservations about a focus on 'special needs', there is likely to be continuing demand for dedicated supported housing, which might be superior to more fully institutionalised and paternalistically controlled accommodation. The lack of adequate provision following deinstitutionalisation has probably contributed to homelessness. As so often in UK housing, there is a shortage of affordable accommodation or services in the right places and under the right conditions. Claims have been voiced about large numbers of 'chronically mentally ill' people becoming homeless, with 'backlash' in the shape of "disproportionate concerns about the dangerousness of recently discharged psychiatric patients" (see McNaught and Bhugra, 1996; Joseph, 1996, p 92).

The Labour government is making alterations under the title 'Supporting People', described as "the most radical change in the funding of housing and support services to date" (Raynsford, 2000a; cf DETR, 2000). The claim is that this will put funding and development of housing and support services on a more secure and coordinated basis, separating funding for support services from housing benefit, and allowing councils a "single pot of money to spend on services needed by vulnerable people in their area" (Raynsford, 2000a, p 16). There is endorsement for cross-service integration, a wider range of support services, greater flexibility, and the breaking of the link of support services to accommodation. Government clearly acknowledges the importance of people being helped to remain in their own homes if they wish, and of helping people leaving care and institutions (DETR, 2000). Policy reflects understanding that issues run across tenures and types of accommodation. It remains to be seen how far budgetary constraints diminish, and whether changes in channels of funding will damage interests of any independent or politically unpopular projects.

People-centred approaches

Strategies which are more definitely people-centred have developed, indicated by the terms 'assisted' or 'supported' living, with diverse innovations moving away from providing specific properties (or a pre-determined package based around this) towards more recognition of individual choice and support in existing homes (see for example JRF, 1997). It is accepted that often people should not need to move accommodation in order to gain support, although progress may depend on how far revenue funding becomes adjusted to user-centred forms of provision (JRF, 1994). Approaches have included 'floating support' (moving intensive support in and out of self-contained accommodation or a mainstream tenancy as and when needed), outreach care teams (offering home care to older people), the 'home-link model' (providing permanent housing and low-level practical support to people with enduring mental health problems, and including mutual support networks), and reliance on non-disabled 'support tenants' (sharing the home with the disabled person and able to provide or seek assistance as necessary) (for example see Franklin, 1998, pp 176-7; Herklots, 1991). Other approaches have involved small distributed groups supported by someone living 'round the corner' (or 'living support networks'), or 'life-sharing' based on enabling people with learning difficulties to live with non-disabled people on an equal basis (JRF, 1995a; JRF, 1993b). The innovations imply some separating out of housing and support, flexible combinations of the two, and less dependence on a particular residential model. Simons and Ward (in JRF, 1997) indicate that people's links – their family, friends, community – can be the starting point in designing services, not an afterthought.

Integral with the ideal of people-centred services is the theme of independence (see Watts and Galbraith, 1998). This does not imply performing every task directly for oneself, but involves having control over one's life, having assistance as and when required, and exercising control over the way help is planned and delivered (cf Fiedler, 1991, p 87). The home is important here. Franklin refers to the importance people attach to events which demonstrate the significance of the attainment of 'self actualisation', giving examples such as an instance when someone leaves an institution to be rehoused in the community, and may have a sense of satisfaction conveyed by such markers as being given one's own key, or having privacy to see visitors (Franklin, 1998, p 165). There may be professional or financial constraints on self-determination, but limits to personal physical independence need not imply loss of control over living. Disabled people are the same as most others in wanting independent control of accommodation and services. Independence may mean people putting together and managing their own care packages, provided that funding mechanisms are adequate, and that monies offered them do not reflect attempts to get services provided 'on the cheap' (Kestenbaum, 1996, p 23). Users might be involved individually or collectively, or through a representative agent, in controlling and managing personal assistance, with managing organisations actively involving disabled people themselves (and relatives and private carers when appropriate). Collaborative care can mean a scheme run collectively on an independent basis, such as one described by Tennyson (1991), self-managed in a housing cooperative, with a diverse membership including people with physical and mental impairments. For many people relatively 'low-level' support is the prerequisite for independence. Means and Smith, citing earlier work, illustrate what could be required to achieve maximum independence; such as giving detailed thought to housing maintenance, personal safety, and access from the dwelling to other facilities or places (Means and Smith, 1996, p 7).

An important development in the late 1980s was the setting up of the Independent Living Fund, to provide regular monthly payments to a small number of disabled people who had personal assistance requirements (for this and prior developments see Oliver and Barnes, 1998, pp 83-7; also Morris, 1993, p 5). Direct payments have proved popular and increased quality of life (for discussions of practices and issues relating to personal assistance and direct payments see Kestenbaum, 1996; Laurie, 1991; DeJong, 1984, pp 64-6). Subsequent legislation gave councils power to make payments to community care users for purchasing their own support. Cash payments to disabled people can be seen as being in lieu of community care services they have been assessed as needing, enabling them to appoint and manage carers and have direction of support staff (Bull and Watts, 1998, p 25) (albeit that success might be subject to adequacy of available personnel, or employment and management arrangements). As Morris points out, the issue of personal assistance has been a key focus within the aims of the Independent Living Movement (Morris, 1993, p 7), which works to enable disabled people to participate fully in society (see Oliver and Barnes, 1998; Priestley 1999). This movement (with international connections) has created specific successes through centres for independent (or integrated) living, has a holistic response to disability which includes demands for human and civil rights, and has developed an integrated living philosophy around various core areas of need. Expectations include having control over the basic parts of daily living, but reach beyond these to aspects of social and community life. The movement has several centres in the UK (see generally Priestley, 1999, pp 69-80; Kestenbaum, 1996; contributions in Laurie, 1991).

Disabled people can also be involved as users in development or running of more 'traditional' services by provider organisations, with channels ranging from conventional participation practices to professional, volunteer or peer advocacy support for people who are unable fully to represent their own interests directly (Kestenbaum, 1996, pp 28-34). Disabled people's organisations have pressed for more involvement, self-determination and self-management, which are logical elements of people-centred approaches. User-centred approaches are essential if providers want to meet real needs sensitively. With consumers sometimes geographically dispersed, and socially or culturally varied, their preferred solutions "are personal and particular to them" (Sapey, 1995, p 83), making consultation crucial. Furthermore, disabled people often develop high levels of expertise about impairments, knowing what they need and how it should be delivered (cf Bury, 1997, pp 126-7). Community care clients can be at the centre of the assessment process, and encouraged to articulate needs and express choice, even though this may conflict with professional preoccupations (for aspects of professional dominance see Franklin, 1998, p 166). Various writings have looked at participation, at principles which might produce more sensitive approaches, or at approaches aimed at involving specific carers and users (see for example Means, 1996, pp 215-18; Carpenter and Sbaraini, 1997; Means and Smith, 1996). For households the issue may not be just about small details, but also about rights which everyone may expect to have in regard to choice, lifestyle and social contacts.

Yet Bochel and Hawtin observe that involving disabled people at service delivery level is "not altogether commonplace" (see Bochel and Hawtin, 1998, pp 293-8). There is still stereotyping and paternalism, with assumptions that people with learning difficulties must accept the combination of housing and support which service providers deem appropriate, with security of tenure and choice of housing not recognised as applicable (JRF, 1996), or with practitioners placing high value on their own professional judgements, leading them to devalue the views of users and carers (JRF, 1993). One report notes that consultation rights are often not afforded to supported housing tenants (JRF, 1996b). Sensitivity to diversity remains underdeveloped. For example, assumptions about sexuality may be made in provider organisations, limiting people's freedoms overtly or thoughtlessly (see Smailes, 1994, pp 154-5). Or stereotypes related to 'race' and ethnicity may be invoked. Practitioners might overestimate preparedness of service users' relatives and social networks to provide informal care, and "could be particularly insensitive to members of minority ethnic communities" (JRF, 1993). There may be under-provision of culturally sensitive services for some groups, and neglect of problems experienced by minority ethnic disabled people (note for instance Analysis, *Black Housing*, March/April 1996, reporting Radia; also Macfarlane and Laurie, 1996, p 21). Cultural diversity is receiving more recognition, but government ministers (in a foreword to CRE, 1997) acknowledge that despite pockets of good practice there may be problems of access, inappropriate assessments, and services that do not adequately reflect ways of life and aspirations (CRE, 1997, p 5). It is observed that 'typically', where 'care' is more akin to control "and brings restrictions on users' autonomy, ethnic minorities are overrepresented", while when the service is 'caring' they tend to be underrepresented (CRE, 1997, p 9) (cf Chakrabarti, 1998, p 155). For older people a stereotype of diminished capacities may affect practitioner thinking on their involvement in community development as well as in community care, although Wistow indicates that the community development approach implies partnerships between agencies and community groups, active community centres and clubs, and a preventative and inclusive approach (see Wistow, 1999, p 57). There are also possibilities of hierarchy among disabled people in regard to consultation, with those most able to articulate their needs, and who present the "socially acceptable face of disability" (without speech problems or visible disfigurement), being responded to more fully (see Fiedler, 1988, p 31).

Universal and inclusive standards

Alongside ideas about specialised support or accommodation, we can also consider possibilities of raising general standards for new dwellings across the different tenures, and enhancing existing houses. There are inherent problems in designing for specific impairments, since occupiers may move on, other impairments may become more significant, and a design may tie up investment inflexibly. In recent years ideas for user-friendly accommodation have been underpinned by the theme that better universal standards are an alternative to designs focused tightly on particular impairments. The aims are to accommodate changes over people's lifetimes and raise mandatory or expected standards for new dwellings in general. This means considering a range of illnesses and conditions when designing. It also points to having at least a 'visitability standard' (Goodchild and Karn, 1997; cf Rowe, 1990, p 4; Madigan and Milner, 1999), so that disabled people would be able to go into most houses with ease, just as any non-disabled person could, and not be restricted to a narrow range of dwellings where they live. Visitability implies, as a minimum, ground-floor accessibility and access to a toilet and living room (see Dodd, 1998, pp 148-9; see also discussion below of Part M). This kind of thinking can be extended to improving quality of life in local neighbourhoods by creating barrier-free environments. Ideally, dwelling design modifications aimed at convenience, safety and comfort should be responses to specific user understandings of detailed needs, but against a backcloth of much enhanced universalistic but flexible standards. Specific cultural or religious needs might also be considered (cf Dodd, 1998, p 163), while particular thought should be given to children's requirements including play space, storage for specific items, and downstairs toilets. Future research might also consider materials used in dwellings or local environments, in view of the possibility that some people may react adversely more than others.

A set of ideas which has gained ground is about 'Lifetime Homes' (Rowe, 1990; Dodd, 1998, pp 157-9), or multi-generational housing. Adopting Lifetime Homes standards would reduce the cost of future adaptations while enhancing independent living. The central idea is for ordinary housing to be built with enough flexibility and space to facilitate comfortable living over a family life-cycle. An occupier whose needs change can remain in the same house, because it is more readily adaptable to change than a traditional dwelling. Standards cover access, internal design, internal amenities, fixtures and fittings. The Rowntree Foundation has sponsored work in this field, including an evaluation of Lifetime Homes in Hull (Cooper and Walton, 1995). The features can be incorporated into new dwellings, making them more flexible, adaptable and accessible, but are not aimed solely at disabled people. This is an alternative to designing 'special needs' housing, and at the very least can be complementary to tailor-made specialised accommodation. It can benefit people growing older, and help at other stages (for example for parents with prams and young children, pregnant women, or people recovering from injury). Organisations' responses to Lifetime Homes standards seem to have varied, some no doubt being affected by financial implications. Crawford and Foord are critical, suggesting that many opportunities to encourage Lifetime Homes have been lost, and indicate that some Registered Social Landlords have been resistant (Crawford and Foord, 1997, pp 99-100; although note Heywood and Smart's comments on the Housing Corporation in relation to Lifetime Homes standards, 1996, p 84).

Ideas certainly have changed. For example, a recent weighty 'handbook of building and interior design solutions to include the needs of visually impaired people' comments critically on the earlier idea of an 'architecture for the blind', and looks towards more inclusive approaches helping everyone (Barker, Barrick and Wilson, 1995, pp 14-20). One reason for changes in thinking is clearly the reaction against segregated environments to which specialist facilities and buildings often contributed. Another reason may be the diversity of impairment itself. It is all too easy to plan solutions aligned to a broader group's assumed requirements, while in fact the design may not fit any actual user's needs (cf Fiedler, 1988, p 22, on adaptations). Only 5% of those who are visually impaired have no sight at all, and the remainder "will have varying degrees of sight which will enable them to function visually to different degrees" (Barker, Barrick and Wilson, 1995, p 21). As these authors show, this does not mean that design principles cannot be worked out; for instance covering logical and readily memorable layouts, use of colour and tone contrast to raise visibility, adequate and evenly distributed lighting, and so forth.

The Labour government has appeared more sympathetic to raising standards generally, and this has been reflected in regulations. Changes were announced in March 1998, extending Part M of the Building Regulations to new domestic developments, providing for new homes to be built with a level entry, an entrance door of adequate width for wheelchair access, WC provision on the entrance level or first habitable floor, and improved internal arrangements including adequate circulation, door widths, and switches and sockets (see Madigan and Milner, 1999; Scotland and Northern Ireland have separate provisions). The immediate response from private housebuilders was apparently unwelcoming, since it was felt that 'starter homes' would become a "larger and more expensive product" (*Housing Today,* 12 March 1998). Nonetheless, advocates for raised standards have noted limitations in the regulations approved, and the DETR has apparently promised a review of Part M (Disability Rights Task Force, 1999, pp 153-6; Crowther, 2000, pp 118-19; also p 122 for planning guidelines).

It is essential to think about older dwellings too. As Sapey explains, the needs of disabled people are not primarily for newbuild dwellings, yet they are experiencing "considerable problems with the adaptation of their own homes" (Sapey, 1995, p 83). He suggests that one of the clearest needs is for an improvement in the adaptation of homes for wheelchair use. Derbyshire indicates, however, that the historical focus on wheelchair users or mobility issues has raised concerns about sight impairment being marginalised, while few professionals carrying out assessments have the requisite knowledge to evaluate the needs of a person with impaired sight (Derbyshire, 1998, p 52). There is certainly a case for a broad focus and response to diverse needs, and to the possibility of a combination of impairments. More expenditure on adaptations to assist people could have a preventative effect, slowing down tendencies towards increased dependency, and reducing pressures for an unwilling move out of a person's home. Although available adaptations may not always match people's needs (and in some instances more space or a changed locality might be preferable), aids and adaptations are very important, and difficulties faced in obtaining them help isolate people. Opportunities to make access improvements have not been taken enough in refurbishment and modernisation programmes, but some analysis has been carried out on achieving Lifetime Homes standards through refurbishment (see JRF, 1996a).

Adaptations have been a key focus for debate. As Heywood and Smart put it, housing adaptations allow people to come and go from their own homes, to move around within them, turn on lights, open windows, cook for a friend, or put a child to bed. They allow an older person to have a bath if they so choose "and not only when someone else decides" (1996, pp viii-ix). In effect, adaptations can help to make ordinary activities easier (for the adaptation process see Bradford, 1998). Among the commonest adaptation requests have been those related to rails (grab rails and stair rails), bathing or central heating (for details of these and others see Heywood and Smart, 1996, pp xx-xxi; see also Derbyshire, 1998, pp 53-4). Equipment is also important; it may be less effective in a non-adapted house, while adaptations may only work well with appropriate equipment (Oldman and Beresford, 1998, p 62).

Legislation potentially involved local authorities with housing modifications through the 1970s and 1980s (see Bull and Watts, 1998, pp 21-30; Smith, 1989, pp 314, 378-9). In 1990 the Disabled Facilities Grant (DFG) arrived, following legislation which "introduced for the first time a grant for adaptations to which disabled people were statutorily entitled" and also the "discretionary but still important" Minor Works grants for older people, along with strong support for the use of Home Improvement Agencies (Heywood and Smart, 1996, p viii; for points on the legislative framework see Crowther, 2000, pp 124-6). These agencies (Care and Repair or Staying Put) were established to help older people who wished to stay in their own homes, but have expanded to provide help and support for both older people and disabled people on low incomes with homes in need of repair, potentially contributing to the prevention of ill-health and accidents (Building and Social Housing Foundation, 1999, pp 24-5). Various other forms of assistance are becoming available (Disabled Persons Housing Services, keeping of adapted properties registers, and so forth), and provisions on grants were amended in 1996 (see Parsons, 1998; also Age Concern and Radar, 1999, on limited progress with registers; Bull and Watts, 1998, pp 27-30).

Against the backcloth of the drive towards community care, adaptations issues have come into the forefront of housing improvement policy, with rising demand in the private sector and council housing, where many disabled people live (see Heywood and Smart, 1996, p xiv). Housing associations have seen increased spending on adaptations in England, although Heywood and Smart suggest that low dwelling standards (in the Conservative period) meant that adaptation costs were being created for the future "with almost every new housing association property" built (Heywood and Smart, 1996, p xix). For the DFG, criticisms have been made of delays, shortage of occupational therapists, funding limits, selectivity, tests of people's resources or means, lack of available information, lack of user consultations, and subjective interpretation of rules with a gap between officials and disabled people as to what is practical and necessary (for instance Sapey, 1995, pp 79-81; Watson, 1997, p 4; Macfarlane and Laurie, 1996, pp 14-16; Heywood and Smart, 1996, pp xii-xiii, xvi, xxii; Oldman and Beresford, 1998, pp 46-50). Even a *Guardian* contribution has reported on the problems whereby what a family could supposedly afford was calculated without considering outgoings, notably mortgage costs (S. Davies, 17 December 1997).

Crawford and Foord suggest that access to funds depends on tenure rather than severity of need (Crawford and Foord, 1997; cf Macfarlane and Laurie, 1996, pp 14-16; Bradford, 1998, pp 93-4), although the DoE

(1996) claims effective targeting on those in greatest need, albeit infrequently reaching families with disabled children. DFG is paralleled by other sources, and for council tenants funding may come "from a council's own resources" (see Oldman and Beresford, 1998, pp 60-1). Preferences may not always be met well, with some people being encouraged to move rather than have the adaptations they want, or being offered adaptations rather than a desired move. One revealing finding shows that a minority of councils have not considered adaptations for their tenants where the property was deemed to be 'underoccupied', or have looked for an alternative via a transfer (Age Concern and Radar, 1999, pp 2-3). Although there can be problems with any dwelling if higher levels of adaptation make its use difficult for subsequent occupiers (and although some tenants might welcome a move), the notion of 'underoccupation' imposes a narrower functional meaning of home on tenants than applies to owner-occupiers (ignoring locality associations, memories, or relatives' visits). This old local authority idea reflects the notion that non-market provision is a gift subject to measurement, re-measurement and conditionality, as well as being tied to the problem of rationing space between people in need that attends upon a limited supply. On a related general point, it is worth noting that a move chosen by a household might be a positive alternative to adaptations in any tenure context, and that a genuinely comprehensive policy would probably cater for substantial financial assistance towards such moves for owner-occupiers or private renters with limited resources, and for crossing tenure divides (cf DoE, 1996). (For some issues about moving see Oldman and Beresford, 1998, pp 53-6, who also illustrate the effect on a family with a disabled child of the assumption that people are 'overhoused' according to housing benefit regulations. This parallels 'underoccupation' ideas.)

Change, citizenship and self-management

This chapter has discussed the movement of thinking away from institutionalised accommodation towards more flexible packages or dwelling designs, and general rights to an environment that accommodates differences. Political and practitioner thinking acknowledges more often than it did that most people with an impairment would want their needs met within conventional housing, or ordinary housing that has been adapted. Fiedler notes that some key principles – choice, consultation, information, participation, autonomy, and "recognition that long-term disability is not synonymous with illness" – have made their way into the policy documents of many social services and health authorities (Fiedler, 1991, p 87). Disabled people are consulted more frequently, and their organisations have challenged established discourses with considerable effect. The needs of carers have also begun to be acknowledged more fully (Johnson, 1999, pp 88-9). Yet people still face important constraints and barriers. To conclude the chapter we offer an overview of constraints related to market and non-market practices, and present a citizenship perspective on struggles against barriers, highlighting the importance of universality alongside self-management or self-determination.

Market and non-market practices; characteristics of social regulation

At the heart of social regulation lie relationships with markets and paid employment, and constant pressures to contain costs outside the market while stimulating consumption within it. We touched on this contrast before in Chapter Four. Discourses associated with market dominance also help push the politics of disability away from rights claims (which imply adapting markets and environments to create more equality), and towards family and community 'duties', which may incorporate concepts of disability as dependency predominantly confined to separate private or 'welfare' realms. Market mainstream housing providers have responded minimally to impairment. Even taken along with social rented dwellings, what is on offer overall in terms of types and characteristics of houses is still restricting, and does not match requirements of a population that is diverse, and in which impairment is frequent. Citing a well-known apt quotation, we can say that in effect mainstream dwellings seem on the whole to have been designed explicitly for non-disabled people, especially for the minority who are "male, fit and aged between 18 and 40", not very tall or short, with good sight and hearing, and right handed (see C. Smart, in Rowe, 1990, p 3).

Allen suggests that Britain is characterised by the hegemony of a "market complemented by the state" ideological welfarism (Allen, 1997, p 91). Clearly, non-market support is frequently cast as 'added on' to a mainstream of household consumption founded in paid employment (albeit confirmed and enhanced by the state), and reflects this in its selectivity, paternalism, tendencies for surveillance, cost-minimising, and pressures for 'normalisation'. Many social costs associated with markets (including numerous illnesses, injuries, pollutions, insecurities and neighbourhood economic effects) are passed over to public welfare services or private households to cope with. There can be assumptions that many in older age are primarily 'spent workers' or a 'burden' (and thus no longer full citizens), and may be treated less respectfully. It may be assumed that people of 'working age' are incomplete citizens if they cannot obtain regular work, and that encouraging paid work (however menial) is the solution to social exclusion. There is a longstanding link with disciplinary practices, where a regulatory goal is to classify legitimate as against non-legitimate income dependency, creating a lever keeping reluctant but apparently capable workers' noses to the grindstone. Just as owner-occupation casts a shadow across social renting (see Chapter Four), so the dominance of employment markets casts a shadow across some of the support available for disabled people, with its rationing and supervision.

Yet discriminatory practices limit work roles for many people with impairments, effectively disabling them. This is often grounded in the organisation and objectives of labour markets, in notions of risk, in employers' reservations about people who seem different, or in demands of profitability. Finkelstein comments on the exclusion of disabled people from work, suggesting that disability itself has come to mean unable to work, and that as non-earners disabled people are identified as incapable home makers and unsuitable love partners (Finkelstein, 1991, p 29). For Vernon, employment is "the means to life", enabling "our physical survival as well as being a key determinant of our sense of mental well-being". Work may be a way of "offsetting disabling attitudes and situations which undermine self-esteem" and hamper independence (Vernon, 1996, pp 53-4). Furthermore, as we have seen already, weak positions in relation to labour markets often mean dependent positions in housing markets.

Provision outside the market mainstream offers support and recognition of needs that are vital to people. Nonetheless, attitudes and provider interests – though much changed – have continuity with the paternalism of the past. The medical model, and traditional discourses about caring for clients, still influence ways in which provider organisations are focused, and transmission and use of ideas day to day. As Macfarlane and Laurie explain, in the main, traditional large institutions are "being replaced by a range of mini-institutions dispersed in the community", while the "use of the language and practices of 'special needs' housing provision continues to segregate disabled people both within housing services and within the community" (Macfarlane and Laurie, 1996, see p 1). There are gaps in the perceptions of practitioners. For example, Oldman and Beresford found that housing and social services professionals had little awareness of the impact of unsuitable housing on families with disabled children, and that "child-specific policies and procedures were rare" (JRF, 1998d, p 1). At the same time there are continuing questions about 'caring', associated with the cost-containing role of partners, relatives and friends who provide unpaid assistance, expectations being buttressed by discourses about women's roles.

Clearly it can be tempting for governments to legitimate low expenditure by invoking ideas about family and community caring responsibilities, while understating disabled people's rights claims on broader society. Personal assistance, however, need not imply passive recipients or 'burdens' and paternalistic 'carers', but can actively involve both (or multiple) 'parties', and may occur in varied settings, sometimes as part of family, kinship or friendship relationships and sometimes not (for discussion see Morris, 1993). Providing unpaid assistance is not necessarily an undesirable burden or unrewarded, and might not restrict the provider (although it may do so), but can generate an unequal relationship, potentially oppressive to either party, particularly if the financial and physical environment is a very disabling or unsupportive one and creates or exacerbates dependency (cf Morris, 1991, pp 140-4, 1993). Perhaps the dominance of economic liberalism contributes to underdevelopment of organisational and financial support for wider networks of participation and interaction which could facilitate independence. Individualistic concepts of 'care' activities say little about the social inclusion, prevention, mutuality and solidarity that could be assumed implicit in the term community care (cf Wistow, 1999, p 57). Nonetheless, although Bytheway and Johnson (1998, p 252) conclude that "care should be reconceived as part of ordinary family and community life", one crucial issue remains the degree to which people requiring assistance are accepted to have rights to claim help, regardless of whether family support is available. Barriers persist here.

Citizenship and self-management

Chapter Three noted that struggles around citizenship rights help shape regulatory practices in the welfare state. Disability provides key examples. Battles are both about particular individual or group needs, and more universalised targets of rights, equal opportunities, or barrier-free environments linked to the goal of the independent citizen. Separatism (in facilities or organisations) or precisely tailored packages can be positive ways forward, but the right to use what other people use or be accorded equivalent status is important too. Discussing independent living, rights and housing, Hurst observes that "the whole question of independent living as the tool for our empowerment" is part and parcel "of our struggle for equal opportunities" (in Laurie, 1991, p 9). Rather than being stereotyped as dependent, disabled people will want that level of acceptance, dignity, security and self-management that non-disabled people expect. Seeing decent housing as part of citizenship claims might mean arguing that all individuals have rights to choose appropriate accommodation or adapt what they have, to enjoy it on affordable terms, and to be free of conditions placing them as mere clients of professionals or recipients of charity. From a user perspective, the design, planning, alteration, allocation, and management of dwellings ought to make this possible. Universalistic and inclusive standards (discussed above) are vital. Going further, disabled people ought to be as free as anyone else to determine what the home means to them, to relate it to aspirations on privacy, conviviality, family, support networks, choice of neighbours, tenure and costs. Continuity may be as significant for a disabled person or someone whose capacities are changing in older age as it is for anyone else, so that staying in a familiar dwelling may be an important preference. Self-management of housing circumstances may be preferred to 'client care', even though the latter remains significant. Help with daily living tasks means disabled people participating in society and personal relationships in ways that non-disabled people take for granted. Flexible, good quality housing has preventative aspects, helping households maintain independence and health (cf Building and Social Housing Foundation, 1999, p 11), while rights of access to finance sustain people in their own homes.

There are two aspects to rights claims. First, the goal of an overall universalistic framework of rights, expectations and status that puts people on more of an equal footing, whether it be in terms of the physical environment, legal protection, or access to resources. Equal opportunities legislation is one foundation. Chadwick indicates that the Disability Discrimination Bill (later the 1995 Act) was based on the individual rather than social model of disability (1996). A medical model focused on impairment determines who can use the legal provisions (see Crowther, 2000, pp 97-9). Nonetheless, the ability to challenge unfair provision or less favourable terms, coupled with duties placed on service providers, is different from a client receiving individualised selectivist treatment, and may be construed as at least a step towards universality of status. Despite limitations in the legislation (see Oliver and Barnes, 1998, p 90; Priestley, 1999, pp 205-9), the Act has made discrimination unlawful against a disabled person when selling or renting property. For Registered Social Landlords a guide has been produced by the RNIB and Housing

Corporation (Crowther, 2000), indicating how to comply with the legislation and develop an action plan to overcome discrimination. Providers have a duty to make 'reasonable' adjustments to enable disabled people to access their services, although there is as yet no requirement to make adjustments to properties that are being sold, let or managed (see Derbyshire, 1998, pp 21-2; Crowther, 2000, p 101; Disability Rights Task Force, 1999, pp 132-6). Service providers have a duty to provide auxiliary aids and services enabling disabled people to use facilities, and to change practices which make it unreasonably difficult for disabled people to use services or facilities (Crowther, 2000, p 103).

Looking beyond this legislation, a set of rights can provide a focus for collective solidarity, is a point of reference for individual defence, may erode overbearing professional determination of needs, can reduce vulnerability to loss of resources as political conditions change, and will enhance user independence. Individual or collective private property rights can be a part of this (see for example JRF, 2000c, p 3; 1995a; King, 1998). Bricks and mortar still have roles to play, not least for social renting, where under-investment and inadequate support services have hastened environmental deterioration that is immensely damaging to the interests of many low-income people with impairments or ill-health. There is an evident disconnection "between the positive and upbeat aspirations of community care" and thinking which "views social rented housing as a stigmatised and residual sector catering for those who have no other choices"; for many people needing extra support or care services, the 'opportunity' for living independently is represented by "a dilapidated flat in an unpopular and run-down area" (Watson, 1997, p 3). Rights to choice and inclusion imply far more adequate resources.

Second, rights claims reflect differences at the micro level, and often the goal of inclusion on the basis of distinct individual or collective needs rather than integration, absorption, or reliance on standard universal services. Services need to be sensitive to diversity and cultural issues (for example making information accessible and facilitating exchanges of views through Braille, signers, advocates, and so forth). Varied preferences generate a complex agenda. A mix of available forms of provision and packages of housing and care seems the ideal, but with flexibility built in whenever feasible. For many people the goal may be ordinary homes (ideally with personal, domestic and social support if needed), although some might perhaps want shared social experiences, networks or accommodation to avoid isolation or loneliness (cf JRF, 2000a). Although we have referred to the social model of disability and the importance of constraints, specific impairments are highly significant, medical support is vital, and people's identities and material interests may well be shaped strongly by their very individual sense of illness and health, barriers or needs. One thing, however, dividing social model theories from those built around individual experience of impairment is the claim that disability has collective existence in the socioeconomic world "beyond the existence or experience of individual disabled people". Thus, while there is diversity of interest and identity, "there remains an essential level of commonality in the collective experience of discrimination and oppression" (Priestley, 1998, p 83). The task for a set of citizenship claims is to combine effectively the universalistic with the particular, bridging the two domains of difference to which we have referred in this book. Collective mobilisations arise in varied contexts and relate to many dimensions of commonality or affiliation (while cultural expectations, functional needs and political commitments may interact distinctively for any group or individual). A common theme, however, is that independence may require *individual or group self-management*, or more precisely *self-determined* living (Macfarlane and Laurie, 1996, pp 9-10). What is available today, of course, does not match up to the diversity of needs and preferences, offers limited choice, may be badly located, or may sometimes bring more supervision or less support than is desired (cf Bochel and Hawtin, 1998, p 300). Major physical, social, and economic barriers persist. It is fundamentally these constraints that the claim for citizenship rights confronts.

SIX

Ethnicity, 'race' and housing

We now turn to ethnicity and 'race'. Building on earlier chapters our account rests on the themes that there is difference within difference, and that difference is regulated. Thus diverse individual and group experiences and strategies among minorities are set within broader patterns of difference linked to structural factors which condition ongoing practices of social regulation. In this chapter we touch on diversity and the defining of needs, and note questions about particularism and ownership. Most of our discussion concerns 'non-white' minority ethnic people, although certain white groups clearly have also been subject to racist discrimination (notably Irish and Jewish people, some refugees, and gypsies and travelling people).

The first section below provides selected information about housing and black minority ethnic households, noting diversities of experiences alongside continuing commonalities of adverse circumstances. The chapter then turns to selected aspects of 'human agency'. Black and minority ethnic communities resist racisms and pursue a variety of housing strategies, albeit in difficult economic and political environments. Their achievements have included not only individual successes for households, but also creation of black-run housing organisations. We then comment on policies and practices of government and provider organisations, where it is important to acknowledge change. As well as being affected by general ideas about 'race', black and minority ethnic households have been subject to specific regulation through the negative and positive practices of numerous housing and allied institutions. A discussion of housing need follows, covering the potentially contested nature of the concept, its links with security, empowerment and ownership, and issues of ethnic managerialism, particularism and universalism. Finally we draw brief conclusions.

Experiences, preferences and constraints

In reviewing housing experiences we must look not only beyond a simple black/white divide, but also beyond assumptions about broad distinctions between (say) Asians and African/Caribbeans. There have been marked differences between various minority ethnic communities "in terms of household size/structure, tenure patterns, dwelling types, amenity levels and density of occupation" (Ratcliffe, 1997, p 130). Phillips notes that there are "forces for both minority ethnic inclusion and exclusion from competition for economic rewards and social status", and that these forces "produce different outcomes for different groups and a variable experience within minority ethnic groups according to generation, gender and class" (Phillips, 1998, p 1681). To provide a picture of circumstances we summarise below from important analyses provided by scholars using census data (albeit sometimes now outdated), supplemented with findings taken from other studies where appropriate. It is worth observing that there have now been many local research exercises focused on minority ethnic housing needs (for instance Davis and Salam with Jones and Paterson, 1996; Ratcliffe, 1996; Gidley, Harrison and Robinson, 1999), while several reports have focused specifically on elders (Bright, 1996; Carlin, 1994; Lemos, 1998; Shah and Williams, 1992; Turkington and Dixon, 1997; Jones, 1994).

In 1991, Indians constituted the largest non-white minority ethnic group in Britain (with a population of approximately 877,000), the two other largest groups being Black Caribbeans and Pakistanis. Differing groups have different population growth rates and potential for new household formation (see Phillips, 1996, pp 51-2), with implications for the pattern of future local housing needs. Where growth occurs in communities that are very poor, there may be particular difficulties in meeting those needs. In fact many black minority ethnic households have relatively low incomes, and specific groups are over-represented in declining industries (see discussion in Green, 1997; also Modood, 1997; Berthoud, 1997). There are substantial variations in unemployment rates, the Black African, Pakistani and Bangladeshi groups being in the worst positions in 1991 (Phillips, 1996, p 56). The unemployment position of Indians has been closer to that of whites. Modood indicates a general pattern of inequality, but "also of a divergence in the circumstances of the main minorities" (cf JRF, 1998f). He explains the diversities, but acknowledges continuing possibilities of 'ethnic penalties', whereby all non-white groups (regardless of qualifications and positions in jobs hierarchies), suffer disadvantage which leads them to fare less well than similarly qualified whites (Modood, 1997, pp 138, 144-5; cf Karn on housing, 1997, p 276). Berthoud (1997) locates Pakistanis and Bangladeshis among the poorest, with "four times the poverty rate found among white people" (JRF 1998f). A recent Birmingham study reinforces impressions of poverty for Bangladeshi, Black African-Caribbean/Black Other and Pakistani groups, and includes the remark that "we can calculate that 56% of all Bangladeshi children under the age of 16 are living in poverty" (Platt and Noble, 1999, see pp 20-3). Local studies deepen evidence of disadvantage for specific minority communities, highlighting large proportions of people with long-term illness or impairment, or noting effects of practical problems such as inability to use central heating fully because of costs (Ratcliffe, 1996; Gidley, Harrison and Robinson, 1999). Law comments from an analysis in Leeds that "racial inequality in terms of housing needs has widened", with black minority ethnic households over-represented in groups defined as having the highest levels of housing need (see Law, 1996, pp 100-2).

Average household size is largest among the South Asian (Indian subcontinent) groups, and smallest among whites. This is influenced by differing age structures, with effects from old people living in small units and dependent children in large households (see Murphy, 1996, p 219). As Warnes points out, "the ethnic minority populations of Great Britain are presently young", although age profiles differ between groups, reflecting distinctive settlement histories and "contrasts in the contemporary social and demographic processes that affect them" (see Warnes, 1996, pp 151, 172). Murphy notes that although the prevalence of extended family living is 'relatively low' at a specific moment, such arrangements are likely to be experienced at some stage by much higher proportions of the population (Murphy, 1996, p 229). There are higher proportions of female-headed, lone-parent families among Black people and more extended household structures among the South Asian groups (Murphy, 1996, pp 235-6). Marriage and family formation (and dissolution) are areas for ethnic diversity (Berrington, 1996, pp 178, 204). None of the black minority ethnic groups has a very high representation of 'pensioner only' households (see Phillips, 1996). This reflects a youthful age structure but also the greater tendency for Asian elders to live within extended family households. It is hard to assess how far this may have been changing, but growth in numbers of elders raises significant issues when combined with "social processes leading to the formation of smaller households, in different ways, across different minority ethnic groups" (see Law et al, 1996, pp 10-15).

There is a high degree of geographical concentration of the minorities within parts of urban England, and there has been an apparent tendency for the growing black minority ethnic population to be "increasingly spatially concentrated" (Owen, 1992, p 9). Many areas of settlement have high unemployment and/or low pay, poor services and difficult housing. In Greater London, households are competing for housing in a market "where decent, affordable accommodation in an acceptable location is in short supply" (Phillips, 1996, p 53). More generally, there has been some selective movement into higher status property outside "deprived areas", albeit "characterised by new nodes of ethnic minority concentration" (Phillips and Karn, 1992, p 358). Although some black and minority ethnic households (particularly Indian) may be relocating in outer urban areas of better quality housing, the larger families and extended family structures of some households mean that suburbanisation is not always associated with lack of overcrowding (Phillips, 1996, pp 54, 62; 1997, p 187). There may be generational as well as ethnic group differences in propensity to migrate (with youth unemployment constraining spatial dispersal), but development of a minority ethnic middle class is associated with reduced exclusion, including the choice of a degree of suburbanisation, since the "benefits of capital clearly outweigh the negative attributes of ethnicity" (Phillips, 1998, p 1699). Each minority ethnic group, however, has its own specific settlement geography and its own potential for class polarisation.

Although it can be argued that residential segregation has been "a medium for the reproduction of racial inequality" (Smith, S., 1989, p 105), geographical concentration in itself does not necessarily indicate disadvantage (see Harrison, 1995, pp 57-9). There is much that has been positive in clustering based on cultural and religious ties, although changes in labour markets and other forces may have left many households "trapped in marginal urban areas in regions of industrial decline" (Phillips, 1998, p 1683; cf Smith, S., 1989, pp 43-4). It is being restricted in housing and environmental quality or job choice which is damaging, not people's location close to other minority ethnic households. Discriminatory practices and disproportionate reliance on public transport may restrict job choices, as may nervousness about journeys to or through white-dominated areas (cf Moore, 1997, p 88). Nonetheless, while segregation may be partly a product of regulatory practices, separation also results from individual strategies. Local spatial patternings are an adjunct, catalyst or symptom of socioeconomic practices, rather than the central causative ingredient. Some minority households certainly face poor quality environments, limited job markets, and under-resourced facilities, while white people tend to live (with exceptions) in wards with a lower level of deprivation (for recent analysis see JRF, 1998b, reporting Dorsett). Yet, as

Dorsett's study confirms, "economic progress is not inevitably tied to geographic dispersion" (JRF, 1998b, p 4). Earlier worries about spatial concentration may have reflected white apprehension or paternalism rather than minority ethnic need (cf Lewis, 1998, pp 105-10, on education). As with disability, it is often inclusion rather than assimilation which is crucial, although locality housing experiences are significant, and it is important to be aware that black minority ethnic people are least represented in the higher status growth areas and more rural parts of Britain.

Despite diversity, black and minority ethnic people in Britain tend to be relatively poorly housed, even though most have been resident for a long time, many having been born here (Owen, 1993, p 12). There have been frequent commentaries on the concentration of minority ethnic households in apparently inferior dwelling types such as flats or inner city terraces (see discussion in Ratcliffe, 1997, pp 139-40), and information on overcrowding, on lack of exclusive use of bath or WC, and on households not living in self-contained accommodation, has indicated relatively disadvantaged circumstances (Owen, 1993a). Although overcrowding persisted throughout the 1970s, 1980s and into the 1990s, there is a little uncertainty about recent trends. Lakey indicates that levels of overcrowding have decreased for all ethnic groups, although differences between groups persist (Lakey, 1997, p 223; but cf Phillips, 1996, p 61, and Ratcliffe, 1997, p 142). Pakistanis and Bangladeshis seem to be living in the most deprived housing conditions (Phillips, 1996, pp 60-1), both groups being affected by high levels of overcrowding, with many in 1991 having no central heating. The pressure on housing space experienced by these groups may increase as populations grow against a backcloth of poor socioeconomic circumstances. Housing types also vary between ethnic groups, with low proportions of Black, Pakistani and Bangladeshi households living in detached or semi-detached properties, but increasing representation of Indian households in such housing (see Phillips, 1996).

For most South Asian groups owner-occupation represents the dominant tenure. Although differences have existed between minority ethnic groups in the proportions of households owning, buying, and in different tenure categories, Ratcliffe points to a narrowing of ethnic differentials in tenure patterns (Ratcliffe, 1997, p 135; cf Phillips, 1997, pp 171, 175-6, 186; Howes and Mullins, 1997, p 214). Low income home ownership persists as a feature of minority ethnic experience generally (Phillips, 1997, p 186). The census showed owner-occupation highest among those of Indian origin, followed by Pakistani households, whites and the Chinese

(Ratcliffe, 1997, p 133). Phillips indicates possible tendencies for Pakistani families to buy properties for their children, for purchases still to be made on short-term loans, and for complexities concerning the head of household and ownership in extended families (Phillips, 1997, p 172). Although private renting is less common than owner-occupancy, more than a tenth of black and minority ethnic households in 1991 rented privately, "with nearly a fifth of Chinese and others in this tenure category" (Owen, 1993a, p 8; see also Lakey, 1997, p 200).

The Indian and Pakistani populations are significantly under-represented within the council housing sector, "despite the low socioeconomic status of the Pakistanis in particular" (Phillips, 1996, p 58). The individual ethnic groups "most dependent upon" public sector housing in 1991 were Black-Africans and Bangladeshis (Owen, 1993a, p 8). (See Ratcliffe, 1997, p 136, for explanation of Bangladeshi involvement with social rented housing.) A recent London report gives a figure of 58% of Bangladeshis in council housing, while black and minority ethnic groups generally constituted 30% of London local authority tenants and 28% for RSLs (Housing Corporation London, 1999, pp 16, 19). It also suggests that ethnic groups leaving council housing (whites and Black Caribbeans) may be being replaced in London by groups such as Bangladeshis and Africans with a greater need for large dwellings (cf Howes and Mullins, 1997, p 194). The total number of black minority ethnic social renting tenants in London increased from around 90,000 in the late 1970s to 244,000 in the mid 1990s (despite overall decline in numbers of such tenancies) (see Housing Corporation London, 1999, p 19). Housing associations have become important for minority households, some groups being well represented here and some (notably Indian and Pakistani) less so (see Howes and Mullins, 1997, p 192). One effect of penetration of social renting has been access to basic housing amenities:

> Black-Caribbeans have scored quite highly on basic amenities largely on the grounds that, irrespective of structural condition, publicly owned housing will almost inevitably have such things as a fixed bath, running hot water and an inside WC. (Ratcliffe, 1997, p 130)

The history for council housing practices, however, should not be forgotten. Since disproportionate numbers of black applicants were allocated into less popular locations and inferior dwellings, some estates they live in may consequently be of low status. Several 'classic' studies highlighted the impact of discrimination against minorities in the council sector, and not all problems have disappeared (Henderson and Karn, 1987; Phillips, 1986; Simpson, 1981; CRE, 1984; cf more recently Jeffers and Hoggett, 1995; Law, 1996, pp 101-2).

Tenure on its own is an unreliable indicator of housing experience for minority ethnic households, telling us little about the social and economic costs involved, the interaction with culture, or the meanings attached to the home. Phillips observes that being denied access to council housing in the earliest years of settlement and confronted by discrimination in the private rented sector, many immigrants – but particularly those from India and Pakistan – opted to buy cheap inner city housing shortly after their arrival, with implications in terms of substandard accommodation and investment risks associated with this (Phillips, 1997, p 170; cf Smith, S., 1989, pp 62-3). She notes that English House Condition Survey data confirm that owner-occupation for Asians is still often associated with poor housing quality (Phillips, 1996, p 62). Lakey indicates that the poor condition of many properties may make them "a liability rather than an asset" (Lakey, 1997, p 206, but see also pp 222-3). There is variation, however, related to cultural preferences, local housing market conditions, institutional discrimination, and employment experiences. Social class effects remain important for housing status and conditions, despite significant differences between ethnic groups. Ratcliffe has found clear differentials in levels of serious overcrowding between those of professional and intermediate background and the semi-skilled/unskilled, even among the Indian cohort. In relation to central heating, he found a "now familiar social class gradient" (Ratcliffe, 1997, pp 142-3). Phillips notes that of all the minority groups of home owners, the Indian population emerged in 1991 data as the one to have been making the greatest strides. She suggests that trends here are consistent with the emergence of an Indian middle class, although Indian households were also strongly represented within poorer inner city areas, pointing to an increasing divergence within the group (Phillips, 1997, p 187). Indian and African Asian households appear to have been reaping some reward from their investment in owner-occupation in terms of detached or semi-detached properties (Lakey, 1997, p 222), but up to a fifth of the Indian group nonetheless lives in poor housing conditions, and many still experience overcrowding (see Phillips, 1996, p 64).

Gender and age are significant for lifestyles and housing outcomes. Disadvantage is experienced by female heads of household, whether single or head of a family. While white women fared better than minority ethnic women who purchased housing, they were worse off in terms of housing type and condition than were white men, and this difference held across social classes (Phillips, 1997, p 180). There may be effects from differences in family structure and disposable income (for instance, male-headed households may incorporate a second adult earner) as well as from disadvantages in raising finance. Phillips observes that data indicate that male heads of households in three broad ethnic groups (white, Indian and Black Caribbean) are significantly more likely to own property than female heads and less likely to be represented in the local authority sector (Phillips, 1996; see also 1997, p 175). Council accommodation is especially important for Black Caribbean and white single parents (39% and 32% respectively were living in council accommodation in 1991). Even for South Asian groups with high ownership rates overall, the public sector "features significantly" when the household is female-headed (Ratcliffe, 1997, p 135). Indian and Black Caribbean female heads of households were more likely to be living in terraced housing than were the male heads of households within their own ethnic group (Phillips, 1996, p 64). Lakey states that younger Caribbean households in the Fourth PSI study had particularly low rates of owner-occupation and high rates of social renting, compared both with older Caribbean households and with younger households from other groups. She indicates that this reflects partly the high proportion of lone parent families among young Caribbean households (see Lakey, 1997, p 221). About half of Black women in their thirties are 'heads of household' compared with about one in ten South Asian women (Murphy, 1996, p 221).

Homelessness illustrates general patterns of disadvantages carried through into housing deprivation, with minority ethnic over-representation noted among homeless families and young single persons in London and other large urban areas (Greve, 1997, p xvi). Harrison (1999) summarises from a range of reports dealing with black and minority ethnic homelessness (including Davies and Lyle with Deacon, Law, Julienne and Kay, 1996; CRE, 1988; Steele, 1997). Specific individual experiences – such as inter-generational conflicts, domestic violence, shortage of funds for this month's rent, or losing one's job – play a part in generating homelessness, but interact with structural factors and the localised practices of organisations. Labour market disadvantage among black youth in some places limits their capacity for independent living, forcing some into a choice between a parental home with severe frictions, temporary refuge with friends, or some other precarious solution. Conditions such as overcrowding contribute directly to likelihood of homelessness, and overcrowding remains a significant area of relative disadvantage for black and minority ethnic groups. Some hidden general financial and social costs falling on homeless people may have strongly affected minority ethnic households (see Edwards, 1995). Also, while there is diversity between communities in the incidence of homelessness, running across this is the impact of racist practices or threats (see Chahal and Julienne, 1999). This not only makes getting and keeping a decent home difficult, but may also create reluctance to approach homelessness services or to remain in white-run facilities such as hostels or refuges.

Strategies from the grass roots

Individuals or groups acquire and use dwellings diversely. People also campaign about their housing through direct political channels, or make common cause in other ways. Human agency is therefore important both in terms of household or small group strategies, and collective activity within the policy arena based on notions of common interests, which may be temporary and context-specific or more longlasting. Channels of political representation or incorporation differ across localities, communities and countries, and a sense of exclusion and oppression may provoke responses ranging from protest to "full-scale confrontation" on the streets (see Smith, S., 1989, pp 163-7). Minority ethnic groups, however, should not be seen as a deprived 'underclass' supposedly sharing a common experience of deprivation which dominates their perceptions and confers upon them a specific shared identity or culture. Some groups have rich cultural capital, with ethnicity often being a source of strength. Perhaps ethnicity is a product as well as a resource in processes of resistance, new ethnicities being generated through resistance to dominant, racialised constructions of English ethnicity. Ballard suggests that strategies deployed by the excluded tend to be particularly effective when those involved have ready access "to a moral, linguistic and conceptual order whose premises differ radically from those which underpin the hegemonic norm" (in this case the 'mainstream' white norm). He notes increasingly varied "trajectories of adaptation, and hence of upward mobility" (Ballard, 1998, p 35). One important variable in cultural resources is religion, but there are others related to locality, gender, age, employment, capital and shared community origins. Commitment to culture does not imply a fixed position, and many members of minorities (especially younger British-born people) have become skilled 'cross-cultural navigators' with a wide range of cultural and linguistic competencies appropriate in a variety of contexts.

At household level, strategies vary widely. At one end of the spectrum is a drive for family incorporation within the upwardly-mobile professional/managerial owner-occupier category. Here wealth may reduce inhibitions on spatial choice posed by harassment, for instance, by providing "a shield in the form of private transport and home security systems that the inner-city poor cannot afford" (Phillips, 1998, p 1697). At the other end of the spectrum we might find a strategy of resistance to the treatment that accompanies homelessness, through non-participation in white-led solutions (Harrison, 1999). The 'home' itself is the object of varying ideals and goals (see Chapter Two), and housing decisions within it, naturally enough, sometimes follow interactive processes involving more than one household member. Stereotypes can mislead here. Those of Asian women may stress passivity or lack of involvement in housing decisions, but this may not hold in reality (see Bowes, Dar and Sim, 1997a, p 114). These authors also found a considerable range of experiences and actions within the Pakistani households being studied in Glasgow. Although facing some similar limitations, interviewees might pursue a variety of possible housing careers, their strategies varying over time bearing in mind the relative importance of different constraints and cumulative effects of earlier choices (Bowes, Dar and Sim, 1997a, pp 118-21). Certainly it is difficult to 'read off' households' choices and housing careers from ethnicity, material positions, or racisms in a simple way. Black and minority ethnic households face common problems in terms of discrimination, and also tend to be materially disadvantaged, but this commonality is overlaid or cross-cut by gender, ethnicity, disability and age, and by highly specific differences between households and their goals. Furthermore, cost, tenure and quality preferences intersect with locality effects, such as a local predominance of terraces (see Howes and Mullins, 1997, pp 213-14).

One constraint households confront is the threat of harassment, with locality effects in terms of 'no-go' areas, and even sometimes a sense of being besieged (for example see 'Besieged in a racist stronghold', *Black Housing*, November/January, 1996/97; Williamson, 1993). There may be general associations between experiencing racist abuse or assault, and ill-health (Karlsen and Nazroo, 2000) as well as effects on family relationships, social isolation or children's play. Yet those on the receiving end of active racist behaviour will not passively accept what is happening. Chahal and Julienne's important study (1999) shows that people create strategies to halt or prevent harassment, with methods ranging from physical deterrents to complaints to official agencies. In some instances, however, a household's strategy might be to move to a safer area, even if this resulted in overcrowding, a change of tenure, and – potentially – the loss of a place on the council's waiting list.

Group action and organisation may help to erode specific practical difficulties, and may also help towards "a positive sense of individual and collective identity" linked to particular ideals (see Hylton, 1999, p xiii). Despite disagreements or divergence, and problems about representativeness within their organisations, people may make common cause across barriers of ethnicity. In housing, black and minority ethnic participation in national and local politics and professional networks has aimed at influencing provision, practices and legislation, and offering an effective voice on needs and problems. Key individual activists and groups have acted as spokespeople for larger constituencies, and battled for change. On the other hand there has been direct involvement in provision of dwellings or services, and the creation of organisations which can parallel or work with the white 'mainstream' or offer a culturally sensitive alternative. Many organisations and groups have focused on needs in the social support field or on socio-medical care, with a link across into housing services. Provision has included refuges, hostels, advocacy and advice, and schemes or services for groups such as elders or people with specialised health needs.

Since housing expenditure creates jobs, there have been efforts to establish better training opportunities for black and minority ethnic people, to help them compete for housing posts, and attempts to create organisations to help secure a fairer share of the indirect benefits arising from investment in social rented housing. For example, self-build solutions with allied training programmes have been pursued in some places, although unreceptive political and financial environments have led to a low UK level of involvement in such enterprises (for a recent discussion see Black Housing, 2000). People from minority communities have often cooperated with white-run organisations or funders to develop schemes and services, such as the London Equal Opportunities Federation (concerned with minority ethnic, disabled and female contractors) and PATH schemes (Positive Action Training in Housing). (See for example Haibatan, 2000.) In political terms, however, the most significant collective achievement has been the creation and development of housing associations run by black and minority ethnic people. The term Black Voluntary Housing Movement has been used to refer to these organisations, a crucial element in the history of the black and minority ethnic housing movement in Britain. The number of officially-recognised black and minority ethnic associations grew from 18 in 1986 to 62 in 1996, and substantial funds have been channelled through them (see Housing Corporation, 1998).

Detailed material on the associations and their activities is available in *Black Housing*, published by the Federation of Black Housing Organisations (FBHO), a body that has supported and represented associations serving diverse ethnic communities. Writings by the present principal author chronicle events in England from the early 1980s onwards (see 1991, 1995, 1998), and we only summarise key points now (see also Julienne, 1998; Royce, Hong Yang, Patel, Saw and Whitehead, 1996; and for Scotland Bowes, Dar and Sim, 1998 and R. Qureshi, in *Housing Today*, 6 July 2000). First of all, although the associations have varied in focus, community connections, and so forth, they have nonetheless generally shared an understanding about combating various kinds of exclusion. That is to say, they came into existence to make good deficiencies that were perceived in opportunities for participation and voice in local housing policy networks, in the availability of appropriate and sensitive provision (both in general terms and in specialised dwellings), and in the chances for self-management and community control of housing. They have been a reaction to racist practices and to material and political disadvantage. Their potential has also been noted in relation to specific problems such as difficulties facing refugees (see for example Means and Sangster, 1998, p 32; Gidley, Harrison and Tomlins, 2001).

Second, their development has provided valued role models and examples of minority ethnic business success, contributed to thinking within white-run organisations, and confirmed and stimulated concerns about 'housing plus' issues going beyond basic housing services (see Harrison, Karmani, Law, Phillips and Ravetz, 1996, pp 17-19). Their impact has been greater than their dwelling stock size would suggest, and many have been involved in local partnerships or relationships with other organisations (although this has raised questions about limited autonomy and dependency on larger bodies). There have been many 'spin-offs' from their presence in particular localities, including research projects on conditions. The FBHO has contributed significantly to discussions about housing policies, apparently playing an enhanced role with government since 1997 (see for example Federation of Black Housing Organisations, 1999).

A third point is that there have been complex interactions with official bodies, especially with the Housing Corporation (which encouraged the associations' development in England through allocating funds and through other forms of assistance), but also with councils and white-run housing associations. The Housing Corporation's programmes in the 1980s and 1990s for the black and minority ethnic associations stand out historically within UK social policy as a unique strategy for separatism in organisational development funded within a major mainstream budget. This is not to suggest an untroubled history, since there have been financial and other difficulties to overcome, and some minority ethnic associations in England have remained precarious or have not succeeded in becoming independent players (for a recent report indicating difficulties over maintaining independence, see *Housing Today*, 4 May 2000). Funding has been an ongoing concern, especially since most of these associations remain relatively small in assets terms. Some have also faced the possibility of a shift from advocacy to managerialism, if they have become more incorporated into the housing establishment in their localities, and no longer seem so close to the arena of protest and campaigning. Nonetheless, the achievements have been extremely important. Black and minority ethnic organisations have engaged actively in the micro- and national-level politics of housing need, putting empowerment, ownership of assets, cultural sensitivity, design, and anti-racist practice firmly into the agenda. They have challenged many entrenched assumptions about organisational strategies and public policies to meet needs.

Strategies and ideas within provider organisations

The Conservative period witnessed an increase in official rhetoric favouring citizens as individual consumers, and some parallel growth in apparent support for collective user involvements (see earlier chapters). At the same time equal opportunity remained on the official agenda (even though government was not strongly preoccupied with this), supplemented by growing acknowledgement of ethnicity. Codes and guidance on equal opportunities and non-racist practice became more pervasive over the period as part of the regimes for performance regulation (see for example CRE, 1991, on co-ops). Areas closely connected to housing saw changes in thinking, sometimes accompanied by significant shifts in practices. For instance, interactions between urban planning and minorities were scrutinised more fully (notably in Thomas and Krishnarayan, 1994), and more sensitive approaches began to emerge (for a good recent illustration see G. Woodward, in *Planning*, 18 February 2000; for an overview of issues see Thomas, 2000). Meanwhile, increasing stress on privatisation, producer competition and contract relationships created practice environments which militated against the success of small enterprises such as minority ethnic housing associations, and altered the agenda facing housing providers. After 1997 the now-favoured goals of regenerating communities and tackling social exclusion were accompanied by more talk of 'making consumers count', although explicit concern for tackling minority ethnic exclusion remained limited. The Housing Corporation, however, has shown strong commitment in its policy statements and comments since 1997, including its *Black and Minority Ethnic Housing Policy* (1998) but also in other statements (for instance, in its *Corporation News*, January 2000). Interest in combating racism has been stimulated in housing as elsewhere by the political impact of the Stephen Lawrence Inquiry (see for example *Housing Today*, 4 March 1999, with comments from H. Beider and A. Mayer; and Macpherson, 1999).

When reflecting on recent trends it is useful to keep in mind the background in terms of entrenched ideas. Regulatory housing practices reflect ideas about 'nation', risk, respectability, being deserving, and needs, as well as about ethnicity, and can exclude, pathologise and classify people as well as sustaining households. Negative discrimination has been apparent in all tenures, although reported most extensively for council housing. Institutional practices in private markets encouraged reliance on word-of-mouth communications and private funding arrangements, steered particular groups in specific directions, and limited potential purchases. Adding to economic constraints, this contributed to some groups occupying the "very worst housing" in the poorest locations, with subsequent implications for choice (Phillips, 1998, pp 1695, 1697). In council house allocation there was sometimes a combination of racist thinking, conventions that worked against newcomers, resource constraints (such as shortages of appropriate dwellings), and hostility from white tenants (for a summary see Harrison, 1995). White people might pursue exclusive strategies such as prioritising allocation of tenancies to 'sons and daughters' of existing estate residents (cf Moore, 1997, p 117, for employment). In any event, for a combination of reasons, black minority ethnic households were placed well down the queue alongside single mothers, unemployed poor households, and other 'undeserving' people. When able to obtain tenancies, they might fare badly in locational or dwelling type terms (cf Howes and Mullins, 1997, pp 198-200, 209-11).

Although some households still face barriers, racist discrimination may have become harder to find in formalised housing practices, as equal opportunities requirements and minority needs have become more recognised. Black minority ethnic groups overall are now "well represented in the social rented sector" (Phillips, 1998, p 1691; although see also our earlier discussion). Housing association activity is important to them in a variety of ways, and current national policies here acknowledge the need for services to be "culturally competent and inclusive", while the term 'empowerment' has come into the official vocabulary (see Armstrong, in Housing Corporation, 1998; and Housing Corporation London, 1999). We should not suggest that RSLs are entirely effective in meeting minority ethnic needs or implementing adequate equality policies (for critical analysis see Tomlins, 2000), but expectations about good practice do include better performance here. Developing a more ethnically varied workforce has also been on the housing agenda for some time, with interest in better practice (for example see Somerville and Steele, 1998; cf Hajimichael, 1988), although employment of black people at higher levels remains limited. Black and minority ethnic households have also taken advantage of the right-to-buy (Lakey, 1997, pp 202-4). In some instances, allocations systems may appear today to be more satisfactory for minority ethnic applicants, although quality of accommodation remains a problem (for discussion see Jeffers and Hoggett, 1995). All this has followed a period of powerful criticism from activists, from the Commission for Racial Equality, and from researchers, especially of local authority and housing association approaches, but also of the private sector.

Explicit racisms have little purchase in official housing discourses today, yet difficulties remain. Educational, welfare and health institutions are not necessarily adapted or receptive to needs of minority ethnic populations (Warnes, 1996, pp 174-5), and this may affect community care and housing. Housing activities still draw criticism. For example, research in Birmingham apparently suggests that segregation between areas has been accentuated by the council's nominations to housing associations (cited in Howes and Mullins, 1997, p 211). Furthermore, public sector investment (including estate regeneration funding) may favour areas of established white settlement, with consequences for differential access to training and employment opportunities as well as housing (see Gidley, Harrison and Robinson, 1999; Law, 1996, pp 104-9). More generally, harassment continues. Development of proactive responses here has been slow, with for a long time little firm action against perpetrators (for landlord practice see DoE, 1996a). Chahal and Julienne (1999) indicate the limitations of support (and the desirability of independent community-based agencies and the opening up of access points for people to report and receive sympathetic treatment). Another persisting issue concerns regulatory practices built around notions of nationality and belonging. Immigration and asylum laws have affected partners and dependents of people already living in Britain, eroded citizenship standing of some settled people in respect of their families, inflicted humiliations, criminalised some people, and distinguished between men and women (see for example Anthias and Yuval-Davis with Cain, 1992; Cook, 1998). Concerns about illegal settlement and 'abuse' of welfare systems have led to some citizens being subjected to checks and restrictions in the housing field, such as having to produce passports (for instance see Henderson and Karn, 1987, p 201; for general housing effects see Waddington, 1998). For refugees there is an element of deterrence (reflecting assertions that many people are in reality economic migrants), and housing rights for asylum-seekers have been reduced. Means and Sangster note that housing problems of refugees are often associated with poverty, and many are able "to pull themselves out of poverty with the support of their refugee community and especially where they have high educational and/or labour market skills" (Means and Sangster, 1998, p 8). Although the idea of dispersing asylum-seekers geographically may be attractive to government, it might work against self-sufficiency (for recent comment on dispersal and so forth see Benjamin, 1999).

To conclude this part of our discussion we return to residualisation. For some tenants there has been an unfortunate coincidence of circumstances. When council housing was a relatively better status form of provision than today, it was difficult for many black and minority ethnic households to obtain good accommodation within it, while other similarly 'less deserving' or 'less respectable' households were also not treated as priorities (for a forceful comment on history see Jacobs, 1985). Today – when some council estates are less sought after – the formerly excluded groups have become more important as potential tenants. Meanwhile, economic and demographic pressures mean that many minority ethnic households have to consider social renting as a possibility, either long- or short-term. Writing in the 1980s, Hamnett and Randolph speculated that the increasing proportion of black people in parts of the council sector perhaps provided "indirect evidence of growing residualisation", given the generally disadvantaged position of these groups in the housing market (Hamnett and Randolph, 1987, p 48). It is worth remembering also that "the housing options of a disproportionately high number of female-headed households in all groups are tied to the policies and practices of institutions in the social rented sector" (Phillips, 1998, p 1692). Affordability problems do not always vanish when households obtain housing here, and difficulties might arise with rents in minority ethnic as well as white-run RSLs (see JRF, 1998a). In a study of affordable childcare and housing, focused through a minority ethnic housing association, Third notes struggles to pay rent among tenants in employment, and consequential rent arrears (Third, 1995, p 48). For many minority ethnic groups, including female-headed households, future conditions and costs of social rented housing are far from marginal matters. The impact of new landlords following stock transfer may also prove significant, whether or not transfer "continues to be a very white experience" (involving relatively few minority ethnic households), as it so far appears to have been (Mullins and Revell, 2000, p 31).

Need

As indicated in earlier chapters, need enters variously into housing policies, ideologies and practices. In recent years there has been growing interest in surveying or analysing housing needs of black minority ethnic households, and it has become more expected that councils will consider such needs when developing housing strategies. Defining need, however, tends to be political rather than simply technical, there is mismatch between available policy levers and needs, public policy emphases reflect dominant market ideas, and universalistic and particularistic approaches may be in tension.

The agenda for a local needs study can be influenced by a range of apparently technical concerns. There may be a wish to assess difficulties experienced by households, physical standards and dwelling deficiencies, present and predicted failures in supply or affordability, relative claims to priority among households, people's preferences, or effectiveness and sensitivity of existing services (cf London Research Centre and Lemos and Crane, 1998, p 3, 1.3). Whether a specific indicator appears relevant depends upon political decisions made about definitions of need, and perhaps on anticipated 'remedial' action. For example, physical deficiencies are only a direct guide to need if we have a predetermined standard against which to appraise a dwelling, and have decided that everyone needs to have this quality of accommodation. Likewise, desires and needs are not necessarily the same thing; preference surveys do not measure need unless we have decided that what people want is clear evidence of what they should have. The key point is that explicit or implicit decisions must be made about defining need when we choose indicators, and that the specific policy environment plays a big part. Traditionally, deficits or shortfalls in physical provision were measured, because policy was frequently concerned with remedying these (cf Harrison and Law, 1997; Gidley, Harrison and Tomlins, 2001). Standard answers included building new affordable dwellings to meet a shortfall, or investing in improving old dwellings to raise quality.

In considering minority ethnic households we might wonder how desirable a traditional approach via social rented newbuild is. Council house design has not always offered appropriate dwellings in terms of size, or the flexibility to accommodate cultural or religious expectations (see Bowes, Dar and Sim, 1998, p 100, for applicability of lifetime homes flexibility for minority ethnic groups). Measures of households' relative need might downplay issues such as isolation or potential harassment in favour of other criteria (although cf Bowes, Dar and Sim, 1998, pp 89-90), while black households could be underrepresented among groups such as medical priority cases or in nominations to housing associations. Beyond these 'technical' issues lies a deeper problem. Black households have been prepared to sacrifice dwelling quality to achieve more security from harassment or to become owner–occupiers, and some council housing has been seen as having a negative utility (Harrison and Law, 1997; Cameron and Field, 1998; although cf Third, Wainwright and Pawson, 1997). For example, although Pakistani households have more experience of applying for and living in council housing than national statistics suggest, many reject the tenure by curtailing the application process or leaving (Bowes, Dar and Sim, 1998, p ii). Along with responding to direct experiences of harassment, minority ethnic households may wish to distance themselves from what is perceived as a crime-prone, less respectable, and 'rough' (generally white) estate culture, just as many white people wish to do. More attractive white estates may be further from core areas of settlement, and (despite appearing less rough or environmentally neglected) may present problems because of having few existing black tenants. (Even a move to the private suburbs could be problematic, perhaps especially for some women; cf Phillips, 1998, p 1698.) Housing association areas may have a better image, but available appropriate lettings are limited, with few acceptable substantial 'outliers' or nodes of development away from established settlement. These issues are important for the pace, character and directions of outward movement from existing areas of settlement (although alongside employment, cultural facilities, family and friends). Neighbourhood security is vital, and there are complex locality residence and movement patterns of relative safety and hazard, although there may also be general (less locationally-focused) feelings that changes in community life, crime and so forth are making independent living more difficult, for instance for elders (cf Turkington and Dixon, 1997, pp 81-3).

In a forward-looking study Cameron and Field suggest that housing providers should prioritise "block allocation as opposed to a process of single house allocation" for the minorities, and that models of shared equity "should form part of the strategic process" (Cameron and Field, 1998, p 43). Elsewhere they indicate that if new housing opportunities are to be found for lower income households, especially in the Bangladeshi community, this may have to involve "mediated mobility through public policy interventions of some kind" (Cameron and Field, 1999, p 12). Elements tailored to community needs and preferences might include conversions to create larger dwellings and opportunities for low-cost home ownership. Perhaps there is potential in some towns for black minority ethnic block social rented housing allocations or large targeted shares of nominations, linked with management and ownership structures facilitating involvement of black-run collective or representative housing organisations. Programmes are unlikely to be straightforward, however, when attempting to bring minority ethnic households into existing areas of white settlement, even with supportive community development strategies (for relevant analysis see Hawtin et al, 1999).

We have touched on a general issue that producer approaches to need may be derived from traditional policy preoccupations which may not suit all groups of households. One effect of misalignments between policies and consumers is that available policy levers locally or nationally may be inadequate for responding to changing understandings of needs or preferences. This is one way of interpreting continuing underdevelopment of public policy responses to 'down-market' owner-occupation and the problems of quality and maintenance faced in this sector. Black minority ethnic communities in some localities may have been passed by, through focusing of local authority mainstream capital programmes on white-occupied areas of social renting, while improvement grant spending has become low despite its potential merits (cf Bowes, Dar and Sim, 1998, pp iv-v, 69-73, 101-6; also Law et al, 1996, pp 55-6). Leather refers to the situation in the 1990s by saying that "grant aid was residualised", leading to a "dramatic reduction in the number of home-owners receiving state assistance" (Leather, 2000, p 149). When funds have been available (and have been assisting minority households) further questions have arisen about sensitivity in terms of advice in appropriate community languages and staffing (see Davis and Salam with Jones and Paterson, 1996, pp 24-5). Beyond grant support and regeneration lie questions about facilitating choice through shared ownership or other methods of equity acquisition, about sustainability in a range of senses, and about tackling difficulties experienced by households in becoming owners. Government's recent housing green paper favours expanded support for low cost home ownership, help for 'key workers' to buy in high demand areas, grants changes, and "reform of benefit help with mortgage interest payments" (DETR and DSS, 2000, chapter 4). At the time of writing it is difficult to say how far future policies will take account of possibilities for rethinking need, but selectivist or safety-net ideology is evidently still influential.

In discussing private housing we are not suggesting that social rented housing does not require investment, and we have already observed the sector's salience. What is at issue is the way need is defined. As we have noted before, the private market is often assumed to be an arena where needs are met by individuals choosing, and where risk belongs to the purchaser rather than to wider society. Producer definitions noted above are tied into a selectivity that has disadvantaged minority ethnic communities disproportionately because of their difficulties in the social rented sector and their weak positions in the owner-occupier spectrum. In a more ideal world there would be mechanisms for assistance regardless of tenure, with risk-minimising or risk-sharing structures, possibilities for easier tenure shifts in more than one direction, and emphasis on connecting resources and support more effectively with people's collective plans and individual housing strategies or housing 'careers'. The dominance of market institutions and thinking has inhibited the emergence of anything of this kind, despite a history of some assistance via improvement grants, council mortgages, and so forth. A further consequence of market dominance is the narrowness and (sometimes) oppressiveness of selectivity in non-market provision. For example, rather than stressing affordable housing supply, national homelessness policy has placed more weight on a traditional welfarist approach of selective aid linked to personal disaster or demonstrable failure to obtain accommodation, qualified by notions of who is 'deserving' in terms of intentionality and local connections. People unwilling to approach certain white-run organisations for help can be discounted officially as not really needy or deserving, while cultural stereotypes can be invoked to pathologise minority ethnic households in need. Homeless people may feel stigmatised as "defective citizens" (Steele, 1997, p 42), but, more specifically for some, family structures or cultural preferences may be highlighted as if these were the cause of homelessness.

Other needs issues are important too. Assumptions about the

applicability of universalistic forms of services provision have been challenged because of lack of inclusiveness in terms of reaching black people and representing them in staffing. This has strengthened demands for alternative provider organisations run by black minority ethnic people (see our section above on strategies), as well as calls for workforces to include people with relevant language skills, cultural knowledge, and understanding of the impact of harassment. Such concerns have arisen not only in mainstream social renting but also in more specialised work related to impairment. Begum concludes that outreach work here should be undertaken by bi-lingual or multi-lingual staff to make contact and assess needs (Begum, 1992, p 85). A CRE report on 'race', culture and community care sets out good practice principles, including respect for religion and cultural heritage, and the recommendation that statutory authorities should work in partnership with minority ethnic organisations (CRE, 1997, pp 14-15).

One reason for white-run RSLs working with minority ethnic ones has been the latter's apparent capacity to offer an approach in which 'housing plus' is part and parcel of practice expectations; this overlaps with issues of cultural sensitivity and broader community ideas about need, which do not necessarily compartmentalise housing, employment issues, social services, and community development. The argument has been carried into the arena of contracting, where the relative exclusion of black-run firms from the benefits of work created by social rented housing investment can be seen as disempowering (see Harrison, 1995). Getting spin-off from investment remains difficult in a competitive environment, where there cannot be an equal playing field, but could be construed as an aspect of 'housing need'. 'Need' from some community perspectives goes far beyond renting bricks and mortar or taking fuller account of minorities' cultures in service provision. Having organisations controlled by minority ethnic people connects with ownership, raising the question of how far empowerment in a marketised society requires individual or collective community control of assets, and how far this should be conceived of as an aspect of housing need today.

Further issues arise in relation to age and gender. For the latter the intersecting of economic disadvantage, harassment and relationship breakdown can create distinctive vulnerabilities and problems of location. The legitimate emphasis on larger households when looking at groups such as Pakistanis may mask such problems, as well as difficulties of other small households. As Bowes, Dar and Sim explain, Pakistani council tenants could often be women alone, older people "who had fallen on hard times, families who had lost their homes, or families with disabled members who needed specially adapted accommodation" (Bowes, Dar and Sim, 1998, p iii). For elders, broad notions of cultural sensitivity must not rely too heavily on stereotypes about extended families, and should take account of very particular needs and problems of isolation, as well as the possibility that low take-up of services can be a poor indicator of real levels of needs. (For interesting findings on differing use of services by older people from majority and minority ethnic groups see Bowes and MacDonald, 2000.) There is likely to be considerable growth in demand for services, and responses should take account of the combination of cultural preferences with 'multiple jeopardies' arising for some elders as a consequence of older age, racisms, class, and a legacy of inadequate provision (cf Blakemore and Boneham, 1994, chapter 4). For some elders, schemes crossing the housing/social care boundaries are beneficial when developed with a specific capacity in cultural knowledge, community links, and language, and this may apply to services focused on helping people in existing dwellings as well as in newbuild.

We have said enough to indicate the contested nature of needs-definition, and the obstacles that inhibit policies connecting effectively with some of the strategies pursued by households. Nonetheless, a great deal has been achieved by activists, concerned professionals and politicians, in altering thinking, and in securing acceptance of diversity alongside equality of opportunities. Governments have no doubt been influenced by an interest in the "formal incorporation of black residents into British society", and by the wish to respond to urban unrest (Moore, 1997, pp 5, 11). 'Race' equality perspectives have been incorporated into "regulatory definitions of need", particularly in the housing association sector (Howes and Mullins, 1997, p 213), and there has been interest in the dwelling design and management implications of cultural sensitivity. There is a duality of concerns, taking account of specific religious and language requirements, but also of the common experience of racist harassment. Diversity has moved more firmly onto the agenda for politicians and practitioners, even if doubts remain about 'deviant' family arrangements or cultures. (Murphy suggests that development of living arrangements and wider societal reactions to these is likely to remain a sensitive issue; see 1996, p 238.)

One interpretation of trends, however, has been in terms of a shift towards an ethnic managerialism privileging the idea of ethnicity in public service management (Law, 1997). This sees policy focusing on particularistic expectations and cultures, while perhaps potentially de-emphasising more universalistic strategies designed to combat racist practices by improved rights and equalities. Ethnic managerialism can be seen to have negative as well as positive potential. Racist stereotypes may distinguish between different minority ethnic groups (and ethnic categorisation may place people by rather selective reference to aspects of their lives). This connects with the shift towards culture, religion and ethnicity that has, to some extent, displaced overt racist commentary built on notions of colour. Praise or condemnation may arise on the basis of alleged cultural traits (where religious affiliations may be perceived as important) (Modood, 1997, p 149). This may have become an ingredient in new forms of managerialism which categorise, monitor or applaud types of cultural allegiance in a model that can overlook other commonalities (cf Mama, 1989a, p 43). Successful grass roots actions might bring at least some risk if – through the elevation of particularistic concerns – pressure for general standards, equal rights and financial support were to be diluted. A recent discussion of Northern Ireland by Gray and Paris reminds us that grass roots participation, and housing organisations identified with particularistic interests, are by no means necessarily unproblematic (Gray and Paris, 1999, pp 160-3).

Conclusions

The material in this chapter vindicates our *difference within difference* framework. On the one hand we see fragmentation and divergence of some of the trajectories of minority groups and households. Minority ethnic access to better types and locations of housing reflects improved socioeconomic circumstances for some, as well as a decline of overt discriminatory practices by institutions, and what Phillips refers to as "an improved ability to negotiate the housing market" (Phillips, 1997, p 187). There are complexities of household experiences and strategies because of the overlapping and interaction of racisms and ethnicity with disability, gender, sexuality, locality, class and age. On the other hand, widespread economic disadvantage persists, and racisms still affect most black people. Many households are constrained by low incomes, but obtaining higher status dwellings can remain more difficult than for white households even where social class is not a factor. Established areas of settlement may be safer and offer more satisfactory facilities than other localities. As Hylton puts it, material wealth or educational success does not completely mitigate or change attitudes to an individual's ethnic origins (Hylton, 1999, pp 24-5). Despite the merits of increased awareness of diversity, it is important not to lose sight of the big picture. The patterns it contains continue, even though specific racist practices and cultural insensitivity have been strongly challenged, and some of today's gatekeepers may play roles as 'change activists' (Tomlins, 1999).

In reviewing social regulation we have seen potential for changes inspired partly from the grass roots, and have noted complications for conceptions of needs in public policies. Processes of incorporation into some policy networks have occurred through involvement of black and minority ethnic housing associations with governmental programmes, while established assumptions about needs have been challenged. White-run services still attract many criticisms. General constraints also persist for providers, reflecting effects which economic liberal and paternalistic values have on non-market provision as well as practical problems of resources and commitment (inadequate monitoring and audit, communications problems, and so forth). There are questions to be asked, also, about what can be expected from particularistic strategies such as those emphasising cultural needs and separatist development. The continuing big patterns of disadvantage cannot be challenged solely through particularistic approaches. One's ethnic or community positioning may provide means of interpreting the world, but people are multi-faceted, with housing options conditioned by a range of structural factors which help locate them in many differing ways. It is clear from the housing press (especially *Black Housing*), that battles to confront broader structural factors and their specific housing manifestations continue, alongside demands for greater sensitivity.

Universalistic principles remain important for households in terms of rights systems, equalities of status, access to resources, and comprehensive governmental programmes for helping people sustain adequate housing. One argument for emphasising universality is that (as explained earlier in this book) the welfare state differentially incorporates and excludes on a constant basis across a wide range of dimensions, confirming, influencing or generating the relative positions of groups. Without fairly generalisable citizenship conventions it may be difficult to achieve sustainable success within these systems on the basis of particularism (or locality) alone. Regulatory practices respond to powerful political interests and to grass roots demands, within other structural constraints and trends. Divisions at the grass roots – whether along intra-class, inter-ethnic, gendered or other lines – are to some extent externally constructed, but reflect or may generate perceived material or cultural interests, as evidenced in competition over housing areas and better quality dwellings. The continuing threat of harassment illustrates the importance of strong universalistic concepts of need expressed in a right to quiet enjoyment and choice of localities.

SEVEN

Gender and housing

Cathy Davis

Women and men differ in their housing opportunities, resources or strategies, and these differences are to a degree systematic and persistent. Earlier chapters touched on the impact which market relationships and labour market positions have on women's housing, and also referred to the realm of ideas, where expectations about family and respectability have played a part. We explored the diverse meanings and functions of home, where gender can be a highly significant variable. Our task now is twofold. First we summarise key points relevant to an analysis of gender in relation to housing and comment on relationship breakdown, as well as on social landlords and homelessness. Second we offer insights into the specific area of rehousing for women who have experienced domestic violence, drawing on new research. This deserves space below because – despite changing labour market opportunities – women in general are still affected strongly by ideologies or discourses that cast them and men in particular domestic and work roles, and that continue to exert influence on social regulation and the activities of practitioners. Women's difficulties in living with and leaving violent men reflect societal outlooks and a lack of autonomy that have changed only slowly, and entrenched expectations about partnering and childcare, as well as financial constraints. The topic highlights how competing ideas are manifested in daily practice.

As in previous chapters we can observe that there is *difference within difference*, and that difference is regulated. Experiences and strategies among women are diverse (and perhaps even somewhat polarised), but still set within broader patterns of difference linked to structural factors that condition ongoing practices of social regulation. Although women are "separated by country, class, race, marriage, maternity and a lot more" (Pascall, 1997, p 22), they nonetheless tend to share low pay, limited political voice, and demanding domestic responsibilities. They confront influential patriarchal traditions and practices, and meet resistance to change. There are complex relationships with other patterns or bases of disadvantage, and effective feminist accounts acknowledge these. Disability, racism and class can be set alongside gender in a more general overview of the kind we are working towards in this book, taking account of the manner in which many differences are regulated. In any event, understanding women's circumstances is essential if we are to get to grips with how housing systems operate, how inequalities are sustained, and how areas of social tension are dealt with.

Disadvantage, change, and public policies

It has been argued with some force that the realm of 'the personal' has often been designated as a private sphere and treated as being of less concern to some social science than the public territories of paid employment, class relations and civic participation. Feminist research and publications have been important in "putting family work on the social policy map", and in drawing attention to welfare state effects that have supported relations of dependency within families, put women "into caring roles", and controlled the work of reproduction (Pascall, 1997, pp 1, 3). As Thomas points out, in the 1970s and 1980s many feminist writers invoked 'experience' (both their own and other women's), "as a way of getting women's voices heard and challenging mainstream (malestream) social science" (Thomas, 1999a, p 69). Light has been cast on ways of living, on needs, and on interactions between home and family forms. Diversity and agency have been celebrated. Both within theoretical debates and in the practical policy arena, feminists have challenged exclusion of concerns focused on unpaid work and inequalities of power or resources within families. They have shown how dependency of women in marriage, difficulties of living in less traditional family forms, and assumptions about caring roles have interlocked to restrict labour market choices. Women's collective actions have played key parts in shifting the policy agenda, and raised ongoing questions about transforming citizenship status to acknowledge unpaid labour and the nurturing activities of women or men, to support autonomy, and to reduce dependencies.

One outcome has been recognition that apparently personal issues are frequently political ones too, and that ideologies and discourses about family, duty, and care (albeit challenged through resistance and counter-discourses) have persistently affected women's opportunities and restricted their effective citizenship. Gendered role responsibilities in domestic contexts may be confirmed by public policies and the ways in which markets operate, as well as influencing these. Public and private life are "reflected in one another"; private life is "not private from social policy, and public life reflects the division of labour in the home, especially in terms of time" (Pascall, 1997, p 12). Structural factors may be seen manifested via material and ideological effects operating in the domestic arena, while the local and particular shed light on structure's interactions with diverse human agency. We can argue that although the personal may be perceived as the political, it is the political (in the broadest sense) which enters into the terrain of the apparently personal. Ideas of women's dependency rooted in longstanding patterns of employment, power, and cultural practice, enter into daily transactions and the very language that is used. Given what we have said about welfare systems in earlier chapters, it is no surprise that services and support systems can have contradictory effects for women. While mothers have been seen as having legitimate claims on resources to counter deprivation for children, welfare systems may also display "judicial and therapeutic aspects that can be experienced as deeply hostile" (Pascall, 1997, p 27).

Fundamental transformations of gender relations have been taking place, with increases in women's education and paid employment, and "new forms of political representation of women's interests" (Walby, 1997, p 1). As Walby indicates, in one third of Britain's local labour markets women form the majority of those in work (Walby, 1997, p 1). Yet much of women's employment is not carried out under conditions equal to those of men, and part-time jobs with few rights or fringe benefits are common. Although women are today less confined to domestic spheres, they still encounter obstructions to their progress in occupational hierarchies. Many jobs held by women "do not provide a secure household income", and cannot take single women or lone mothers out of poverty, while horizontal and vertical occupational sex segregation persist (see Duncan and Edwards, 1999, pp 182-3). Walby points also to polarisation between women of different generations as young women improve their qualifications and labour market situations, but also to disadvantages affecting those younger women lacking educational qualifications, perhaps especially if they are mothers without a supporting partner (Walby, 1997, p 2). Women may be more independent of men, but poorer, although there is variation by ethnicity, locality, and so forth.

It is important to remember agency. For example, lone mothers have variable understandings and capacities for social action, and there is variety in the social and material contexts in which identities are negotiated. Individuals decide what is morally right as regards parenting and work, and respond to the diversity in neighbourhoods, labour markets, social networks and local expectations, as well as to the national framework of law and finance (for many insights see Duncan and Edwards, 1999, pp 2, 5, 11, 22). Nonetheless, conformity to a two-parent (or two-earner) norm is, to an extent, still privileged, and personal relationships, identifications, and jobs remain affected by continuities in expectations about male and female roles. Women remain under-represented in senior posts (including jobs in housing), have participation problems in civic life (because of childcare and other responsibilities), and control only limited resources collectively through female-run voluntary organisations and firms. Governmental responses to transformations in patterns and practices of family formation have been slow, while the longstanding goal of protecting children seems to take second place to the making of profits, and paid work remains prioritised over supportive activity in the home or neighbourhood.

Women and housing

Gender is "an important dimension for understanding how access to housing is structured, how economic disadvantage translates to housing disadvantage", and how "housing disadvantage reinforces economic dependency" (Wasoff, 1998, p 127). This is not to deny diversity among women and among men, nor the specific housing effects that societal reactions to impairment, age, marital status, sexual orientation, ethnicity, or family composition may have. Furthermore, we must acknowledge that social stratification linked to class and wealth remains crucial. In effect, gender distinctions are cross-cut, complicated, reinforced or modified by other lines of division in housing and, in turn, influence those other divisions. For example, disability may reinforce limitations on housing choice associated with being a female-headed household, making dependence on social renting even more likely for lone parents with disabled children than for lone parents in general (see Graham, 1997, pp 196-8). Similarly, racist practices mean that some black women have choices more limited than those of comparable white women, and may be at a disadvantage across the tenures (Woods, 1996, p 80).

Despite experiential diversity associated with this complexity, persistent patterns of housing disadvantage exist for women and may be manifested especially for single women: they can encounter poorer quality environments than men (run-down estates, and terraced housing and flats rather than detached dwellings), lack of choice, and insecurity.

Although homelessness defined narrowly (sleeping rough) involves men more than women, many women are in insecure accommodation (with friends/relatives, in hostels, and so forth) and the scale of their problems may be under-estimated. For young women, sexual and physical abuse from guardians or partners may contribute to their leaving home. Owner-occupation is more readily accessed by married or cohabiting couples, and women without a partner may experience difficulty in sustaining owner-occupancy. Against a backcloth of persisting stereotyped gender roles and continuing influence from the nuclear family model, household forms remain salient for access to (and exit from) the different tenures, even though non-traditional forms have become more accepted. In fact many women's access to a social rented dwelling depends on having the primary care of children. Many women on low incomes depend on social renting, where operating practices of landlords are crucial and will in some instances determine if a woman can form a separate household. Women in older age who lack occupational pensions or a partner's income may be reliant on this non-market provision. For women of 'working age' the level of rents may affect susceptibility to the poverty trap, high levels making it difficult to take a job (given the consequential loss of benefit support for paying that rent).

We have touched on barriers in the market sectors of housing in earlier chapters. Differentials in income and wealth remain crucial, despite women's increasing success in labour markets. Since women in general earn "significantly less than men", while many work part-time or have intermittent or insecure employment, they may be "simply not able to afford owner occupation", and when they can, "they must commit more of their earnings to do so" (see Woods, 1996, pp 71-3). Although direct discrimination by mortgage lenders and other market actors has diminished, some indirectly disadvantaging practices may continue. Furthermore, women may experience harassment from private landlords (Woods, 1996), while some landlords may be reluctant to accept children. Most women are in owner-occupation, many living with male partners (see Wasoff, 1998, for relevant data summary), but having a partner does not eliminate potential insecurities or make marginal the issue of independent access. A high proportion of women will at some point in their lives live in a female-headed household (Wasoff, p 128). Woods indicates that governmental encouragement for low-cost housing for sale and part-buy/part-rent schemes has potential advantages for women (Woods, 1996, p 82). Perhaps this point might be expanded to argue that women could benefit from financial support for housing being more readily available and transferable across the tenures, from easier movement between tenures, and from governmental recognition that many owner-occupiers as well as tenants do need assistance.

Apart from questions about access and affordability, feminists have suggested that design and planning have worked systematically and importantly to disadvantage women. This is less easy to demonstrate in a universal way, given the diversity of meanings and functions attached to the home (see Chapter Two). Even so, assumptions about lifestyles may have worked against women's preferences, while inadequate estate safety and lack of services can be crucial. Roles important to women may be inadequately catered for, with insufficient attention given to home-working, privacy, transport problems, use of domestic space, and organisation of domestic life. Women are often at the forefront of campaigns to get improvements and better resources for their areas.

Relationship breakdown

The ending of a relationship can create considerable housing problems for a woman. Given low earnings and lack of housing options, some women have to choose between continuing difficult domestic relationships in good housing, or better relationships in poorer housing. Domestic violence is more common than has often been acknowledged, and plays an important part in conditioning women's housing strategies; it may be associated with conflict over allocation of domestic labour, monetary or sexual resources (see Duncan and Edwards, 1999, p 259). Leaving a violent partner, however, is not necessarily straightforward, and can be expensive as well as stressful (in terms of time, delays, legal costs, moving and fitting out a home, or security worries). There will be additional financial implications if there are unpaid rents or mortgage costs (particularly if a woman has to pay simultaneously for accommodation in two places). If the change means becoming a lone parent, this might well mean living more insecurely in housing terms, with frequent moves, disrupted schooling for children, overcrowded conditions, and sometimes sharing (cf Pascall, 1997, p 147). Nonetheless, women are not passive in the face of these difficulties. Collective action by women has had a big impact through the provision of refuges, with the prospect of mutual support rather than charity, and the opportunity to rebuild self-confidence and plan for the future.

Accommodation changes following separation or divorce may well involve moving downward in housing quality terms. They may also involve women seeking help from a social landlord on becoming homeless. Women's homelessness (along with rent and mortgage arrears) may be linked to relationship breakdown and domestic violence. The responses of social landlords can be crucial, both in respect of the housing solutions offered, and in terms of sensitivity to the social tensions of the situation, and to specific difficulties facing the woman.

Recent years have seen significantly more attention given in public policy to the policing of male violence against women and children. Traditional family ideas have become less important in housing allocation, although this is offset by the deteriorating choice of social rented dwellings associated with residualisation processes. Since social renting is important to many women, and potentially important for many more (should they come into difficulties in domestic relationships), how this housing is rationed and obtained is crucial. The homelessness legislation has long incorporated the goal of protecting children, so that women could "access shelter where they had a permanent right to live and to care for themselves and their children" (Smith, 1999, p 109); although during the Conservative period rhetoric was for supporting traditional two-parent families rather than single-parent households. In any event, supplementing the tradition of support for children, increasing pressure has fallen on councils to meet housing needs for women escaping violence or dealing with relationship breakdown. The present government's *Break the Chain* leaflet campaign (Home Office, 1999) and *Living Without Fear* report (The Women's Unit, Cabinet Office/Home Office, 1999) are some of the most recent indications that official attitudes towards relationship-based violence and abuse are changing. It is currently recognised that between one in eight and one in 10 women will be abused in any one year (Mooney, 1993; Stanko et al, 1998) and that two women a week are murdered by partners or ex-partners (Home Office, 1998). It is the intention of the government to encourage people to obtain help and to make this type of violence unacceptable.

Social landlords, homelessness and rehousing

One important activity for local authority and housing association landlords in recent years has been housing homeless people. The Housing Act 1996 Part VII changed the statutory obligations of local authorities in relation to homelessness. The current Act represents a weakening of the responsibilities of local authorities towards homeless people. Statutory assessment is not now linked automatically to an obligation to provide a permanent home, which was the case with the preceding Housing Act 1985 Part III (despite the anomalous case of *R v LB Brent, ex parte Awua* [1996][1] which determined that only temporary housing need be provided). At the time of our research drawn on below, national guidance prevented local authorities from including homelessness per se as a 'housing need' priority in their housing registers although the authority in this study used "living in temporary and insecure accommodation" as an alternative. The incoming Labour government reintroduced homelessness in 1997 as a legitimate priority for housing registers through amendment of the regulations prescribing preference groups (s167[5]) but the structure of the Act remains in place. This is potentially problematic for homeless applicants for a number of reasons including the continuing legislative split between Part VII, the assessment as homeless (and the provision of temporary accommodation) and Part VI, registration and rehousing from the local authority housing register (Local Government Association, 1999).

Housing associations have no direct statutory obligations towards the homeless although they have been expected to assist local authorities with the provision of housing when requested (Housing Act 1996 Part VII, s170). Neither are associations obliged to have a formal policy and sympathetic practices in relation to women leaving violent men: the Housing Corporation would not consider including detailed recommendations about this as part of their Performance Expectations when approached informally by the National Federation of Housing Associations (NFHA) in 1995 (NFHA Women and Violence Working Group minutes). More positively, the NFHA issued good practice guidance, *Women and Violence at Home* (Davis, 1993), and another possible constructive influence on them has been *Domestic Violence: Don't Stand For It,* guidance from the Home Office on inter-agency working (Home Office/Welsh Office, 1995). This recommended that organisations work in a more coordinated and helpful fashion towards women who approached them. Nevertheless, all of this is discretionary guidance.

The current government continues to expect Registered Social Landlords and 'arm's length housing companies' to take over the running of council stock (see Chapter One). Nonetheless, local authorities currently still retain the statutory responsibility for certain groups of homeless people. Most women who become homeless because of domestic violence and who have approached an English local authority for help have been rehoused by local authorities rather than housing associations (Binney, Harkell and Nixon, 1981; Malos and Hague with Dear, 1993). This has not always been the case in Wales where associations have been playing an increasing role (Charles with Jones, 1993; Charles, 1994). One reason for these differences is that local authorities have a degree of discretion in interpreting their statutory obligations towards homeless people. Three important pieces of research – Bull (1993), Charles with Jones (1993) and Malos and Hague with Dear (1993) – were published in the period up to 1996 when the homelessness legislation changed. Other research, conducted more broadly, for example Welsh Women's Aid (1986) and Mama (1989), also contributes to the overall picture.

The research undertaken by Malos and Hague with Dear (1993) illustrated the ways in which local authorities might interpret their responsibilities in relation to homeless women who had left violent men. Authorities might be 'generous' (accepting all women in this situation), 'legal' (keeping within the spirit of the law and the Code of Guidance), or restrictive (with 'minimal compliance' with the legislation). Two circumstances seemed important in accounting for the differences between local authorities: the responsibility for dependent children, and actual physical violence. Another important difference in response lay in whether or not an authority accepted what a woman said, and her wish to live independently, without expecting external corroboration of her statements. The most restrictive authorities expected women to use injunctions/ exclusion orders to exclude violent partners from their previous home as an alternative to giving them statutory homeless priority and rehousing them (Malos and Hague with Dear, 1993, pp 36-7). Many women did not regard obtaining or using injunctions to return to their former home as realistic or safe (Barron, 1990; Law Commission, 1992) but they might be found to be 'intentionally homeless' if they refused to accept the advice of staff in these authorities.

Managing domestic violence: findings from case studies

The analysis below illustrates some of the complexities women face in searching for alternative accommodation to get away from a violent male partner, ex-partner, family member or acquaintance. We concentrate on the process of applying for housing, through examining how three housing associations responded to women who applied for social rented housing, having experienced violence from partners or ex-partners. This draws upon information gathered from staff in these organisations as part of a wider study of associations' responses towards women who had left violent men. First we introduce the case study housing associations, commenting on the changing nature of their housing management, and also introduce the local authority for the area where our study took place. An assessment of women's applications then follows, where we review the types of information which housing staff gathered and considered appropriate, and their views about women's circumstances. There are then some observations on the 'customer' status of women leaving violent men, before we draw conclusions for the chapter as a whole.

The case study organisations

The local authority in our study was one which could be categorised as 'generous'. It had a domestic violence policy which staff were expected to work within. Women were not expected to provide 'proof' or external corroboration of violence which they had experienced, and a broad definition of violence was endorsed involving a range of relationships where violence might occur. Although formal policy was sympathetic, there could be differences between policy and practice; for example, some staff had been known to ask women for 'proof' of violence or to refuse to consider women with rent arrears (contrary to formal policy). This authority had been involved in a consortium with five local housing associations (including our three case-study associations), and several thousand new homes had been built in various locations across the city, owned and managed by the associations. In exchange for 'free land', the authority received increased nomination rights to these properties (75% of new lettings and all relets for the next twenty years).

The three housing associations have been given pseudonyms to ensure anonymity. One was *Bluebell HA*, a local association which had grown from a small, predominantly inner city association and by 1997 managed 1700 properties. Its growth had shifted its geographical focus away from the inner city. The Chief Executive believed that private sector methods could be used to attain social objectives, but changes in the ways in which work was now expected to be undertaken in the association did not sit easily with approaches and attitudes from a previous decade. *Foxglove HA* was a multi-regional association which had built between 400 and 500 rented homes in the five years to 1997, an increase of about a third over the number of homes it had managed in this area in 1988. The association had reorganised in 1997, aiming to increase its competitiveness, improve working relationships with local authorities, improve service to 'customers', and increase "accountability to the local community" (Area Director). The reorganisation followed the "new public management" model (Pollitt, 1990). Several staff remarked that the process of reorganisation had undermined staff morale, and that the association had now lost its 'family feel'. *Tulip HA* had registered as an association in the late 1980s, being established primarily to rehouse black people who were either homeless or living in poor housing conditions. About 500 of the association's 700 homes had been built through the consortium, but the Vice-Chair believed that the association had been given the worst sites to develop. Although Tulip was a black association, some sites were in predominantly white residential areas with a known history of racist attacks. Tulip HA had restructured in 1996, and the Board was trying to create 'a changed ethos' and practice, perhaps similar to the 'competitive regime' outlined by Clarke and Newman (1997). The association's most important priority now was financial; to ensure that rent was paid by tenants and that arrears were dealt with promptly by staff. The association's links with the local community had been put under strain through changes of emphasis in its new building programme and through elements of its housing management practice (for example, evictions). Nonetheless, more women leaving domestic violence were being rehoused by Tulip HA than by the other two associations. Only Tulip HA staff maintained close links with the refuges and the local authority's central homeless service, which may account for its higher rehousing rate.

The housing management service in all three associations had changed a great deal over the preceding 10 years. The growing influence of various forms of managerialism had accompanied the de facto redefinition of Housing Officer/Housing Services Officer jobs. No longer could staff work to build what they regarded as a positive landlord/tenant relationship among association tenants as a whole. Increasingly, their role was to deal as quickly and effectively as possible with arrears, voids and anti-social behaviour to minimise the cost to the association (in rent loss, arrears or damage to property). Applicants' or tenants' requests were either dealt with at the lowest level possible in the organisational hierarchy (by new Customer Services staff) in Foxglove HA and Tulip HA, or had to be squeezed into the time available by hard-pressed Housing Officers working a longstanding Duty Officer rota. Changes in the nature of Housing Officer/Housing Services Officer jobs (in all of the associations) and the introduction of Customer Services staff (in two associations) were reinforced by changes in dominant organisational cultures. All of the recent changes in the three associations were commensurate with becoming more competitive rather than becoming more accessible. There was a focus on maximising rental income and minimising the costs of staff and overheads in housing management. By contrast, there appeared to be less commitment (or an undermining of commitment) and fragmented levels of understanding in relation to 'race', gender and disability equality. As far as staffing was concerned, Tulip HA had recruited mainly black and Asian staff (women and men) to its housing management service, Bluebell HA had white, African Caribbean and Asian staff (women and men), but all Foxglove HA staff were white (although all three associations had inner city offices). Very few staff in the associations were disabled and there were few arrangements in place to make the associations more accessible to disabled people.

Front-line staff revealed that help and advice given to applicants was diminishing; with constraints on their time, they simply gathered information necessary for their purposes. Women would generally be told by staff in all three associations to go to the council for help and a nomination. Women who were distressed or very determined to be interviewed fully might find that personal interviewers spent longer with them, but the trend was not to do so. The emphasis was on introducing ways of working (including standardising procedures) that reduced to a minimum the time spent with each applicant.

Assessing women's applications

Although women who were homeless because of domestic violence would initially receive the highest points total in all of the associations' waiting lists (and/or a priority nomination from the local authority) it could not be assumed that assessment of their housing applications would be straightforward. This section looks at the way in which applications were assessed in relation to a number of features. Some were known to be influential in housing management practice and had been identified in good practice guidance (Davis, 1993), housing management literature (Henderson and Karn, 1987; Parker, Smith and Williams, 1992; Withers and Randolph, 1994) and research on women's access to social housing in these circumstances (Mama, 1989; Bull, 1993; Charles with Jones, 1993; Malos and Hague with Dear, 1993). It also seemed likely that there would be other issues which might be important, including more overtly financial considerations (Ford and Seavers, 1998; Walker, 2000).

In all three associations, a woman applying for accommodation was expected to provide information on an application form about domestic violence, either through writing details in a blank section or ticking a box. All the associations gave high priority to applications from people homeless because of domestic violence, and appeared not to distinguish between lone parents and single women in determining priority. All applicants were independently assessed by the associations whether or not they had already been given priority homeless status and been nominated from the local authority's housing register. (This was contrary to the joint agreement which had been negotiated between the National Federation of Housing Associations and the local government associations; see NFHA, AMA and ADC, 1989). Bluebell HA assessed applications from women leaving violence on the basis of the woman's housing circumstances (having no time or inclination to check further). Foxglove HA and Tulip HA did this *and* expected to be given 'support letters' *and* undertook a 'landlord check' (whether or not the applicant had been nominated by the local authority as statutory homeless).

I. The 'home visit' or equivalent office interview

Prioritising the violence or the homelessness

One key difference between associations concerned whether staff regarded the violence or the homelessness to be the most important feature of a woman's application. Prioritising the violence enabled women who were still living with violent partners to be considered as high priority applicants without their becoming homeless.

Bluebell HA and Tulip HA were most concerned about the violence which had occurred. The staff felt it was a secondary issue whether the woman was actually or about to be homeless as defined in the Housing Act 1996. This potentially enabled more women to be assessed as high priority. This approach had helped a disabled woman (whose alternative home had to be adapted for her before she moved) and an Asian woman who could not use the local refuge (because her eldest son was too old to be accepted). Both made arrangements to move while living with their violent husbands and waited many more months until a suitable property could be offered. Foxglove HA would only prioritise women if they were actually homeless or about to become homeless. Staff would return priority homeless nominations to the local authority for reassessment if they believed the applicant was not homeless. For example, a woman who had left her partner and who lived temporarily in an assured shorthold tenancy would not be regarded as homeless by this association. This narrower interpretation of the circumstances which might be considered a priority pre-empted the possibility of women making any plans to move away from a violent partner: the association would only give a woman sufficient priority to be rehoused if she was effectively homeless.

The 'types' of violence considered

A second difference between associations related to how staff evaluated the violence which had occurred. In recent years, broader definitions of violence have been endorsed: in the Code of Guidance to the homelessness legislation (DoE, 1991); in the NFHA's good practice guide (Davis, 1993); and in a number of local authority housing department policies on domestic violence. Staff in the three associations viewed physical and sexual violence seriously. Bluebell HA and Tulip HA staff also felt that psychological intimidation, threats and abuse were equally damaging. Foxglove HA's formal policy on harassment emphasised the broader view but Housing Services Officers felt that in practice women who were being physically attacked would get priority over women who were being threatened and intimidated. They regarded the former situation as more urgent and possibly more serious. Ironically, they would probably not have to choose between applicants in these circumstances because, unknown to them, the Customer Services staff in Foxglove HA (who were responsible for registering applications and chasing up 'support letters') cancelled applications involving threats and intimidation because, regardless of the policy, *they* did not regard them as serious.

Housekeeping standards

Staff from Foxglove HA and Tulip HA collected information about applicants' housekeeping standards when they visited them at home. The justification for this was that it was a useful indicator of whether an applicant would make a 'good' tenant. At the other end of the spectrum, Bluebell HA staff did not collect such information, regarding it as not relevant to assessing 'housing need'. In the past, local authority housing visitors collected this information and their class and 'race' bias in doing so has been amply illustrated (Burney, 1967; Damer and Madigan, 1974; Gray, 1976; CRE, 1984; Henderson and Karn, 1987). Using an evaluation of housekeeping as part of the assessment process had not been recommended as good practice (Davis, 1993; Institute of Housing, 1990) although the latter survey of local authority waiting list practices acknowledged that a significant number of authorities still assessed housekeeping and/or the state of decoration in the home.

Most women who had left violent men were homeless and living in temporary accommodation. In these circumstances, it would be difficult for staff to make a judgement about their housekeeping (because of shared kitchens and bathrooms and cramped living conditions). In this situation, the Housing Services Officers in Foxglove HA were expected to find out what an applicant's housekeeping had been like in previous tenancies. The Team Leader in Foxglove HA explained that they considered this evidence carefully. It was usually difficult to obtain (especially from private landlords) but he felt that past behaviour was likely to be a good indicator of future behaviour:

> I'm looking at it in terms of the applicant's ability and willingness to care for the property that they're in and I don't necessarily agree that *because the way of life between the partners is of a poor standard that necessarily means the house is kept to a poor standard.* I don't think they go hand in hand at all. [my emphasis] (Foxglove HA Team Leader)

Foxglove HA had a formal policy on harassment (including domestic violence) which expected a reasonably sympathetic response. Nevertheless, this did not appear to have affected staff attitudes as much as might have been expected, as was clear from the comment above (which by implication attributed responsibility for the violence equally between the man and the woman).

2. The role of 'support letters'

Staff varied in whether they required 'support letters' to supplement a woman's account of what had happened. 'Support letters' might be written by doctors, solicitors, advice agencies, social workers, family members or friends. Bluebell HA staff did not need 'support letters'. They believed the woman, and felt that it was difficult for women to approach an organisation for help because of shame, embarrassment and/or fear (Pahl, 1985; Kelly, 1988; Mullender, 1996). They were pragmatic about the possibility of women abusing the system through inventing violence. A Bluebell HA Housing Officer remarked:

> I don't think you can have any doubts. I've seen too many cases, especially girls in here. I mean fine – you may be rehousing someone who may not be experiencing domestic violence, but for every *one*

there's *twenty* that have. It's better doing that than asking people [for proof].

A contrary position was pursued by the senior staff in Foxglove HA and Tulip HA who felt that an applicant was not 'genuine' unless she could supply 'support letters'. They expected staff to insist that women provide such letters. The Team Leader in Foxglove HA believed he was protecting the association from abuse. The Senior Housing Officer in Tulip HA felt similarly. They feared that women would invent violence to gain priority especially if they were not required to supply 'proof'. The staff appeared to have no difficulty with this approach. For example, in Foxglove HA, the status of the formal policy seemed to be barely relevant:

> What occurs to me straightaway when you talk about judgement is the fact that – you can't get away from the fact – that there are women out there who know that it can be a quick route to being rehoused by claiming it. But again, our policy *does* state that women should be *believed* and that's the bottom line. But we know in reality we can't house everybody and we can't transfer everybody so although women should be believed, because of the difficulties involved in rehousing, you've got to go into it in more detail and try and get some hard and fast proof if you can – some more information – something that is the proof that this is a genuine case. I'm not talking about bruises and so on but perhaps doctor's information, information from the police or solicitors or whatever. Those would be the main ones. (Foxglove HA Housing Services Officer)

Some 'support letters' were considered to have greater legitimacy than others, depending on whether they had been written by a family member or friend, a member of staff in an organisation or a professional acting on behalf of the woman. It was felt that the former would necessarily be biased while the latter would not. Foxglove HA entirely disregarded letters from family and friends for that reason and they were given lesser weight in Tulip HA. Having said that, some staff remained suspicious. One Housing Services Officer remarked that she was aware

> ... of the fact that some women are very good at getting support. They're very vocal and they're all too happy to go everywhere to get supporting letters because they know the system ... It's a minefield. (Foxglove HA Housing Services Officer)

The staff in these two associations also believed that letters from agencies or professionals indicated that the woman was, as they put it, 'making an effort' to resolve her problem. This misunderstood the nature of the problem and revealed ignorance of the difficulties which women might experience in obtaining help (Hanmer and Saunders, 1984; Pahl, 1985; Dominy and Radford, 1996; Mullender, 1996; Bewley, Friend and Mezey, 1997) especially if they were black or Asian. For example, in the area of the study, there was a large number of black and minority ethnic-led advice organisations. Black and Asian women might use them although they might worry about whether an organisation could be independent from the pressures/influence of their local community and whether staff could keep private matters confidential (comment from Tulip HA's Housing Services Administrator). Black and Asian women might also be reluctant to use alternative white organisations for fear of the response they might receive, including how their families and community might be perceived (Rai and Thiara, 1997).

In Foxglove HA and Tulip HA, some staff seemed to make a moral virtue out of what, for women, could be a confusing trawl between different organisations (Cavanagh, 1978; Dobash and Dobash, 1992; Bull, 1993; Dominy and Radford, 1996). Others only asked women to supply 'support letters' because they were expected to do so by senior staff. The expectation that women would provide appropriate 'support letters' (even if they had been assessed by the local authority and nominated without the need for them before) revealed an ignorance about the reality of women's circumstances. It showed that staff had little idea of how difficult it was for women to find appropriate help and it also illustrated another aspect of the landlord/tenant relationship. Essentially, staff were educating women applicants into their future 'supplicant role' rather than responding to them as 'customers' or, alternatively, as women with rights to be rehoused. (Earlier chapters have noted distinctions between services provided as a gift and those provided as a right.)

3. The 'landlord check'

In two associations more detailed enquiries were made by staff about an applicant's past housing history. This was designed to give staff some idea of what the applicant might be like as a future tenant: distinguishing those who were potentially 'good' tenants from those who it was felt would be 'poor' tenants. In Foxglove HA, staff routinely called these 'conduct of tenancy' investigations, though the Team Leader also referred to this as 'taking up references'. Tulip HA staff thought similarly: that they were 'taking up references'. Underlying these approaches was the assumption that the past should be used to judge applicants in the present, and a lack of awareness that a woman who had left a violent man might have had no control over the actions of her ex-partner, for example in relation to rent arrears, damage or abusive behaviour to neighbours (see Davis, 1993 and DETR, 1999, for good practice).

Rent arrears

Research has shown that women have faced considerable difficulties in obtaining accommodation from local authorities if they (or their violent ex-partner) had rent arrears (Binney, Harkell and Nixon, 1981; Welsh Women's Aid, 1986, as revised 1989; Bull, 1993; Charles with Jones, 1993). Women who had formerly been joint tenants might have had difficulties if their violent ex-partner had controlled the family finances. Alternatively, their ex-partner may have been the sole tenant but arrears might have been attributed to the woman (especially if her partner disappeared). Recent research has indicated that associations have become more interventionist and less flexible about arrears than they might have been in the past (Ford and Seavers, 1998). The present writer's research indicated what this might mean for some women.

All applicants with rent arrears were expected to be able to show evidence of repaying the debt (whether or not they were legally liable). The reasons why arrears had built up were not important. The two larger associations had a more flexible attitude to rent arrears, possibly because they were financially more secure. In Bluebell HA, women were expected to come to an arrangement about the arrears but this did not affect their housing priority. Officially, this was the same in Foxglove HA. Unofficially, the staff used arrears 'flexibly'. If they wanted to cancel an application, arrears (of rent or other utilities) were used as the justification. Tulip HA, the smallest association in the study, would not rehouse anyone with outstanding rent arrears with another landlord. The view of the Board was that they could not rehouse anyone who might be regarded as a 'poor risk', given the financial circumstances of the association and the fact that their tenants' rent arrears had become unacceptably high in recent years. One woman who lived in fear of a neighbour who had sexually abused her daughter had paid off £100 arrears to the council in a lump sum because she had been told by a Housing Officer in Tulip HA that she could *only* have a particular vacancy if she cleared her arrears within a few days. If she did not, it would be offered to another family. She lived on income support so she borrowed the money, further indebting herself.

'Making up her mind'

Staff in Foxglove HA and Tulip HA were unhappy about applications from women who had returned to a violent ex-partner in the past. They did not want to make an offer of accommodation to a woman who was likely to return to an ex-partner after a short period because it created work for themselves. Senior staff judged that some women could re-establish themselves and their children in a new area with relatively little difficulty and did not want or need extra help from formal sources. Other women were more vulnerable but might not want to ask for help for fear of being stigmatised further. The Team Leader of Foxglove HA believed that 'the greater percentage' of women whom Foxglove HA rehoused were in this situation:

> They bring with them a whole range of vulnerability ... [and] ... have great difficulty in being able to manage their own affairs – [they] probably have a history of not only a single violent relationship but a number of violent relationships – a repeated pattern, if you like, of behaviour. Perhaps it's the social group that people come from that produces that effect ... I do think a lot of our tenancies fail because there are a lot of people who can't make it on their own either financially or because they've lost something. They've lost a partner who, however aggressive and unpleasant that person might have been, he sort of made the decisions and organised the family in whatever slipshod, nasty way that might have been. (Foxglove HA Team Leader)

What the Team Leader was describing here was lack of confidence, insecurity and fear which many women experience and have to come to terms with when they leave a violent partner. The view that many women have multiple violent relationships and that violence only occurs in a particular 'social group' is mistaken (British Medical Association, 1998; Mullender, 1996). These were surprising views to find in this association where the formal policy pointed out that domestic violence extends across social class and ethnic group. Several of the women interviewed for this research spoke of the long-term impact of their experience of violence and how hard it was to establish themselves independently. That did not mean that they could not succeed in that attempt (which was the implication of the Team Leader's comments) although they might need to try several times before succeeding.

Inventing violence

Staff in Foxglove HA and Tulip HA thought that some women invented violence so that they would be able to obtain sufficient priority to be offered a property. They believed this because they could cite examples of women who had been rehoused and who had then been joined by their ex-partner:

> *In many cases*, the length of time between the woman signing up for a property and the man being present in the home is 24 hours. It's as quick as that. So it makes one very distrusting – often to the detriment of the *genuine*. [my emphasis] (Foxglove HA Team Leader)

What can be made of this view? First, it has to be acknowledged that there are women who will lie about violence in order to gain sufficient priority to be rehoused. Nevertheless, it has also to be pointed out that this is a risky strategy. Would a woman make herself and her children deliberately homeless and live in a refuge or hostel for months? Would she run the risk of being offered very poor property? Second, one has to cast doubt on the version of events recounted here. Staff in Foxglove HA were not involved in arrangements made by women to move into new homes and did not visit after they had moved in. The distance between staff and tenants was such that the reality for a woman of being found by and being terrified of their ex-partner and what he might do (and consequently her lack of choice about whether he moved in) was not understood by staff. They believed that a woman could simply end the relationship and leave. They could not deal with a reality where women were likely to have to make many attempts at independent living before finally being free.

Being forced to move

Another issue emerged in discussion with staff in Foxglove HA. Some staff felt that even if a woman was 'genuine', there was the possibility that she might not live in the property long or might bring problems with her (for example, her ex-partner might find her). This might create instability in the neighbourhood through disturbance and possible damage or abandonment of the property. One Housing Services Officer in Foxglove HA remarked:

> ...When I do an application visit, if I see over the last three years that somebody has had six or seven addresses and they'd fled violence from every single one, I would be thinking about that seriously, really. (Researcher: "In terms of cancelling?")
>
> Yes ... because it could be a potential management problem and you can't always do something about it.

These attitudes about women's possible mobility were bedded in a misunderstanding of the nature and seriousness of the violence which men use to intimidate and control women and their persistence in finding women partners who have left them. They also reflected a concern to minimise the risks to property which rehousing some women might entail.

Honesty

One final aspect of the 'landlord check' details was to confirm the accuracy of the applicant's 'housing history', or any other details of their application. If an officer in Foxglove or Tulip HA discovered that there were discrepancies between what they had been told by the woman applicant and what they discovered through their own enquiries, it was possible that the application would be cancelled. Staff believed that the issue here was honesty. An example was given by a Housing Services Officer in Foxglove HA. A woman had failed to give details of one of the homes she had abandoned because she was being tracked by her violent ex-husband. Her former landlord could not immediately confirm this as the reason why she had left. Her application to Foxglove HA was cancelled because she had 'misled the association' (Housing Services Officer) having left a tenancy for no good reason and then covered it up (as they saw it). She subsequently obtained the necessary confirmation and was rehoused by another association.

Why were staff so concerned about something that had happened in the past when the woman had applied because of current fears about her violent ex-partner? It is difficult to be definitive. The reaction might derive from the underlying suspicion of women which was commonplace in Foxglove HA and with some staff in Tulip HA. Alternatively, it might reflect a staff concern that association priorities and their own position were being undermined or challenged by applicants who did not keep to the rules. Again, this reflected a greater concern to establish the 'supplicant role' of the potential tenant rather than to recognise the applicant as a woman trying to find a new home either as a 'customer' or as someone with rights.

'Customers' or gendered management?

It could be argued that the responses which women received from the associations reflected a housing management unease about dealing with a social situation which challenged the dominant view that familial relationships were private and uncontentious (see Bull, 1993). Associations were not obliged to work within the priorities established by homelessness legislation, by its case law or good practice recommendations, and their approaches differed. The most sympathetic responses came from Bluebell HA and some staff in Tulip HA. More staff in these associations had experience of dealing practically with women who had left violent partners/ex-partners/family members/acquaintances and this seemed to be one key to a better understanding. It was also helpful if senior staff gave a lead in relation to attitudes towards women in this situation. Managers' priorities in two associations did not accord with providing a particularly supportive approach.

The relationship between formal policy and actual practice was unexpected. Foxglove HA had a reasonably progressive policy in relation to domestic violence but in practice responses to women were restrictive and moralistic. It 'struggled' to rehouse sufficient nominated households each year (Area Director) and the Team Leader was not particularly sympathetic. The other two associations had no formal policies but provided more sympathetic services. Even so, staff were under pressure from senior management to change their approaches to applicants, with tensions over the length of interview given and the amount of help and advice provided.

It could be argued that although homeless women who had left violent men formally received the highest priority for housing, it was more difficult for them to work through the application process than it might be for women who had not experienced violence. For a homeless woman who had left a violent partner it was not just a case of exercising 'choice' through walking, customer-like, through the office entrance or picking up the telephone. The transaction was not dependent on how much she could pay but her particular personal circumstances and how these were formally and informally assessed by housing management staff. She might find it embarrassing or shameful to relate what had happened or she might be afraid of saying too much, fearing the potential reaction of staff or being concerned to maintain her own safety. The response of the staff member would affect the woman's confidence in giving information about her circumstances, but the possibility of staff providing a supportive helpful response was becoming more difficult because of wider organisational pressures and priorities. Black and Asian women who were homeless because of domestic violence might also have difficulties because of inappropriate staffing, no practical links between the association and local black communities, and a lack of knowledge and understanding about those communities including the situation in which black and Asian women might find themselves. (Only Tulip HA was able to provide a full service for women in these circumstances.)

It is worth adding that none of the associations took action against their male joint tenants whose violence made their partner homeless. The associations' stated reasons for not doing so (through using compulsory transfer or eviction to release a home appropriate for a family) were that such action would be difficult, it had never been done by the association, or that it was not housing management's role to interfere with private relationships in this way. Considering the process which women went through in applying for housing, it is clear that associations were not being gender-neutral.

Conclusions

We began this chapter by noting the significance of gender for understanding housing, reminding readers of the persistence of patterns of disadvantage alongside diversity. There are clear limiting effects on housing choices due to labour market circumstances, and from the relatively low independent incomes available to many women, especially in relation to owner-occupation. Beyond this there are practices and discourses within local authority and housing association housing which influence access. This chapter has described what may happen to women who become homeless because of violent men. Markets play crucial roles in conditioning women's housing 'careers', but for those who come to depend on social renting, the supply of dwellings, the character of rationing and the precise responses to household needs and differences can be vital. Local authorities have statutory responsibilities but, in relation to homelessness, associations do not. Nevertheless, associations and 'arm's-length companies' are due to grow rapidly in the next few years, replacing local authority landlords. The findings set out above illustrate the ways in which association management staff in three associations assessed applications from women who had left or were trying to leave violent men. Some at least were not particularly sympathetic. Our material reveals that they were affected by managerialist concerns, by worries about risk, and by gendered approaches and insensitivities rooted in traditional ideas. Only a profound change in management priorities and attitudes towards men who inflict violence and women and children who survive it will help women to establish new lives for themselves and their families, free from the violence they have known in the past. Some doubt must attach to whether these new and growing organisations will see this as a priority.

Earlier chapters have commented on the positive and negative implications of social regulation and the coexistence of a concern for 'needs' with measurement and social control. The analysis presented here shows that *attempts to respond to complex circumstances, like those arising for the women in this study, may be cut across by institutional traditions and managerial pressures* (linked with ideas about financial risk, controlling costs, maximising income and competition), *as well as by dominant assumptions which relate to gender roles, 'race' and class* (the 'deserving', the 'genuine', and so forth). There can be few more salient tests of the real character of the social regulation of difference than analyses of responses to domestic violence and homelessness.

Note

[1] Regina v London Borough of Brent ex parte Awua (1996) 1 AC 55, 27 HLR 453, HL.

EIGHT

The accommodation of difference

This book has reviewed 'difference' in housing contexts, and touched on relationships with markets, paternalism, inequalities, and discourses about dependencies and economic life. Theoretically-led general analyses of housing policy remain scarce (see Dickens et al, 1985; Kemeny, 1992; King, 1996), and our study has broken new ground. The analysis has messages applicable beyond housing, offering perspectives on the welfare state in general. Experiential diversity can be brought more comprehensively into accounts of welfare systems, but analysts should not be deflected by awareness of differentiation and choice from tackling the big picture. Households vary greatly, but act in contexts which privilege some and substantially disadvantage others in regular and patterned ways. We have used the term *difference within difference* to locate diversity of household experiences, strategies and identities within persistent broader patterns of differentiation.

To provide stepping-stones between the detail of daily events and the idea of more longstanding structural factors, our book has deployed the term *social regulation*. This takes form in an ensemble of overlapping mechanisms, practices and influential assumptions through which people's varied lives and plans may be constrained, facilitated or conditioned, and through which difference is responded to, socially constructed, oppressed or celebrated. Many households are helped by institutions in empowering ways, but wealth and labour market status remain crucial for outcomes, alongside degrees of risk and conformity that households represent. Once achieved, the home itself can influence differential access to services and other resources, conferring as well as expressing status (cf Clapham, Kemp and Smith, 1990, pp 61-2). The realm of ideas is important. While competing discourses are propagated, there is a *structured selectivity* which helps accord some more weight than others (see comments below on property rights). Specific historical circumstances can be crucial. For example, alongside increasing social and spatial polarisation (and weakened labour market ties), discourses about conditionality and social order have gained ground, suggesting growing desires to deter or punish through administrative practices of welfare provision as well as through law and order systems.

As contributors to the social regulation ensemble, housing policies have ambiguous effects, both constraining and facilitating choice, and responding to a variety of participants against a backcloth of differentiations among households in strategies and resources. The role of agency appears here in many important manifestations, including explicit challenges or pressures from the grass roots, individual households' decisions, and actions by professionals. Earlier in the book we indicated that agency and structure are mutually implicated. It is important to keep in mind what this means in housing, considering how the structural becomes the specific (and vice-versa), and roles that people play in interpreting, confirming and reshaping constraints. The social regulation perspective has been meant to help here. We have acknowledged implicitly or explicitly the possibilities of challenge, resistance, conflict, negotiation, representation, intermediation, and re-interpretation, around and within housing institutions and practices. The complexity of interests involved is borne out by the co-existing strands of thinking found in housing management (see Chapter Four).

One crucial tension is about the balance between citizen or consumer rights claims and demands for self-management on the one hand, and paternalistic 'gifts' selectively made on the basis of professional definitions of need and the deserving on the other. Citizenship rights were considered especially in Chapter Five, but have also been a theme elsewhere. Another tension in social regulation concerns the 'fit' (or lack of it) between two kinds of activity or emphasis: support or protection; and control, measurement, conditionality and supervision. Responses to domestic violence described in Chapter Seven illustrate the continuing impact of a range of provider motives and values apart from the concern to assist. These connect with deeply embedded practices and discourses on competition, risk-minimising, and the 'deserving'.

A striking lesson from looking at disability, gender and 'race' is an appreciation of how all three are affected by some similar forces. Private markets bring hopes of a particular kind of equality, insofar as everyone's status is achieved through money, itself not visibly influenced by differences of ethnicity, gender, and so forth. Yet the promise of markets is unfulfilled, for they inevitably measure and rank people according to relative risks, and this – allied with great inequalities of inheritance and earnings – makes equal opportunity an impossibility. The groups we have considered are much affected. Furthermore, dominance of markets influences non-market provision. There are ideological effects from the 'normalisation' of owner-occupation and from ideas about the deserving, risk-free, or less deserving (which connect intimately to organisation of the world of labour markets), and there are related political effects in the constant pressures on public finance and the way that selectivity and conditionality are handled. Additionally, penetration by commercial principles and managerialist practices can inhibit the responsiveness to people's welfare needs of non-market provider organisations; while directly involving private sector investment (rather than using monies from taxation or general national borrowing at cheap rates) turns help for the poor into a highly profitable activity for private investors or landlords.

In summing up on the responsiveness of social regulation to difference, we can stress the shadow increasingly cast over non-market provision by owner-occupation, alongside the characteristics of the fragmented owner-occupation mainstream itself. Housing policy makers have been distracted by the tenure divide from addressing people's strategies, housing 'careers' and conditions in comprehensive and flexible ways which might cross or bridge that divide. Despite the positive achievements of council housing, some of the households we have been concerned with remain in the shadow, lacking rights and resources, sometimes experiencing degrees of involuntary social or spatial segregation from environments enjoyed by the majority, and subject to distinctive forms of supervision. Meanwhile owner-occupation is dominated by practices with few concessions to impairment, low incomes, or lack of household resources. Leather notes authoritatively that what is lacking in Britain "is a coherent philosophy defining the legitimate interest of the state in the condition of private sector housing and the respective responsibilities or duties of the state and private owners in this area" (Leather, 2000, p 165). This is part of a larger matter, embracing the potential roles of public policy in confirming, conferring, reshaping and distributing property rights, in ensuring stability and sustainability, and in connecting with the varying strategies and needs of diverse households in differing locality, cultural and tenure settings.

Strategies and struggles

Fairly early in this book a question was raised about how people make their histories against a backcloth of structural factors. The basic answer – as one would expect – is through a wide variety of collective as well as individual strategies, ranging from resistance or non-participation to campaigns and protest. At the same time actors operate within constraints, some of which they can affect while some (as we have seen) are more fixed. A related question concerns how far and in what ways apparently increasingly diverse collective identities and commonalities of interests can form and operate, seeking to obtain recognition or resources, in relation to structural constraints and opportunities. In policy arenas, perceived *shared material interests* within long- or short-lived groupings can be as important for collective organisation as the highly distinctive (and multiple) identities we all have. Relationships with institutions are important, and may condition mobilisations and the targets set by groups ('interests' perhaps being to some extent constituted through interactions and struggles). Seen in another way, some processes and practices in the organisation of consumption and welfare create grounds and resources for opposition and resistance among consumers; to corporate dominance, market effects, and institutional authority (Harrison, 1990). At the same time politicians and state institutions may mediate and participate in struggles between groups over resources or emergent policies.

Social welfare movements may form and operate in situations where diverse cultures and networks can be seen (and can sometimes be drawn on as resources) alongside continuing commonalities associated with larger patterns in relationships with other groups and institutional power. Such movements may have distinctive characteristics by contrast with those focused on peace or 'green issues'. Their concerns can include material goals related to processes of political inclusion and incorporation, to the running of services, to property rights claims, and to the 'micro-politics' of needs definition (see earlier chapters). Disabled people, black minority ethnic groups, and women's organisations have fought to increase their opportunities for having a say in policy, and battles for representation and inclusion in political senses may thus parallel claims for better shares of resources. Creation and official recognition of some user-led or community-based organisations (such as black and minority ethnic housing associations) might have symbolic as well as practical significance in challenging established traditions or power-holders. Such organisations may enable groups to exert influence over the social construction of problems and needs, of physical facilities and of geographical spaces.

A significant general issue is of course about who in particular makes history, or has the opportunity to do so most independently. Households including 'able-bodied' white men in good jobs have tended to remain relatively advantaged in housing markets, while provision has responded less generously to non-traditional households or people more marginalised in relation to the world of work. Grass roots pressures have helped shift the policy agenda to take more specific account of women, minority ethnic households and disabled people. On the other hand, the declining influence of the labour movement has had implications for the politics of welfare, as have the 'normalisation' of owner-occupancy, increasing social polarisation and the political isolation of the poor (cf Kleinman, 1996, pp 177-81). It is important not to under-rate less obvious forms of ongoing political pressure exerted by those who have already been incorporated within housing provision to a relatively satisfactory degree. Offering a much-simplified example, we can guess that 'Middle England' looks for social order on the streets, social closure and quiet enjoyment in rural settlements, suburbia or gentrified inner area enclaves, favourable systems of finance, transport, and inheritance, and security of possession. Some middle class households may be unworried by the segregation that accompanies parts of non-market provision, and might wish a very strong measure of conditionality to govern social renting. As we noted in Chapter Two, a perspective on agency associating it primarily with the previously disempowered would mislead. Furthermore, the very construction of inter-group boundaries and the categorising of people into supposedly distinct groups clearly involve agency of the past or present.

Particularism and universality

Although specific individuals' or groups' needs are important, focusing on these does not remove the issue of more collective needs and universalistic public policy responses. Policy implementors have to sort, label, and measure between competing requests to some degree, while policies also confirm general standards and entitlements. Particularistic demands may help make universalism more sensitive to diversity and cultural specificity, but might obscure common interests in general rights claims, and potential shared values and mutual obligations (for legal issues see Poulter, 1998). One must remember that while "multiculturalism by definition strives to maintain a respect for differences", differences may "conspire against equity" (L. Green, foreword to Huff and Kline, 1999, p ix). There is more to welfare than potentially competing short-term consumer goals. Bauman suggests that "the idea of the welfare state makes little sense without appealing to the idea of the *sameness* of the human condition, human needs and human rights" (Bauman, 1998, p 59). We must not forget, also, that complex interdependencies mean that numerous anticipated and unanticipated consequences arise for others from the actions of groups or individuals (for informative analysis see Twine, 1994). In any event, we would argue that the constraints on freedom of identity formation and expression are not only "structural and patriarchal" but also part of the "necessary price of combining universalism and difference"; participants may pay this when bringing difference into a universalistic context, because the latter requires some tolerance and mutuality of recognition of claims (see Ranger, 1996, p 23). Furthermore, as noted in Chapter One and elsewhere (Harrison, 1995), particularistic strategies often require underpinning with universalised systems of citizenship rights and access to resources.

Oppressive practices are to an extent contingent on specific relationships that develop around provision of services or funds. Establishing universalistic rights can erode hierarchy, conditionality, dependency, or the sense that people are receiving a gift at the expense of others. This is evident through the struggles to establish disabled people's full rights as citizens. Universalistic services and widespread welfare and consumer rights also influence human agency insofar as commonality of interests – or the sense of this – might mean acceptance of fairness, queues, altruism, mutual obligation, or sharing.

A universalistic emphasis in housing could mean a focus on more equality of status, property rights, or finance. For example, one response to the tenure divide might be to move funding towards greater 'neutrality' in the support available as between similar households in differing settings (see Malpass, 1990, pp 161-2). Assistance could be less dependent upon tenure, and geared more effectively to relative needs (thus making flexible tenure forms and households' tenure shifts less problematic). There might be a more universalised system of financial support (such as a general housing allowance, benefit or tax credits system), possibly varying in relation to local circumstances, and ideally capable of being accessed collectively by groups or community organisations as well as individually. In responding to difficult conditions in all tenures, such a system might accord everyone similar status as a potential user of resources, albeit subject to some measure of income. Perhaps there could be basic assistance and protection that most people received at some times in their lives, enhanced in line with lower income and any specialised needs. Poor or vulnerable people would therefore be enmeshed within a general system that served everyone as and when required and justifiable, thus minimising stigma and visible dependency. Universalistic financial support arrangements could have preventative effects, helping towards increased security and sustainability. Financial mechanisms reducing risks and catering for household change might especially benefit elders, women, and households that included disabled people.

A general allowances system, however, might not be unproblematic. Certain governmental goals – such as better building maintenance or collective acquisition of assets for use by a succession of households – are not about assisting identifiable individuals. There are also questions about beneficiaries and cost effects of a household subsidy, tax relief or credit, which can inflate prices and put money into the hands of investors and managers of building or finance companies, pockets of private landlords, or pay packets of housing managers. Approaches focused directly on supply and improving or controlling quality or pricing remain significant alternatives. Furthermore, there are probably far too many people on low incomes in the UK to make possible a comprehensive, cross-tenure system of allowances, genuinely catering for household necessities and 'careers', except at a cost that central government will not accept. Nonetheless, the principle of universalistic systems accommodating recognition of diversity has much to recommend it, and could be pursued in the territory of property rights, or in relation to rights of voice and participation, as well as affordability, funding, or quality standards for dwellings.

Citizenship, property, and local power

As we have seen, disabled people, minority ethnic households and women do not always enjoy a full citizenship status in terms of housing access, security, and entitlements. Although much has changed (for example through acknowledgement of cultural diversity, or laws on equality), individuals must still on occasion submit themselves to unpleasant procedures of measurement or assessment (such as passport checks, measures of physical capacity, or intrusive enquiries into their personal relationships). Some disabled people have not even been regarded as entitled to become independent property-owners.

Unsurprisingly, rights claims are an important focus of struggles, and here housing raises distinctive questions for citizenship theorists. The meanings and expectations focused on the home, and the defining of needs, are complex. If we take preferences, agency, and self-management seriously, we must be careful about a simplistic approach to social rights. *Welfare rights (and social rights of citizenship) need not be conceived of in opposition to property and the commodification of consumption.* In saying this we may part company with writers such as Dean with Melrose, who present social rights as vulnerable and subordinate to other kinds of rights, "having no distinctive forum for their expression or realisation" (Dean with

Melrose, 1999, p 90; cf Twine, 1994, pp 102-12, referring to Esping-Andersen). Some 'social rights' may indeed be vulnerable to withdrawal. For example, United States welfare provisions for settled immigrants have proved vulnerable to 'rollback' recently in the absence of political support for them, and in a context that provision of social services can be seen as conditional on governmental fiscal capacity to pay as well as on recipients being perceived as deserving national citizens (see Demleitner, 1998; cf Kvistad, 1998, p 146). Yet consumer-focused rights cannot all be demolished so easily. The experience of owner-occupation suggests that property rights carry relatively strong consumer and welfare entitlements.

In effect, property rights arrangements are an important facet of the material experience of citizenship (as they have frequently been in earlier periods of history), a key part in its differentiation, and a potential basis for mobilisations and solidarities. *In housing, effective property claims (in all tenures) can constitute people as rights-holders rather than supplicants.* Leaving property rights out of UK debates about welfare and citizenship is a damaging omission, potentially relegating much argument over extending or defending social dimensions of citizenship (although not universalistic services) to the terrain of the selectively awarded gift confined to the marginalised. *If we wished to envisage a comprehensive housing rights dimension to citizenship claims, then we would need to confront the dominance of economic liberalism, exclusion and markets within the core systems of housing provision, where the characteristics and availability of property rights are central.* Freedom, security, social control and differentiation are important issues here, just as in social renting. If social policy needs to find ways of imparting greater certainty to the meaning of citizenship, as Dean with Melrose perceptively suggest (Dean with Melrose, 1999, p 172), then private property rights (held individually or collectively) have important roles to play. Although frequently helping confirm inequalities, property rights systems also have potential to contribute to evening out the present highly unequal social distributions of risk experienced by households, and to securing many ideals that people now associate with 'home'. Despite the obvious case for interpreting property concepts as ideologically shaped, this cannot excuse dismissing them as building blocks for people's strategies, as if households had some very crude false consciousness about the benefits. That would be to downgrade agency. Furthermore, property rights concern relationships between people in relation to things; a desire for property is far more than a desire for objects, being about ways of living. Indeed, private property rights modify people's relationships to the labour market and dependence on the commodification of their labour (a type of commodification which fits ill with notions of social rights).

None of this argues that there is something innately superior about extensive private ownership. Indeed, large-scale provision of municipal housing was in many ways a strong alternative, while the UK's National Health Service has demonstrated advantages from a heavily socialised system in meeting needs. Crucially, however, claims linked to property are politically difficult to deny in societies in which ideologies and discourses about property rights are so firmly entrenched (and in effect privileged through the structured selectivity to which we referred earlier). Specific historical circumstances gave owner-occupation its attractions in Britain (see for example Cole and Furbey, 1994, pp 40-3), and the notion that owner-occupation is the 'natural' and superior tenure may be "largely the product of the 1920s and 1930s" (Daunton, 1987, p 68), although this might not explain the tenure's attraction for some minority ethnic groups. Yet ownership has long fitted well with the ideal of defensible claims to tangible (and growing) resources free of control by employers, neighbours or bureaucrats. The character and extent of the defensible boundary drawn around assets here continues to be highly salient politically, with questions about how far owners should part with their equity to pay for social support services in older age, or for adaptations for their disabled children or when faced with legal costs, rather than drawing on universalistic services (such as grants, legal aid, and so forth).

In any event, it is easier for governments to sell off public assets, or concede rights over such assets to private investors in return for working capital, than to remove acknowledged private property rights from individuals or organisations. Furthermore, creating effective and sustainable rented alternatives to owner-occupation runs up against contrasts between images of ownership and the paternalism and supervision associated with the notion of a gift for a relatively excluded (albeit large) minority. There is potential for diluting tenure boundaries, developing more individual, collective or community-based property rights for renters, and creating more imaginative forms of affordable home ownership (while also making tenure moves in either direction easier, and tenure itself more flexible; see Cope, 1999, p 343). Governmental strategies for transferring council estates to new landlords could give higher explicit priority to households' rights, assets, funding and collective ownership, rather than inserting tenants as partners or 'stakeholders'. Collective rights to a pooled discount for tenants on estates would have been a logical counterpart of individual right-to-buy discounts in the 1980s, confirming the status of dwellings as held in trust for occupiers by acknowledging tenants' rights to controlling part of the equity (with implications for organisational structures) (Harrison, 1990). Transfer processes may favour the career housing executive and the private investment institution, rather than the tenant. Labour is discarding council estates, but has shown little vision in reviewing alternative tenure possibilities and managerial frameworks. Despite references to tenant-led organisations, nothing suggests government has much interest in prioritising cooperative, mutual or self-help solutions in ways that would create well-resourced and genuinely empowering organisations, where property rights could reside primarily with residents, and where benefits in terms of housing employment might fall locally. It also seems unlikely that organisations run by disabled people, women or black minority ethnic people will end up having much of a share in transferred assets by the time everything has been disposed of.

Of course, more rights over hard-to-let flats on decaying estates cannot solve households' problems. Sustainable neighbourhood improvement requires increased incomes and real wealth, for relative poverty lies at the heart of housing disadvantage. Many people in the groups we have discussed face the severe constraints that low incomes bring. Even a better-developed system of housing allowances (as outlined above) would not resolve this, although it would help. Yet rights might be a complementary route to decreasing dependency, increasing security, and (given political will) entrenching improved access to financial resources and bricks and mortar. Property rights focus around assets, rather than an income flow to the poor that is dependent on daily political manoeuvres, while the enhancement of rights is of concern to everyone in housing, including existing owner-occupiers. Perhaps the distribution, growth, protection and control of assets offers over the long term one of the more secure bases for welfare. In housing, a larger stake in property might also strengthen people's motivations for involving themselves in tenant-led management (see *Housing Today*, 20 July 2000, for apathy among housing association tenants).

Any further developments in collective localised control, however, whether based on enhanced property rights or not, would probably be hedged about by universalistic performance expectations and standards to protect equalities and prevent unfair discrimination. Furthermore, models orientated towards grass-roots empowerment raise questions about the policing of those who are so different as to constitute a threat to others. *Difference is not always something to celebrate,* but (as recent hostilities directed at suspected child-abusers show) grass-roots reactions to deviance are by no means always well-informed. This issue is a reminder that neither a vision of collective local power nor of the sovereign individual customer is enough. Social regulation includes processes for managing tensions and risks, as well as judging between claims for resources. *There is still a great deal of space here for well-trained personnel with commitment to the much-maligned tradition of 'public service'*, and there are plenty of strategic, advisory and service roles that belong with public authorities.

Analysing welfare systems and states

Despite this book's rather specific focus, we conclude with two general messages for theorists who look more broadly at welfare systems. First, the evaluation and interpretation of welfare and social rights arrangements is a complex enterprise. It may benefit from an inclusive notion of welfare and consumption channels and practices, embracing mechanisms of assistance, differential incorporation, and control, and paying attention to market as well as non-market and domestic elements. We have started developing implements for building an overview here, in our ideas of social regulation. Second, in approaching agency and structure it is useful not to over-privilege one specific line of division (class, gender, ethnicity, disability, age, and so forth), given the limitations arising from missing out supposedly 'secondary' divisions, or bolting them on in a marginalising manner (as so often happens with disability). Focusing on mechanisms, practices and unequal patterns of outcomes need not require such a prior privileging, and can improve understandings of interactions between institutions and difference across the range of household diversities.

Bibliography

Abberley, P. (1991) 'The significance of the OPCS disability surveys', in M. Oliver (ed) *Social work: Disabled people and disabling environments*, London: Jessica Kingsley, pp 156-76.

Abberley, P. (1997) 'The limits of classical social theory in the analysis and transformation of disablement', in L. Barton and M. Oliver (eds) *Disability studies: Past, present and future*, Leeds: The Disability Press, pp 25-44.

Abberley, P. (1997a) 'The concept of oppression and the development of a social theory of disability', in L. Barton and M. Oliver (eds) *Disability studies: Past, present and future*, Leeds: The Disability Press, pp 160-78.

Age Concern and RADAR (1999) *Disabled facilities grants – Is the system working?*, London: RADAR.

Allen, C. (1997) 'The policy and implementation of the housing role in community care – a constructionist theoretical perspective', *Housing Studies*, vol 12, no 1, pp 85-110.

Allen, C. (1998) 'Post-modernism and knowledgeable competence', in I. Shaw, S. Lambert and D. Clapham (eds) *Social care and housing*, Research Highlights in Social Work 32, London: Jessica Kingsley, pp 81-108.

Allen, J. and Hamnett, C. (eds) (1991) *Housing and labour markets*, London: Unwin Hyman.

Andersen, H., Munck, R., Fagan, C., Goldson, B., Hall, D., Lansley, J., Novak, T., Melville, R., Moore, R. and Ben-Tovim, G. (1999) *Neighbourhood images in Liverpool*, York: Joseph Rowntree Foundation.

Anderson, I (1993) 'Housing policy and street homelessness in Britain', *Housing Studies*, vol 8, no 1, pp 17-28.

Anthias, F. (1999) 'Theorising identity, difference and social divisions', in M. O'Brien, S. Penna and C. Hay (eds) *Theorising modernity*, London: Longman, pp 156-78.

Anthias, F. and Yuval-Davis, N., with Cain, H. (1992) *Racialized boundaries*, London: Routledge.

Arblaster, L., Conway, J., Foreman, A. and Hawtin, M. (1996) *Asking the impossible?*, Bristol/York:The Policy Press/Joseph Rowntree Foundation.

Archer, M. (1995) *Realist social theory:The morphogenetic approach*, Cambridge: Cambridge University Press.

Armstrong, H. (1999) 'A new vision for housing in England', in T. Brown (ed) *Stakeholder housing:A third way*, London: Pluto Press, pp 122-32.

Balchin, P., Isaac, D. and Rhoden, M. (1998) 'Housing policy and finance', in P. Balchin and M. Rhoden (eds) *Housing: The essential foundations*, London: Routledge, pp 50-106.

Balchin, P., Rhoden, M. and O'Leary, J. (1998) 'Conclusion', in P. Balchin and M. Rhoden (eds) *Housing: The essential foundations*, London: Routledge, pp 309-12.

Ball, M. (1983) *Housing policy and economic power: The political economy of owner occupation*, London: Methuen.

Ballard, R. (1992) 'New clothes for the emperor? The conceptual nakedness of the race relations industry in Britain', *New Community*, vol 18, no 3, pp 481-92.

Ballard, R. (1996) 'Negotiating race and ethnicity: exploring the implications of the 1991 Census', *Patterns of Prejudice*, vol 30, no 3, pp 3-33.

Ballard, R. (1997) 'The construction of a conceptual vision:"ethnic groups" and the 1991 UK census', *Ethnic and Racial Studies*, vol 20, no 1, pp 182-94.

Ballard, R. (1998) 'Asking ethnic questions: some hows, whys and wherefores', *Patterns of Prejudice*, vol 32, no 2, pp 15-37.

Barke, M. and Turnbull, G. (1992) *Meadowell:The biography of an 'estate with problems'*, Aldershot: Avebury.

Barker, P., Barrick, J. and Wilson, R. (1995) *Building sight*, London: HMSO, in association with the Royal National Institute for the Blind.

Barnden, L. (2000) 'Finally coming in from the cold', *Housing Today*, 186, 1 June, pp 14-15.

Barnes, C. (1994) *Disabled people in Britain and discrimination*, 2nd edn, London: Hurst.

Barnes, C. (1997) 'A legacy of oppression: a history of disability in Western culture', in L. Barton and M. Oliver (eds) *Disability studies: Past, present and future*, Leeds: The Disability Press, pp 3-24.

Barnes, C. (1999) 'Disability studies: new or not so new directions?', *Disability and Society*, vol 14, no 4, pp 577-80.

Barnes, C., Mercer, G. and Shakespeare, T. (1999) *Exploring disability: A sociological introduction*, Cambridge: Polity Press.

Barron, J. (1990) *Not worth the paper? The effectiveness of legal protection for women and children experiencing domestic violence*, Bristol: WAFE.

Bartlett, W., Propper, C., Wilson, D. and LeGrand, J. (eds) (1994) *Quasi-markets in the welfare state: the emerging findings*, Bristol: SAUS Publications, University of Bristol.

Bauman, Z. (1998) *Work, consumerism and the new poor*, Buckingham: Open University Press.

Bayley, R. (1999) 'Still locked out', *Roof*, vol 24, no 5, pp 23-5.

Begg, T. (1996) *Housing policy in Scotland*, Edinburgh: John Donald Publishers.

Begum, N. (1992) *Something to be proud of: The lives of Asian disabled people and carers in Waltham Forest*, London: Waltham Forest Race Relations Unit and Disability Unit.

Bengtsson, B. and Clapham, D. (1997) 'Tenant participation in a cross-national comparative perspective', in C. Cooper and M. Hawtin (eds) *Housing, community and conflict: Understanding resident 'involvement'*, Aldershot: Arena, pp 121-49.

Benjamin, A. (1999) 'Learning how to cope', *Roof*, vol 24, no 3, pp 18-19.

Benjamin, A., Roberts, D. and Dwelly, T. (2000) 'What works. New trends in social housing practice: 9 Neighbourhood management', *Roof*, vol 25, no 2, pp 35-40.

Benson, S. (1996) 'Asians have culture, West Indians have problems: discourses of race and ethnicity in and out of anthropology', in T. Ranger, Y. Samad and O. Stuart (eds) *Culture, identity and politics*, Aldershot: Avebury, pp 47-56.

Berrington, A. (1996) 'Marriage patterns and inter-ethnic unions', in D. Coleman and J. Salt (eds) *Ethnicity in the 1991 Census*, Volume 1, Demographic characteristics of the ethnic minority populations, London: HMSO, pp 178-212.

Berthoud, R. (1997) 'Income and standards of living', in T. Modood and R. Berthoud with J. Lakey, J. Nazroo, P. Smith, S. Virdee and S. Beishon, *Ethnic minorities in Britain: Diversity and disadvantage*, London: Policy Studies Institute, pp 150-83.

Best, R. (1997) 'Housing associations: the sustainable solution?', in P. Williams (ed) *Directions in housing policy: Towards sustainable housing policies for the UK*, London: Paul Chapman, pp 103-19.

Bewley, S., Friend, J. and Mezey, G. (eds) (1997) *Violence against women*, London: Royal College of Obstetricians and Gynaecologists.

Bhugra, D. (ed) (1996) *Homelessness and mental health*, Cambridge: Cambridge University Press.

Binney, V., Harkell, G. and Nixon, J. (1981) *Leaving violent men: A study of refuges and housing for battered women*, Leeds: Women's Aid Federation England.

Birchall, J. (1997) 'The psychology of participation', in C. Cooper and M. Hawtin (eds) *Housing, community and conflict: Understanding resident 'involvement'*, Aldershot: Arena, pp 183-200.

Black Housing (2000) 'Our parents and grandparents built their own homes and so can you!', *Black Housing*, 109, December/January, pp 17-18.

Blair, T. (1995) 'The rights we enjoy reflect the duties we owe', *The Spectator Lecture*, 22 March, London: Press Release.

Blair, T. (1999) 'Beveridge revisited: a welfare state for the 21st century', in R. Walker (ed) *Ending child poverty: Popular welfare for the 21st century?*, Bristol: The Policy Press, pp 7-18.

Blakemore, K. and Boneham, M. (1994), *Age, race and ethnicity: A comparative approach*, Buckingham: Open University Press.

BMA (British Medical Association) (1998) *Domestic violence: A health care issue?*, London: BMA.

Bochel, H. and Hawtin, M. (1998) 'Involvement and disablement', in C. Cooper and M. Hawtin (eds) *Resident involvement and community action: Theory to practice*, Chartered Institute of Housing Policy and Practice Series in collaboration with the Housing Studies Association, Coventry: CIH, pp 288-304.

Bonoli, G. (1997) 'Classifying welfare states: a two-dimensional approach', *Journal of Social Policy*, vol 26, no 3, pp 351-72.

Bowes, A. and MacDonald, C. (2000) *Support for majority and minority ethnic groups at home – Older people's perspectives*, Social Work Research Findings No 36, Edinburgh: Scottish Executive Central Research Unit.

Bowes, A., Dar, N. and Sim, D. (1997) 'Tenure preference and housing strategy: an exploration of Pakistani experiences', *Housing Studies*, vol 12, no 1, pp 63-84.

Bowes, A., Dar, N. and Sim, D. (1997a) 'Life histories in housing research: the case of Pakistanis in Glasgow', *Quality and Quantity*, vol 31, pp 109-25.

Bowes, A., Dar, N. and Sim, D. (1998) *'Too white, too rough, and too many problems': A study of Pakistani housing in Britain*, Housing Policy and Practice Unit Research Report No 3, Stirling: Department of Applied Social Science, University of Stirling.

Bradford, I. (1998) 'The adaptation process', in R. Bull (ed) *Housing options for disabled people*, London: Jessica Kingsley, pp 78-113.

Bramley, G. and Morgan, J. (1998) 'Low cost home ownership initiatives in the UK', Policy Review, *Housing Studies*, vol 13, no 4, pp 567-86.

Bright, G. (1996) *Caring for diversity: The housing care and support needs of older black and ethnic minority people*, London: Odu Dua Housing Association.

Brown, P. (1999) 'Redefining acceptable conduct: using social landlords to control behaviour', *Local Government Studies*, vol 25, no 1, pp 75-83.

Brown, T. (ed) (1999) *Stakeholder housing: A third way*, London: Pluto Press in association with the Labour Housing Group.

Brownill, S. and Darke, J. (1998) *'Rich mix': Inclusive strategies for urban regeneration*, Bristol/York: The Policy Press/Joseph Rowntree Foundation.

Buck, N., Gershuny, J., Rose, D. and Scott, J. (1994) *Changing households: The BHPS 1990 to 1992*, Colchester: ESRC Research Centre on Micro-social Change, University of Essex.

Building and Social Housing Foundation (1999) *Adding life to years: New ideas and attitudes to housing for older people*, Coalville: BSHF.

Bull, J. (1993) *Housing consequences of relationship breakdown*, London: DoE.

Bull, R. (1998) 'Making the most of an occupational therapist's skills in housing for people with disabilities', in R. Bull (ed) *Housing options for disabled people*, London: Jessica Kingsley, pp 40-77.

Bull, R. and Watts, V. (1998) 'The legislative and policy context', in R. Bull (ed) *Housing options for disabled people*, London: Jessica Kingsley, pp 13-39.

Burchardt, T. and Hills, J. (1999) 'A numbers game', *Housing Today*, 117, January, pp 17-18.

Burney, E. (1967) *Housing on trial: A study of immigrants and local government*, Oxford: Oxford University Press.

Burrows, R., Pleace, N. and Quilgars, D. (eds) (1997) *Homelessness and social policy*, London: Routledge.

Bury, M. (1997) *Health and illness in a changing society*, London: Routledge.

Byrne, D. (1997) 'Social exclusion and capitalism', *Critical Social Policy*, 17, 1; 50, pp 27-51.

Bytheway, B. and Johnson, J. (1998) 'The social construction of "carers"', in A. Symonds and A. Kelly (eds) *The social construction of community care*, Basingstoke: Macmillan, pp 241-53.

Cairncross, L., Clapham, D. and Goodlad, R. (1997) *Housing management, consumers and citizens*, London: Routledge.

Cameron, S. and Field, A. (1998) *Meeting housing needs and strategies for Asian households in West Newcastle*, Sunderland: Banks of the Wear Community Housing Association.

Cameron, S. and Field, A. (1999) 'Ethnic minority housing needs assessment in West Newcastle', Paper presented at Housing Studies Association Conference, April.

Campbell, J. and Oliver. M. (1996) *Disability politics*, London: Routledge.

Carlen, P. (1996) *Jigsaw – A political criminology of youth homelessness*, Buckingham: Open University Press.

Carlin, H. (1994) *The housing needs of older people from ethnic minorities: Evidence from Glasgow*, Occasional Papers on Housing No 6, Stirling: Department of Applied Social Science, University of Stirling.

Carpenter, J. and Sbaraini, S. (1997) *Choice, information and dignity: Involving users and carers in care management in mental health*, Bristol/York: The Policy Press/Joseph Rowntree Foundation.

Carr, H. (1998) 'The sorting of the forks from the spades: an unnecessary distraction in housing law?', in D. Cowan (ed) *Housing: Participation and exclusion*, Aldershot: Ashgate, pp 107-25.

Cattell, V. and Evans, M. (1999) *Neighbourhood images in East London*, York: Joseph Rowntree Foundation.

Cavanagh, C. (1978) 'Battered women and social control', University of Stirling MA thesis, quoted in C. Hooper (1992) *Mothers surviving child sexual abuse*, London: Tavistock/Routledge, p 120.

Central Housing Advisory Committee (1969) *Council housing purposes, procedures and priorities*, 9th Report of the Housing Management Sub-committee, Ministry of Housing and Local Government/Welsh Office, London: HMSO.

Chadwick. A. (1996) 'Knowledge, power and the Disability Discrimination Bill', *Disability and Society*, vol 11, no 1, pp 25-40.

Chahal, K. and Julienne, L. (1999) *"We can't all be white!": Racist victimisation in the UK*, York: Joseph Rowntree Foundation.

Chakrabarti, M. (1998) 'Race, culture, housing and social services', in I. Shaw, S. Lambert and D. Clapham (eds) *Social care and housing*, Research Highlights in Social Work 32, London: Jessica Kingsley, pp 145-60.

Chamba, R., Ahmad, W., Hirst, M., Lawton, D. and Beresford, B. (1999) *On the edge: Minority ethnic families caring for a severely disabled child*, Bristol/York: The Policy Press/Joseph Rowntree Foundation.

Charles, N. (1994) 'Domestic violence, homelessness and housing: the response of housing providers in Wales', *Critical Social Policy*, 41; 14, 2, pp 36-52.

Charles, N. with Jones, A. (1993) *The housing needs of women and children escaping domestic violence*, Cardiff: Tai Cymru.

Charman, S. and Savage, S. (1999) 'The new politics of law and order: Labour, crime and justice' in M. Powell (ed) *New Labour, new welfare state?*, Bristol: The Policy Press, pp 191-212.

Clapham, D. and Dix, J., with Griffiths M. (1996) *Citizenship and housing: Shaping the debate* , Coventry: Chartered Institute of Housing.

Clapham, D. and Kintrea, K. (1986) 'Rationing, choice and constraint: the allocation of public housing in Glasgow', *Journal of Social Policy*, vol 15, no 1, pp 51-67.

Clapham, D. and Kintrea, K. (1992) *Housing co-operatives in Britain: Achievements and prospects*, Harlow: Longman.

Clapham, D. and Smith, S. (1990) 'Housing policy and "special needs"', *Policy & Politics*, vol 18, no 3, pp 193-205.

Clapham, D., Kemp, P. and Smith, S. (1990) *Housing and social policy*, Basingstoke: Macmillan.

Clarke, J. and Newman, J. (1997) *The managerial state: Power, politics and ideology in the remaking of social welfare*, London: Sage Publications.

Clarke, J. and Saraga, E. (1998) 'Introduction', in E. Saraga (ed) *Embodying the social: Constructions of difference*, London: Routledge in association with the Open University, pp 1-2.

Cole, I. and Furbey, R. (1994) *The eclipse of council housing*, London: Routledge.

Cole, I., Hickman, P., Millward, L., Reid, B., Slocombe, L. and Whittle, S. (2000) *Tenant participation in England: A stocktake of activity in the local authority sector*, Sheffield: Centre for Regional Economic and Social Research, Sheffield Hallam University.

Cole, I., Kane, S. and Robinson, D. (1999) *Changing demand, changing neighbourhoods: The response of social landlords*, Sheffield: Centre for Regional Economic and Social Research, Sheffield Hallam University.

Cook, D. (1998) 'Racism, immigration policy and welfare policing: the case of the Asylum and Immigration Act', in M. Lavalette, L. Penketh and C. Jones (eds) *Anti-racism and social welfare*, Aldershot: Ashgate, pp 149-65.

Cooper, C. and Hawtin, M. (1997) 'Concepts of community involvement, power and democracy', in C. Cooper and M. Hawtin (eds) *Housing, community and conflict: Understanding resident 'involvement'*, Aldershot: Arena, pp 83-119.

Cooper, C. and Hawtin, M. (1997a) 'Community involvement, housing and equal opportunities', in C. Cooper and M. Hawtin (eds) *Housing, community and conflict: Understanding resident 'involvement'*, Aldershot: Arena, pp 245-71.

Cooper, C. and Hawtin, M. (1997b) 'Understanding community involvement in housing', in C. Cooper and M. Hawtin (eds) *Housing, community and conflict: Understanding resident 'involvement'*, Aldershot: Arena, pp 273-91.

Cooper, C. and Hawtin, M. (1998) 'An alternative perspective on the theory and practice of involving residents', in C. Cooper and M. Hawtin (eds) *Resident involvement and community action: Theory to practice*, Chartered Institute of Housing Policy and Practice Series in collaboration with the Housing Studies Association, Coventry: CIH, pp 67-96.

Cooper, C. and Walton, M. (1995) *Once in a lifetime: An evaluation of lifetime homes in Hull*, Hull: University of Humberside, DesignAge, and the Joseph Rowntree Foundation.

Cope, H. (1999) *Housing associations: The policy and practice of registered social landlords*, 2nd edn, Basingstoke: Macmillan.

Corrigan, P. (1997) *The sociology of consumption: an introduction*, London: Sage Publications.

Cowan, D. (1998) 'Reforming the homelessness legislation', *Critical Social Policy*, 18, 4; 57, pp 435-64.

Cowan, D. and Gilroy, R. (1999) 'The homelessness legislation as a vehicle for marginalisation: making an example out of the paedophile', in P. Kennett and A. Marsh (eds) *Homelessness: Exploring the new terrain*, Bristol: The Policy Press, pp 161-85.

Cowans, D. (1999) 'Backdoor', *Roof*, vol 24, no 2, p 48.

Craig, P. (1986) 'The house that Jerry built? Building societies, the state and the politics of owner-occupation', *Housing Studies*, vol 1, no 2, pp 87-108.

Crawford, G. and Foord, M. (1997) 'Disabling by design', *Housing Review*, vol 46, no 5, pp 98-100.

CRE (Commission for Racial Equality) (1984) *Race and council housing in Hackney*, Report of a formal investigation, London: CRE.

CRE (1988) *Homelessness and discrimination*, London: CRE.

CRE (1991) *Achieving racial equality in housing co-ops*, London: CRE.

CRE (1993) *Room for all: tenants' associations and racial equality*, London: CRE.

CRE (1997) *Race, culture and community care*, London: CRE.

Crow, L. (1996) 'Including all of our lives: renewing the social model of disability', in J. Morris (ed) *Encounters with strangers*, London: The Women's Press, pp 206-26.

Crowther, N. (2000) *Overcoming disability discrimination: A guide for registered social landlords*, London: RNIB and The Housing Corporation.

Damer, S. (1974) 'Wine Alley: the sociology of a dreadful enclosure', *Sociological Review*, New Series, vol 22, no 2, pp 221-47.

Damer, S. and Madigan, R. (1974) 'The housing investigator', *New Society*, 29; 616, pp 226-7.

Darke, J. (1994) 'Women and the meaning of home', in R. Gilroy and R. Woods (eds) *Housing women*, London: Routledge, pp 11-30.

Daunton, M. (1987) *A property-owning democracy? Housing in Britain*, London: Faber and Faber.

Davies, C. and Gidley, G. (1998) 'A quiet revolution? Resident involvement in rural areas of Britain', in C. Cooper and M. Hawtin (eds) *Resident involvement and community action: Theory to practice*, Chartered Institute of Housing Policy and Practice Series in collaboration with the Housing Studies Association, Coventry: CIH, pp 201-24.

Davies, J. and Lyle, S. with Deacon, A., Law, I., Julienne, L. and Kay, H. (1996) *Discounted voices: Homelessness amongst young black and minority ethnic people in England*, Sociology and Social Policy Research Working Paper 15, Leeds: University of Leeds.

Davis, C. (1993) *Women and violence at home: Policy and procedure for housing associations*, London: National Federation of Housing Associations.

Davis, C. and Salam, S., with Jones, A. and Paterson, G. (1996) *Black and Asian housing needs – Calderdale*, Leeds: Charitable Trust of Housing Associations in West Yorkshire.

Deacon, A. and Mann, K. (1999) 'Agency, modernity and social policy', *Journal of Social Policy*, vol 28, no 3, pp 413-35.

Dean, H. (1991) *Social security and social control*, London: Routledge.

Dean, H. and Khan, Z. (1997) 'Muslim perspectives on welfare', *Journal of Social Policy*, vol 26, no 2, pp 193-209.

Dean, H. with Melrose, M. (1999) 'Poverty, riches and social citizenship', Basingstoke: Macmillan.

DeJong, G. (1984), *Independent living and disability policy in the Netherlands: Three models of residential care and independent living*, International Exchange of Experts and Information in Rehabilitation, New York: World Rehabilitation Fund.

Demleitner, N. (1998) 'Power, perceptions, and the politics of immigration and welfare', in H. Kurthen, J. Fijalkowski and G. Wagner (eds) *Immigration, citizenship, and the welfare state in Germany and the United States: Part B, welfare policies and immigrants' citizenship*, Stamford: JAI Press, pp 9-28.

Derbyshire, F. (1998) *Better housing management for blind and partially sighted people: A good practice guide*, London: RNIB and The Housing Corporation.

DETR (Department of the Environment, Transport and the Regions) (1999) *Relationship breakdown: A guide for social landlords*, London: DETR.

DETR (2000) *Housing Signpost*, 07, June.

DETR and DSS (Department of Social Security) (2000) *Quality and choice: A decent home for all. The Housing Green Paper*, London: DETR.

DfEE (Department for Education and Employment) (2000) *Disability Statistics*, Analytical Services, DFEE Disability Briefing, February, http://www.disability.gov.uk/disum99.html.

Dickens, P., Duncan, S., Goodwin, M. and Gray, F. (1985) *Housing, states and localities*, London: Methuen.

Disability Rights Task Force (1999) *From exclusion to inclusion*, Report, The Disability Rights Task Force on Civil Rights for Disabled People, London: DfEE.

Dobash, R.E. and Dobash, R.P. (1992) *Women, violence and social change*, London: Routledge.

Dodd, T. (1998) 'Regulations, standards, design guides and plans', in R. Bull (ed) *Housing options for disabled people*, London: Jessica Kingsley, pp 144-71.

DoE (Department of the Environment) (1977, 1983, 1991, 1997) *Homelessness code of guidance for local authorities*, London: HMSO.

DoE (1994) 'Living independently', *Housing Research Summary*, 28, London: DoE.

DoE (1996) 'An evaluation of the disabled facilities grants system', *Housing Research Summary*, 52, London: DoE.

DoE (1996a) 'Racial attacks and harassment: the response of social landlords', *Housing Research Summary*, 53, London: DoE.

Doherty, P. and Poole, M. (2000) 'Living apart in Belfast: residential segregation in a context of ethnic conflict', in F. Boal (ed) *Ethnicity and housing: Accommodating differences*, Aldershot: Ashgate, pp 179-97.

Dominy, N. and Radford, L. (1996) *Domestic violence in Surrey: Developing an effective inter-agency response*, Surrey: Surrey County Council/ Roehampton Institute.

Donnison, D. (1967) *The government of housing*, Harmondsworth: Penguin.

Donzelot, J. (1980) *The policing of families*, London: Hutchinson, translated by R. Hurley.

Dowling. R. (1998) 'Gender, class and home ownership: placing the connections', *Housing Studies*, vol 13, no 4, pp 471-86.

Doyal, L. and Gough, I. (1991) *A theory of human need*, Basingstoke: Macmillan.

Drury, B. (1996) 'The impact of religion, culture, racism and politics on the multiple identities of Sikh girls', in T. Ranger, Y. Samad and O. Stuart (eds) *Culture, identity and politics*, Aldershot: Avebury, pp 99-111.

Duncan, S. and Edwards, R. (1999) *Lone mothers, paid work and gendered moral rationalities*, Basingstoke: Macmillan.

Dupuis, A. and Thorns, D. (1996) 'Meanings of home for older home owners', *Housing Studies*, vol 11, no 4, pp 485-501.

Dwelly, T. (2000) 'Choice words: *Roof*'s guide to the housing green paper', *Roof*, vol 25, no 3, pp 18-21.

Dwelly, T. (2000a) 'Notes: New Labour, new homes?', *Roof*, vol 25, no 4, p 8.

Dwyer, P. (1998) 'Conditional citizens? Welfare rights and responsibilities in the late 1990s', *Critical Social Policy*, 18, 4; 57, pp 493-517.

Eade, J. (1989) *The politics of community*, Aldershot: Avebury.

Eade, J. (1996) 'Ethnicity and the politics of cultural difference: an agenda for the 1990s?', in T. Ranger, Y. Samad and O. Stuart (eds) *Culture, identity and politics*, Aldershot: Avebury, pp 57-66.

Easterlow, D., Smith, S. and Mallinson, S. (2000) 'Housing for health: the role of owner occupation', *Housing Studies*, vol 15, no 3, pp 367-86.

Edwards, R. (1995) 'Making temporary accommodation permanent: the cost for homeless families', *Critical Social Policy*, 15, 1; 43, pp 60-75.

Esping-Andersen, G. (1990) *The three worlds of welfare capitalism*, Cambridge: Polity Press.

Fagan, T. and Lee, P. (1997) '"New" social movements and social policy: a case study of the disability movement', in M. Lavalette and A. Pratt (eds) *Social policy: a conceptual and theoretical introduction*, London: Sage Publications, pp 140-60.

Federation of Black Housing Organisations (1999) *Annual Report 1998/99*.

Fiedler, B. (1988) *Living options lottery: Housing and support services for people with severe physical disabilities*, London: The Prince of Wales' Advisory Group on Disability.

Fiedler, B. (1991) 'Housing and independence', in M. Oliver (ed) *Social work: Disabled people and disabling environments*, London: Jessica Kingsley, pp 86-97.

Finkelstein, V. (1991) 'Disability: an administrative challenge?', in M. Oliver (ed) *Social work: Disabled people and disabling environments*, London: Jessica Kingsley, pp 19-39.

Ford, J. (1999) 'Can owner-occupation take the strain?', in F. Spiers (ed) *Housing and social exclusion*, London: Jessica Kingsley, pp 163-78.

Ford, J. and Seavers, J. (1998) *Housing associations and rent arrears: Attitudes, beliefs and behaviour*, Coventry: CIoH.

Forrest, R. and Williams, P. (1997) 'Future directions?', in P. Williams (ed) *Directions in housing policy*, London: Paul Chapman, pp 200-11.

Forrest, R., Murie, A. and Williams, P. (1990) *Home ownership: Differentiation and fragmentation*, London: Unwin Hyman.

Foucault, M. (1979) *Discipline and punish*, Harmondsworth: Penguin, translated by A Sheridan.

Franklin, B. (1998) 'Discourses and dilemmas in the housing and support debate', in I. Shaw, S. Lambert and D. Clapham (eds) *Social care and housing*, Research Highlights in Social Work 32, London: Jessica Kingsley, pp 161-81.

Franklin, B. (1998a) 'Constructing a service: context and discourse in housing management', *Housing Studies*, vol 13, no 2, pp 201-16.

Franklin, B. and Clapham, D. (1997) 'The social construction of housing management', in *Housing Studies*, vol 12, no 1, pp 7-26.

Garside, P. (1993) 'Housing needs, family values and single homeless people', *Policy & Politics*, vol 21, no 4, pp 319-28.

Giddens, A. (1984) *The constitution of society*, Cambridge: Polity Press.

Giddens, A. (1994) *Beyond left and right*, Cambridge: Polity Press.

Gidley, G., Harrison, M. and Robinson, D. (1999) *Housing black and minority ethnic people in Sheffield*, Sheffield: CRESR, Sheffield Hallam University.

Gidley, G., Harrison, M. and Tomlins, R. (2001: forthcoming) 'The housing needs of black and minority ethnic groups', in P. Somerville and A. Steele (eds) *'Race', housing and social exclusion'*, London: Jessica Kingsley.

Gilroy, R. (1994) 'Women and owner occupation in Britain: first the prince, then the palace?', in R. Gilroy and R. Woods (eds) *Housing women*, London: Routledge, pp 31-57.

Gilroy, R. (1998) 'Bringing tenants into decision-making', in D. Cowan (ed) *Housing: participation and exclusion*, Aldershot: Ashgate, pp 22-40.

Goodchild, B. and Karn, V. (1997) 'Standards, quality control and house building in the UK', in P. Williams (ed) *Directions in housing policy*, London: Paul Chapman, pp 156-74.

Goodlad, R. (1993) *The housing authority as enabler*, Coventry: Institute of Housing and Longman.

Goodwin, J. (1998) 'Locked out', *Roof*, vol 23, no 4, pp 25-9.

Graham, H. (1997) 'Finding a home', in C. Ungerson and M. Kember (eds) *Women and social policy: A reader*, Basingstoke: Macmillan, 2nd edn, pp 187-202.

Gray, F. (1976) 'Selection and allocation in council housing', *Transactions of the Institute of British Geographers*, vol 1, no 1, pp 34-46.

Gray, P. and Paris, C. (1999) 'A vision for Northern Ireland', in T. Brown (ed) *Stakeholder housing: A third way*, London: Pluto Press in association with the Labour Housing Group, pp 156-66.

Grayson, J. (1997) 'Campaigning tenants: a pre-history of tenant involvement to 1979', in C. Cooper and M. Hawtin (eds) *Housing, community and conflict: Understanding resident 'involvement'*, Aldershot: Arena, pp 15-65.

Green, A. (1997) 'Patterns of ethnic minority employment in the context of industrial and occupational growth and decline', in V. Karn (ed) *Ethnicity in the 1991 Census*, Volume 4, Employment, education and housing among the ethnic minority populations of Britain, London: The Stationery Office, pp 67-90.

Greve, J. (1997) 'Preface; homelessness then and now', in R. Burrows, N. Pleace and D. Quilgars (eds) *Homelessness and social policy*, London: Routledge, pp xi-xvii.

Gurney, C. (1990) *The meaning of home in the decade of owner occupation*, SAUS Working Paper 88, Bristol: SAUS Publications, University of Bristol.

Gurney, C. (1999) 'Pride and prejudice: discourses of normalisation in public and private accounts of home ownership', *Housing Studies*, vol 14, no 2, pp 163-83.

Haibatan, S. (2000) 'PATH LA a decade on', *Black Housing*, 109, December/January, p 16.

Hajimichael, M (1988) *The sting in the tail: race and 'equal opportunity' in London housing associations*, London: The Black Caucus/London Race and Housing Research Unit.

Hall, S. (1996) 'Politics of identity', in T. Ranger, Y. Samad and O. Stuart (eds) *Culture, identity and politics*, Aldershot: Avebury, pp 129-35.

Hall, S. (1996a) 'Introduction: who needs "identity"?', in S. Hall and P. Du Gay (eds) *Questions of cultural identity*, London: Sage Publications, pp 1-17.

Hamnett, C. (1999) *Winners and losers: Home ownership in modern Britain*, London: UCL Press.

Hamnett, C. and Randolph, B. (1987) 'The residualisation of council housing in inner London 1971-1981', in D. Clapham and J. English (eds) *Public housing: Current trends and future developments*, London: Croom Helm, pp 32-50.

Hamzah, M.bin, Harrison, M. and Dwyer, P. (2000) *Islamic values, human agency and social policies*, 'Race' and Public Policy (RAPP) Research Working Paper, Leeds: Department of Sociology and Social Policy, University of Leeds.

Hanmer, J. and Saunders, S. (1984) *Well-founded fear: A community study of violence to women*, London: Hutchinson.

Harriott, S. (1998) 'Zero tolerance in housing', *Housing and Planning Review*, vol 53, no 3, pp 28-9.

Harriott, S. and Matthews, L., with Grainger, P. (1998) *Social housing: An introduction*, Harlow: Addison Wesley Longman.

Harrison, L. and Means, R. (1990) *Housing: The essential element in community care: the role of 'care and repair' and 'staying put projects'*, Oxford: Anchor Housing Trust.

Harrison, M. (1987) 'Property rights, philosophies, and the justification of planning control', in M. Harrison and R. Mordey (eds) *Planning control: Philosophies, prospects and practice*, London: Croom Helm, pp 32-58.

Harrison, M. (1990) 'Welfare state struggles, consumption, and the politics of rights', *Capital and Class*, vol 42, Winter, pp 107-30.

Harrison, M. (1991) *Achievements and options: Black and minority ethnic housing organisations in action*, Armley: Leeds.

Harrison, M. (1995) *Housing, 'race', social policy and empowerment*, CRER Research in Ethnic Relations Series, Aldershot: Avebury.

Harrison, M. (1998) 'Minority ethnic housing associations and local housing strategies: an uncertain future?', *Local Government Studies*, vol 24, no 1, pp 74-89.

Harrison, M. (1998a) 'Theorising exclusion and difference: specificity, structure and minority ethnic housing issues', *Housing Studies*, vol 13, no 6, pp 793-806.

Harrison, M. (1999) 'Theorising homelessness and "race"', in P. Kennett and A. Marsh (eds) *Homelessness: Exploring the new terrain*, Bristol: The Policy Press, pp 101-21.

Harrison, M. and Law, I. (1997) 'Needs and empowerment in minority ethnic housing: some issues of definition and local strategy', *Policy & Politics*, vol 25, no 3, pp 285-98.

Harrison, M. and Stevens, L. (1981) *Ethnic minorities and the availability of mortgages*, Department of Social Policy and Administration, Social Policy Research Monograph 5, Leeds: University of Leeds.

Harrison, M., Karmani, A., Law, I., Phillips, D. and Ravetz, A. (1996) *Black and minority ethnic housing associations: An evaluation of the Housing Corporation's black and minority ethnic housing association strategies*, London: The Housing Corporation.

Hawksworth, J. and Wilcox, S. (1995) 'The PSBR handicap', in S. Wilcox (ed) *Housing finance review 1995/96*, York: Joseph Rowntree Foundation, pp 9-15.

Haworth, A. and Manzi, T. (1999) 'Managing the "underclass": interpreting the moral discourse of housing management', *Urban Studies*, vol 36, no 1, pp 153-65.

Hawtin, M. and Lowe, S. (1998) 'Frameworks for resident involvement', in C. Cooper and M. Hawtin (eds) *Resident involvement and community action: Theory to practice*, Chartered Institute of Housing Policy and Practice Series in collaboration with the Housing Studies Association, Coventry: CIH, pp 21-37.

Hawtin, M. Kettle, J., and Moran, C. with Crossley, R. (1999) *Housing integration and resident participation*, York: Joseph Rowntree Foundation.

Henderson, J. and Karn, V. (1987) *Race, class and state housing: Inequality and the allocation of public housing in Britain*, Aldershot: Gower.

Herklots, H. (1991) 'Community care in sheltered housing', *Housing Review*, vol 40, no 5, pp 99-100.

Heywood, F. and Smart, G. (1996) *Funding adaptations: The need to cooperate*, Bristol/York: The Policy Press/Joseph Rowntree Foundation.

Hills, J. (1998) *Income and wealth: The latest evidence*, York: Joseph Rowntree Foundation.

Hills, J. (1999) 'Beveridge and New Labour: poverty then and now', in R. Walker (ed) *Ending child poverty: Popular welfare for the 21st century?*, Bristol: The Policy Press, pp 35-47.

Holmes, C. (2000) 'Tide turning?', *Roof*, vol 25, no 4, pp 18-19.

Home Office (1998) *Criminal statistics*, London: Home Office Research and Statistics Department.

Home Office (1999) *Domestic violence break the chain*, London: Home Office (leaflet).

Home Office/Welsh Office (1995) *Domestic violence don't stand for it: Inter-agency co-ordination to tackle domestic violence*, London: Home Office.

Honoré, A.M. (1961) 'Ownership', in A.G. Guest (ed) *Oxford essays in jurisprudence*, Oxford: Oxford University Press, pp 107-47.

Hood, M. (1997) 'The governance revolution from the tenants' perspective', in P. Malpass (ed) *Ownership, control and accountability: The new governance of housing*, Coventry: Chartered Institute of Housing, pp 95-108.

Hood, M. (1999) 'Tenants as stakeholders', in T. Brown (ed) *Stakeholder housing: A third way*, London: Pluto Press, pp 173-82.

Housing Corporation (1998) *Black and minority ethnic housing policy*, London: The Housing Corporation.

Housing Corporation London (1999) *Black and minority ethnic housing strategy for London*, London: The Housing Corporation London Region.

Howes, E. and Mullins, D. (1997) 'Finding a place – the impact of locality on the housing experience of tenants from minority ethnic groups', in V. Karn (ed) *Ethnicity in the 1991 Census*, Volume 4, Employment, education and housing among the ethnic minority populations of Britain, London: The Stationery Office, pp 189-220.

Hudson, J., Watson, L. and Allan, G. (1996) *Moving obstacles: Housing choices and community care*, Bristol/York: The Policy Press/Joseph Rowntree Foundation.

Huff, R. and Kline, M. (eds) (1999) *Promoting health in multicultural populations: A handbook for practitioners*, London: Sage Publications.

Hughes, G. (1998) 'A suitable case for treatment? Constructions of disability', in E. Saraga (ed) *Embodying the social: Constructions of difference*, London: Routledge in association with the Open University, pp 43-90.

Hughes, G. (1998a) '"Picking over the remains": the welfare state settlements of the post-second world war UK', in G. Hughes and G. Lewis (eds) *Unsettling welfare: The reconstruction of social policy*, London: Routledge in association with The Open University, pp 3-37.

Hunter, C. and Nixon, J. (1998) 'Better a public tenant than a private borrower be: the possession process and the threat of eviction', in D. Cowan (ed) *Housing: Participation and exclusion*, Aldershot: Ashgate, pp 84-106.

Hutchinson, J. and Smith, A. (1996) 'Introduction', in J. Hutchinson and A. Smith (eds) *Ethnicity*, Oxford: Oxford University Press, pp 3-14.

Hutson, S. and Clapham, D. (eds) (1999) *Homelessness: Public policies and private troubles*, London: Cassell.

Hylton, C. (1999) *African-Caribbean community organisations*, Stoke on Trent: Trentham Books.

Imrie, R. (1996) *Disability and the city: International perspectives*, London: Paul Chapman.

Institute of Housing (1990) *Housing allocations. Report of a survey of local authorities in England and Wales*, Coventry: Institute of Housing.

Jacobs, K. and Manzi, T. (2000) 'Performance indicators and social ·constructivism: conflict and control in housing management', *Critical Social Policy*, 20, 1: 62, pp 85-103.

Jacobs, S. (1985) 'Race, empire and the welfare state: council housing and racism', *Critical Social Policy*, 5, 1; 13, pp 6-28.

Jarvis, H. (1999) 'Housing mobility as a function of household structure: towards a deeper explanation of housing-related disadvantage', *Housing Studies*, vol 14, no 4, pp 491-505.

Jeffers, S. and Hoggett, P. (1995) 'Like counting deckchairs on the Titanic: a study of institutional racism and housing allocations in Haringey and Lambeth, *Housing Studies*, vol 10, no 3, pp 325-44.

Jessop, B. (1982) *The capitalist state*, Oxford: Martin Robertson.

Johnson, N. (1999) 'The personal social services and community care', in M. Powell (ed) *New Labour, new welfare state?*, Bristol: The Policy Press, pp 77-100.

Jones, A. (1994) *The numbers game: Black and minority ethnic elders and sheltered accommodation*, Oxford: Anchor Housing Trust.

Jones, C. (1998) 'Setting the context: race, class and social violence', in M. Lavalette, L. Penketh and C. Jones (eds) *Anti-racism and social welfare*, Aldershot: Ashgate, pp 5-26.

Jones, C. and Murie, A. (1999) 'Stability and change in council estates: the right to buy', *Housing and Planning Review*, vol 54, no 2, pp 11-12.

Jones, C. and Novak, T. (1999) *Poverty, welfare and the disciplinary state*, London: Routledge.

Joseph, P. (1996) 'Homelessness and criminality', in D. Bhugra (ed) *Homelessness and mental health*, Cambridge: Cambridge University Press, pp 78-95.

JRF (Joseph Rowntree Foundation) (1989) 'The housing finance implications of an ageing society', Joseph Rowntree Memorial Trust, *Housing Research Findings*, 3, November, York: JRF.

JRF (1991) 'Disabled people and institutional discrimination', *Social Policy Research Findings*, 21, November, York: JRF.

JRF (1992) 'The experience of young people with arthritis', *Social Care Research Findings*, 26, September, York: JRF.

JRF (1993) 'Involving disabled people in assessment', *Social Care Research Findings*, 31, March, York: JRF.

JRF (1993a) ' Ageing with a disability', *Social Care Research Findings*, 34, June, York: JRF.

JRF (1993b) 'Community living for people with learning difficulties', *Social Care Research Findings*, 41, October, York: JRF.

JRF (1994) 'Financing user choice in housing and community care', *Housing Summary*, 6, October, York: JRF.

JRF (1995) 'Housing needs of people with physical disability', *Housing Research Findings*, 136, February, York: JRF.

JRF (1995a) 'Housing and support for people with learning difficulties', *Social Care Research Findings*, 66, April, York: JRF.

JRF (1996) 'Housing, support and the rights of people with learning difficulties', *Social Care Research Findings*, 81, March, York: JRF.

JRF (1996a) 'Incorporating lifetime homes standards into modernisation programmes', *Housing Research Findings*, April, 174, York: JRF.

JRF (1996b) 'Tenant participation in supported housing', *Housing Research Findings*, April, 177, York: JRF.

JRF (1997) 'The early years of supported living in the UK', *Social Care Research Findings*, 94, June, York: JRF.

JRF (1998) 'Assessing housing needs in community care', *Findings*, March, York: JRF.

JRF (1998a) 'Rents, viability and value in black and minority ethnic housing associations', *Findings*, May, York: JRF.

JRF (1998b) 'Ethnic minorities in the inner city', *Findings*, September, York: JRF.

JRF (1998c) 'Ethnic minority families', *Findings*, September, York: JRF.

JRF (1998d) 'Housing, disabled children and their families', *Findings*, October, York: JRF.

JRF (1998e) 'The impact of housing benefit restrictions on young single people living in privately rented accommodation', *Findings*, October, York: JRF.

JRF (1998f) 'The incomes of ethnic minorities', *Findings*, November, York: JRF.

JRF (1998g) 'Reviewing the right to buy', *Findings*, December, York: JRF.

JRF (1998h) 'Homes unfit for children', *Findings in focus*, July/August/September, York: JRF.

JRF (1999) 'Low intensity support: preventing dependency', *Foundations*, January, York: JRF.

JRF (1999a) 'Current practice in housing sex offenders', *Findings*, October, York: JRF.

JRF (1999b) 'Young Caribbean men and the labour market: a comparison with other ethnic groups', *Findings*, November, York: JRF.

JRF (1999c) 'Older owner-occupiers' perceptions of home-ownership', *Findings*, September, York: JRF.

JRF (2000) 'Neighbourhood management's role in tackling social exclusion', in *Findings in focus*, January/February, York: JRF.

JRF (2000a) 'The views of young black disabled people on independent living', *Findings*, March, York: JRF.

JRF (2000b) 'Planning for older people at the health/housing interface', *Findings*, April, York: JRF.

JRF (2000c) 'The impact of independent advice and information about housing and support options for people with learning difficulties', *Findings*, June, York: JRF.

JRF (2000d) 'Social landlords' use of legal remedies to deal with neighbour nuisance', *Findings*, July, York: JRF.

Julienne, L. (1998) 'Talking about a revolution: a brief history of the black housing movement', *Black Housing*, 100, April/June, pp 11-13.

Karlsen, S. and Nazroo, J. (2000) 'The relationship between racism, social class and health among ethnic minority groups', ESRC, *Health Variations*, Newsletter 5, January, pp 8-9.

Karn, V. (1997) '"Ethnic penalties" and racial discrimination in education, employment and housing: conclusions and policy implications', in V. Karn (ed) *Ethnicity in the 1991 Census*, Volume 4, Employment, education and housing among the ethnic minority populations of Britain, London: The Stationery Office, pp 265-90.

Kearns, A. and Stephens, M. (1997) 'Building societies: changing markets, changing governance', in P. Malpass (ed) *Ownership, control and accountability: The new governance of housing*, Coventry: Chartered Institute of Housing, pp 14-30.

Kearns, A., Hiscock, R., Ellaway, A. and Macintyre, S. (2000) '"Beyond four walls". The psycho-social benefits of home: evidence from West Central Scotland', *Housing Studies*, vol 15, no 3, pp 387-410.

Kelly, L. (1988) *Surviving sexual violence*, Cambridge: Polity Press.

Kemeny, J. (1992) *Housing and social theory*, London: Routledge.

Kemp, P. (1999) 'Housing policy under New Labour', in M. Powell (ed) *New Labour, new welfare state?*, Bristol: The Policy Press, pp 123-47.

Kemp, P. (2000) 'Housing benefit and welfare retrenchment in Britain', *Journal of Social Policy*, vol 29, no 2, pp 263-79.

Kemp, P. and Williams, P. (1991) 'Housing management: an historical perspective', in S. Lowe and D. Hughes (eds) *A new century of social housing*, Leicester: Leicester University Press, pp 121-41.

Kennett, P. (1998) 'Differentiated citizenship and housing experience', in A. Marsh and D. Mullins (eds) *Housing and public policy: Citizenship, choice and control*, Buckingham: Open University Press, pp 30-56.

Kennett, P. and Marsh, A. (eds) (1999) *Homelessness: Exploring the new terrain*, Bristol: The Policy Press.

Kestenbaum, A. (1996) *Independent living: A review*, York: JRF.

King, N. (1998) 'Buying is an option for folk like Tony', *Housing Today*, 82; 7 May 1998, p 17.

King, P. (1996) *The limits of housing policy: A philosophical investigation*, London: Middlesex University Press.

Kleinman, M. (1996) *Housing, welfare and the state in Europe*, Cheltenham: Edward Elgar.

Kleinman, M. (1997) 'A European perspective', in P. Malpass (ed) *Ownership, control and accountability: The new governance of housing*, Coventry: Chartered Institute of Housing, pp 142-56.

Kleinman, M. (1999) 'A commentary on "housing policy: does it have a future?"', *Policy & Politics*, vol 27, no 2, pp 229-30.

Kvistad, G. (1998) 'Membership without politics? The social and political rights of foreigners in Germany', in H. Kurthen, J. Fijalkowski and G. Wagner (eds) *Immigration, citizenship, and the welfare state in Germany and the United States: Part B, welfare policies and immigrants' citizenship*, Stamford: JAI Press, pp 141-57.

Lakey, J. (1997) 'Neighbourhoods and housing', in T. Modood and R. Berthoud with J. Lakey, J. Nazroo, P. Smith, S. Virdee and S. Beishon, *Ethnic minorities in Britain: Diversity and disadvantage*, London: Policy Studies Institute, pp 184-223.

Laurie, L. (1991) *Building our lives: Housing, independent living and disabled people*, London: Shelter.

Law Commission (1992) *Family law: Domestic violence and occupation of the family home*, London: HMSO.

Law, I (1996) *Racism, ethnicity and social policy*, London: Prentice Hall/ Harvester Wheatsheaf.

Law, I. (1997) 'Modernity, anti-racism and ethnic managerialism', *Policy Studies*, 18, 3/4, pp 189-205.

Law, I., Davies, J., Phillips, D. and Harrison, M. (1996) *Equity and difference: Racial and ethnic inequalities in housing needs and housing investment in Leeds*, 'Race' and Public Policy Research Unit, Leeds: School of Sociology and Social Policy, University of Leeds.

Leather, P. (2000) 'Grants to home-owners: a policy in search of objectives', *Housing Studies*, vol 15, no 2, pp 149-68.

Lee, P. (1998) 'Housing policy, citizenship and social exclusion', in A. Marsh and D. Mullins (eds) *Housing and public policy: Citizenship, choice and control*, Buckingham: Open University Press, pp 57-78.

Lee, P. and Murie, A. (1997) *Poverty, housing tenure and social exclusion*, Bristol/York: The Policy Press/Joseph Rowntree Foundation.

Lemos, G. (1998) *Not as in the hour of thoughtless youth*, Bristol: United Housing Association.

Levitas, R. (1998) *The inclusive society?*, Basingstoke: Macmillan.

Lewis, G. (1998) 'Welfare and the social construction of "race"', in E. Saraga (ed) *Embodying the social: Constructions of difference*, London: Routledge in association with the Open University, pp 91-138.

Liggett, H. (1997) 'Stars are not born: an interpretive approach to the politics of disability', in L. Barton and M. Oliver (eds) *Disability studies: Past, present and future*, Leeds: The Disability Press, pp 179-94.

Lister, R. (1997) 'Citizenship: towards a feminist synthesis', *Feminist Review*, vol 57, Autumn, pp 28-48.

Lister, R. (1997a) *Citizenship: Feminist perspectives*, Basingstoke: Macmillan

Local Government Association (1999) *Report of the LGA allocations and homelessness task group*, circular 488/99, London: Local Government Association.

London Research Centre and Lemos and Crane (1998) *Assessing black and minority ethnic housing needs*, report for Housing Corporation London Region, London: The Housing Corporation.

Lund, B. (1996) *Housing problems and housing policy*, London: Longman.

Lund, B. and Foord, M. (1997) *Towards integrated living? Housing strategies and community care*, Bristol: The Policy Press, in association with the Joseph Rowntree Foundation.

Lusk, P. (1997) 'Tenants' choice and tenant management: who owns and who controls social housing?', in C. Cooper and M. Hawtin (eds) *Housing, community and conflict: Understanding resident 'involvement'*, Aldershot: Arena, pp 67-81.

MacEwen, M. and Third, H. (1998) 'Tenure choice and ethnic minorities in Scotland: recent research and some legal conundrums', in D. Cowan (ed) *Housing: participation and exclusion*, Aldershot: Ashgate, pp 147-67.

Macfarlane, A. and Laurie, L. (1996) *Demolishing 'special needs'*, Derby: The British Council of Organisations of Disabled People.

Maclennan, D. (1997) 'The UK housing market: up, down and where next?', in P. Williams (ed) *Directions in housing policy*, London: Paul Chapman, pp 22-53.

Macnicol, J. (1987) 'In pursuit of the underclass', *Journal of Social Policy*, vol 16, no 3, pp 293-318.

Macpherson, W. (1999) *The Stephen Lawrence inquiry: Report of an inquiry*, by Sir William Macpherson advised by T. Cook, J. Sentamu and R. Stone, Cm 4262-I, London: The Stationery Office.

Madigan, R. and Milner, J. (1999) 'Access for all: housing design and the Disability Discrimination Act 1995', *Critical Social Policy*, 19, 3; 60; pp 396-409.

Malik, K. (1996) *The meaning of race*, London: Macmillan.

Malos, E. and Hague, G. with Dear, W. (1993) *Domestic violence and housing: Local authority responses to women and children escaping violence in the home*, Bristol: WAFE and the School of Applied Social Studies, University of Bristol.

Malpass, P. (1990) *Reshaping housing policy: Subsidies, rents and residualisation*, London: Routledge.

Malpass, P. (1996) 'The slippery slope to rent control', *Roof*, vol 21, no 2, p 13.

Malpass, P. (1997) 'The local governance of housing', in P. Malpass (ed) *Ownership, control and accountability: The new governance of housing*, Coventry: Chartered Institute of Housing, pp 82-94.

Malpass, P. (1999) 'Housing policy: does it have a future?', *Policy & Politics*, vol 27, no 2, pp 217-28.

Malpass, P. and Murie, A. (1999) *Housing policy and practice*, 5th edn, Basingstoke: Macmillan.

Mama, A. (1989) *The hidden struggle. Statutory and voluntary sector responses to violence against black women in the home*, London: London Race and Housing Unit.

Mama, A. (1989a) 'Violence against black women: gender, race and state responses', *Feminist Review*, vol 32, Summer, pp 30-48.

Mann, K. (1992) *The making of an English 'underclass'?*, Milton Keynes: Open University Press.

Marsh, A. (1998) 'Processes of change in housing and public policy', in A. Marsh and D. Mullins (eds) *Housing and public policy*, Buckingham: Open University Press, pp 1-29.

Marsh, A. and Mullins, D. (eds.) (1998) *Housing and public policy: Citizenship, choice and control*, Buckingham: Open University Press.

Marsh, A. and Riseborough, M. (1998) 'Expanding private renting: flexibility at a price?', in A. Marsh and D. Mullins (eds) *Housing and public policy: Citizenship, choice and control*, Buckingham: Open University Press, pp 99-123.

Marshall, T. and Bottomore, T. (1992) *Citizenship and social class*, London: Pluto Press.

McCrone, G. and Stephens, M. (1995) *Housing policy in Britain and Europe*, London: UCL Press.

McCulloch, A. (1997) '"You've fucked up the estate and now you're carrying a briefcase!"', in P. Hoggett (ed) *Contested communities: Experiences, struggles, policies*, Bristol: The Policy Press, pp 51-67.

McNaught, A. and Bhugra, D. (1996) 'Models of homelessness', in D. Bhugra (ed) *Homelessness and mental health*, Cambridge: Cambridge University Press, pp 26-40.

McPeake, J. (1998) 'Religion and residential search behaviour in the Belfast urban area', *Housing Studies*, vol 13, no 4, pp 527-48.

Means, R. (1996) 'From "special needs" housing to independent living?', *Housing Studies*, vol 11, no 2, pp 207-31.

Means, R. and Sangster, A. (1998) *In search of a home: An evaluation of refugee housing advice and development workers*, Bristol: The Policy Press.

Means, R. and Smith, R. (1996) *Community care, housing and homelessness*, Bristol: The Policy Press.

Modood, T. (1997) 'Employment', in T. Modood and R. Berthoud with J. Lakey, J. Nazroo, P. Smith, S. Virdee and S. Beishon, *Ethnic minorities in Britain: Diversity and disadvantage*, London: Policy Studies Institute, pp 83-149.

Mooney, G. (1997) 'Quasi-markets and the mixed economy of welfare', in M. Lavalette and A. Pratt (eds) *Social policy: A conceptual and theoretical introduction*, London: Sage Publications, pp 228-44.

Mooney, J. (1993) *The hidden figure: Domestic violence in North London*, Islington: Islington Council Police and Crime Prevention Unit.

Moore, R. (1997) *Positive action in action: Equal opportunities and declining opportunities on Merseyside*, Aldershot: Ashgate.

Morris, J. (1991) *Pride against prejudice*, London: The Women's Press.

Morris, J. (1993) *Community care or independent living?*, York: Joseph Rowntree Foundation.

Morris, J. (ed.) (1996) *Encounters with strangers*, London: The Women's Press.

Morris, J. and Winn, M. (1990) *Housing and social inequality*, London: Hilary Shipman.

Muir, J. and Ross, M. (1993) *Housing the poorer sex*, London: London Housing Unit.

Mullender, A. (1996) *Rethinking domestic violence: The social work and probation response*, London: Routledge.

Mullins, D. (1997) 'From regulatory capture to regulated competition: an interest group analysis of the regulation of housing associations in England', *Housing Studies*, vol 12, no 3, pp 301-19.

Mullins, D. (1998) 'More choice in social rented housing?', in A. Marsh and D. Mullins (eds) *Housing and public policy: Citizenship, choice and control*, Buckingham: Open University Press, pp 124-52.

Mullins, D. and Niner, P. (1998) 'A prize of citizenship? Changing access to social housing', in A. Marsh and D. Mullins (eds) *Housing and public policy: Citizenship, choice and control*, Buckingham: Open University Press, pp 175-98.

Mullins, D. and Revell, K. (2000) 'Third way on trial', *Roof*, vol 25, no 4, pp 29-31.

Muncie, J. (1999) 'Institutionalized intolerance: youth justice and the 1998 Crime and Disorder Act', *Critical Social Policy*, 19, 2; 59, pp 147-175.

Munro, M. and Madigan, R. (1993) 'Privacy in the private sphere', *Housing Studies*, vol 8, no 1, pp 29-45.

Murie, A. (1987) 'Social polarisation and housing provision', in D. Clapham and J. English (eds) *Public housing: Current trends and future developments*, London: Croom Helm, pp 12-31.

Murie, A. (1997) 'Beyond state housing', in P. Williams (ed) *Directions in housing policy*, London: Paul Chapman, pp 84-102.

Murie, A. (1998) 'Secure and contented citizens? Home ownership in Britain', in A. Marsh and D. Mullins (eds) *Housing and public policy: Citizenship, choice and control*, Buckingham: Open University Press, pp 79-98.

Murie, A. (2000) 'Allocation policies: facts and fantasies', *Axis*, April/May, pp 6-7.

Murphy, M. (1996) 'Household and family structure among ethnic minority groups' in D. Coleman and J. Salt (eds) *Ethnicity in the 1991 Census*, Volume 1, Demographic characteristics of the ethnic minority populations, London: HMSO, pp 213-42.

National Federation of Housing Associations, Association of Metropolitan Authorities, and Association of District Councils (1989) *Joint statement by the NFHA, AMA and ADC on local authority nominations to housing associations*, London: National Federation of Housing Associations.

Neale, J. (1997) 'Theorising homelessness: contemporary sociological and feminist perspectives', in R. Burrows, N. Pleace and D. Quilgars (eds) *Homelessness and social policy*, London: Routledge, pp 35-49.

Newman, J. (1998) 'Managerialism and social welfare', in G. Hughes and G. Lewis (eds) *Unsettling welfare: The reconstruction of social policy*, London: Routledge in association with The Open University, pp 333-74.

Niner, P. (1998) 'Charters in housing: enhancing citizenship, promoting choice or reinforcing control?', in A. Marsh and D. Mullins (eds) *Housing and public policy: Citizenship, choice and control*, Buckingham: Open University Press, pp 199-220.

Nixon, C. and Hunter, C. (2000) 'Hard cases', *Roof*, vol 25, no 2, pp 32-3.

Oldman, C. (1998) 'Joint planning: why don't we learn from the past?' in I. Shaw, S. Lambert and D. Clapham (eds) *Social care and housing*, Research Highlights in Social Work 32, London: Jessica Kingsley, pp 63-79.

Oldman, C. and Beresford, B. (1998) *Homes unfit for children: Housing, disabled children and their families*, Bristol: The Policy Press.

Oldman, C. and Beresford, B. (2000) 'Home, sick home: using the housing experiences of disabled children to suggest a new theoretical framework', *Housing Studies*, vol 15, no 3, pp 429-42.

Oliver, M. (1990) *The politics of disablement*, Basingstoke: Macmillan.

Oliver, M. and Barnes, C. (1998) *Disabled people and social policy: From exclusion to inclusion*, London: Longman.

Owen, D. (1992) 'Ethnic minorities in Great Britain; settlement patterns', 1991 *Census Statistical Paper* 1, National Ethnic Minority Data Archive, Centre for Research in Ethnic Relations, Warwick: University of Warwick.

Owen, D. (1993) 'Ethnic minorities in Great Britain; age and gender structure', 1991 *Census Statistical Paper* 2, National Ethnic Minority Data Archive, Centre for Research in Ethnic Relations, Warwick: University of Warwick.

Owen, D. (1993a) 'Ethnic minorities in Great Britain; housing and family characteristics', 1991 *Census Statistical Paper* 4, National Ethnic Minority Data Archive, Centre for Research in Ethnic Relations, Warwick: University of Warwick.

Özüekren, S. and Van Kempen, R. (eds) (1997) *Turks in European cities: Housing and urban segregation*, Utrecht: ERCOMER.

Pahl, J. (1985) 'Violent husbands and abused wives: a longitudinal study', in J. Pahl (ed) *Private violence and public policy*, London: Routledge and Kegan Paul, pp 23-94.

Papps, P. (1998) 'Anti-social behaviour strategies – individualistic or holistic?', *Housing Studies*, vol 13, no 5, pp 639-56.

Parrillo, V. (1998) 'The strangers among us: societal perceptions, pressures and policy', in H. Kurthen, J. Fijalkowski and G. Wagner (eds) *Immigration, citizenship, and the welfare state in Germany and the United States: Part B, welfare policies and immigrants' citizenship*, Stamford: JAI Press, pp 47-66.

Parker, J., Smith, R. and Williams, P. (1992) *Access, allocations and nominations: The role of housing associations*, London: HMSO.

Parsons, J. (1998) 'Ways of obtaining appropriate or adapted housing', in R. Bull (ed) *Housing options for disabled people*, London: Jessica Kingsley, pp 114-43.

Pascall, G. (1997) *Social policy: A new feminist analysis*, London: Routledge.

Passaro, J. (1996) *The unequal homeless: Men on the streets, women in their place*, New York, NY: Routledge.

Pawson, H. and Kearns, A. (1998) 'Difficult to let housing association stock in England: property, management and context', *Housing Studies*, vol 13, no 3, pp 391-414.

Pearl, M. (1997) *Social housing management: A critical appraisal of housing practice*, Basingstoke: Macmillan.

Penketh, L. and Ali, Y. (1997) 'Racism and social welfare', in M. Lavalette and A. Pratt (eds) *Social policy: A conceptual and theoretical introduction*, London: Sage Publications, pp 101-20.

Penoyre and Prasad Architects, with Audley English Associates, Matrix Feminist Architectural Co-op, Elsie Owusu Architects, and Safe Neighbourhoods Unit (1993) *Accommodating diversity; the design of housing for minority ethnic, religious and cultural groups*, London: National Federation of Housing Associations and North Housing Trust.

Phillips, D. (1986) *What price equality?*, GLC Housing Research and Policy Report No 9, London: Greater London Council.

Phillips, D. (1996) 'Appendix 2: an overview of the housing needs of black and minority ethnic households; census analysis', in M. Harrison, A. Karmani, I. Law, D. Phillips and A. Ravetz, *Black and minority ethnic housing associations: An evaluation of the Housing Corporation's black and minority ethnic housing association strategies*, London: The Housing Corporation, pp 50-65.

Phillips, D. (1997) 'The housing position of ethnic minority group home owners', in V. Karn (ed) *Ethnicity in the 1991 Census*, Volume 4, Employment, education and housing among the ethnic minority populations of Britain, London: The Stationery Office, pp 170-88.

Phillips, D. (1998) 'Black minority ethnic concentration, segregation and dispersal in Britain', *Urban Studies*, vol 35, no 10, pp 1681-702.

Phillips, D. and Karn, V. (1992) 'Race and housing in a property owning democracy', *New Community*, vol 18, no 3, pp 355-69.

Pinder, R. (1997) 'A reply to Tom Shakespeare and Nicholas Watson', in L. Barton and M. Oliver (eds) *Disability studies: Past, present and future*, Leeds: The Disability Press, pp 274-80.

Pinderhughes, H. (1997) *Race in the hood: Conflict and violence among urban youth*, Minneapolis: University of Minnesota Press.

Piven, F. and Cloward, R. (1972) *Regulating the poor: The functions of public welfare*, London: Tavistock.

Platt, L. and Noble, M. (1999) *Race, place and poverty*, York: Joseph Rowntree Foundation.

Policy Action Team 8 (2000) *Report of Policy Action Team 8: Anti-social behaviour*, National Strategy for Neighbourhood Renewal, Norwich: The Stationery Office.

Pollitt, C. (1990) *Managerialism and the public services: The Anglo-American experience*, Oxford: Blackwell.

Poulter, S. (1986) *English law and ethnic minority customs*, London: Butterworths.

Poulter, S. (1998) *Ethnicity, law and human rights: The English experience*, Oxford: Clarendon Press.

Powell, M. (1999) 'Introduction', in M. Powell (ed) *New Labour, new welfare state? The 'third way' in British social policy*, Bristol: The Policy Press, pp 1-27.

Priestley, M. (1998) 'Constructions and creations: idealism, materialism and disability theory', *Disability and Society*, vol 13, no 1, pp 75-94.

Priestley, M. (1999) *Disability politics and community care*, London: Jessica Kingsley.

Rai, D. and Thiara, R. (1997) *Re-defining spaces: the needs of black women and children in refuge support services and black workers in women's aid*, Bristol: WAFE.

Randolph, B. (1993) 'The re-privatization of housing associations', in P. Malpass and R. Means (eds) *Implementing housing policy*, Buckingham: Open University Press, pp 39-58.

Ranger, T. (1996) 'Introduction', in T. Ranger, Y. Samad and O. Stuart (eds) *Culture, identity and politics*, Aldershot: Avebury, pp 1-25.

Ratcliffe, P. (1996) *'Race' and housing in Bradford*, Bradford: Bradford Housing Forum.

Ratcliffe, P. (1997) '"Race", ethnicity and housing differentials in Britain', in V. Karn (ed) *Ethnicity in the 1991 Census*, Volume 4, Employment, education and housing among the ethnic minority populations of Britain, London: The Stationery Office, pp 130-46.

Ravetz, A. with Turkington, R. (1995) *The place of home: English domestic environments, 1914-2000*, London: E and F.N. Spon.

Raynsford, N. (2000) 'Under orders: Nick Raynsford reveals the findings of Policy Action Team 8 on anti-social behaviour', *Housing Today*, 177, 30 March 2000, pp 14-15.

Raynsford, N. (2000a) 'Supporting people – supporting independence', *Black Housing*, 111, pp 16-17.

Reeve, K. (1999) (unpublished) *The squatters' movement in London 1968-1980*, Thesis for PhD, University of Leeds.

Reid, B. (1995) 'Interorganisational networks and the delivery of local housing services', *Housing Studies*, vol 10, no 2, pp 133-49.

Reid, B. (1997) 'Interorganisational relationships and social housing services', in P. Malpass (ed) *Ownership, control and accountability: The new governance of housing*, Coventry: Chartered Institute of Housing, pp 109-30.

Rhoden, M. (1998) 'Equal opportunities and housing', in P. Balchin and M. Rhoden (eds) *Housing: The essential foundations*, London: Routledge, pp 107-21.

Riseborough, M. (1998) 'More control and choice for users? Involving tenants in social housing management', in A. Marsh and D. Mullins (eds) *Housing and public policy: Citizenship, choice and control*, Buckingham: Open University Press, pp 221-45.

Roof (2000) *Catalyst: an update on housing issues in Scotland*, Edinburgh: *Roof* with Scottish Homes, July.

Rosenberg, J. (1998) *Against the odds: Walterton and Elgin from campaign to control*, London: Walterton and Elgin Community Homes.

Rostron, J. (1995) *Housing the physically disabled*, Aldershot: Arena.

Rowe, A. (ed) (1990) *Lifetime homes*, London: Milgate for The Helen Hamlyn Foundation.

Royce, C., Hong Yang, J., Patel, G., Saw, P. and Whitehead, C. (1996) *Set up to fail? The experiences of black housing associations*, York: Joseph Rowntree Foundation.

Sandhu, H. (1999) 'Housing needs of Asian elders', *Axis*, June/July, p 17.

Sapey, B. (1995) 'Disabling homes: a study of the housing needs of disabled people in Cornwall', *Disability and Society*, vol 10, no 1, pp 71-85.

Saraga, E. (1998a) 'Abnormal, unnatural and immoral? The social construction of sexualities', in E. Saraga (ed) *Embodying the social: Constructions of difference*, London: Routledge in association with the Open University, pp 139-88.

Saraga, E. (ed) (1998) *Embodying the social: Constructions of difference*, London: Routledge in association with the Open University,

Sarre, P., Phillips, D. and Skellington, R. (1989) *Ethnic minority housing: Explanations and policies*, Aldershot: Avebury.

Saunders, P. (1989) 'The meaning of "home" in contemporary English culture', *Housing Studies*, vol 4, no 3, pp 177-92.

Scott, S. and Parkey, H. (1998) 'Myths and reality: anti-social behaviour in Scotland', *Housing Studies*, vol 13, no 3, pp 325-45.

Secretaries of State for the Environment and Wales (1995) *Our Future Homes: opportunity, choice, responsibility*, Cm 2901, London: HMSO.

Shah, L. and Williams, P. (1992) *The housing needs of the Asian elderly in Cardiff*, Research Report, Centre for Housing Management and Development, Department of City and Regional Planning, Cardiff: University of Wales College of Cardiff.

Shaw, I., Lambert, S. and Clapham, D. (1998) 'Boundaries of change in social care and housing', in I. Shaw, S. Lambert and D. Clapham (eds) *Social care and housing*, Research Highlights in Social Work 32, London: Jessica Kingsley, pp 7-26.

Shaw, K. (1990) 'Ideology, control and the teaching profession', *Policy & Politics*, vol 18, no 4, pp 269-78.

Short, J. (1982) *Housing in Britain: The post-war experience*, London: Methuen.

Showstack Sassoon, A. (1987) *Gramsci's politics*, London: Hutchinson.

Simons, B. (2000) 'Three cheers, three fears', *Roof*, vol 25, no 4, p 17.

Simpson, A. (1981) *Stacking the decks*, Nottingham: Nottingham and District Community Relations Council.

Sinfield, A. (1978) 'Analyses in the social division of welfare', *Journal of Social Policy*, vol 7, no 2, pp 129-56.

Smailes, J. (1994) '"The struggle has never been simply about bricks and mortar": lesbians' experience of housing', in R. Gilroy and R. Woods (eds) *Housing women*, London: Routledge, pp 152-72.

Smith, J. (1997) 'Transforming estates', in C. Cooper and M. Hawtin (eds) *Housing, community and conflict: Understanding resident 'involvement'*, Aldershot: Arena, pp 165-82.

Smith, J. (1999) 'Gender and homelessness', in S. Hutson and D. Clapham (eds) *Homelessness: Public policies and private troubles*, London: Cassell, pp 108-32.

Smith, M. (1989) *Guide to housing*, 3rd edn, London: The Housing Centre Trust.

Smith, N. (1998) 'Bureaucracy or death: safeguarding lives in houses in multiple occupation', in D. Cowan (ed) *Housing: participation and exclusion*, Aldershot: Ashgate, pp 168-88.

Smith, S. (1989) *The politics of 'race' and residence*, Cambridge: Polity Press.

Smith, S. and Mallinson, S. (1996) 'The problem with social housing; discretion, accountability and the welfare ideal', *Policy & Politics*, vol 24, no 4, pp 339-57.

Smith, S. and Mallinson, S. (1997) 'Housing for health in a post-welfare state', *Housing Studies*, vol 12, no 2, pp 173-200.

Social Exclusion Unit (2000) *National strategy for neighbourhood renewal: A framework for consultation*, Report, London: Cabinet Office.

Somerville, P. (1998) 'Empowerment through residence', *Housing Studies*, vol 13, no 2, pp 233-57.

Somerville, P. (2000) 'The meaning of home for African-Caribbean-British people', in F. Boal (ed) *Ethnicity and housing: Accommodating differences*, Aldershot: Ashgate, pp 263-72.

Somerville, P. and Steele, A. (1998) *Career opportunities for ethnic minorities*, Salford: University of Salford.

Spicker, P. (1987) 'Concepts of need in housing allocation', *Policy & Politics*, vol 15, no 1, pp 17-27.

Spicker, P. (1989) *Social housing and the social services*, Coventry: Institute of Housing and Longman.

Spink, B. (1998) 'Housing management 1800 to 2000: a practice in search of a policy', in C. Cooper and M. Hawtin (eds) *Resident involvement and community action: Theory to practice*, Chartered Institute of Housing Policy and Practice Series in collaboration with the Housing Studies Association, Coventry: CIH, pp 38-66.

Squires, P. (1990) *Anti-social policy: Welfare, ideology and the disciplinary state*, London: Harvester Wheatsheaf.

Stanko, E., Crisp, D., Hale, C. and Lucraft, H. (1998) *Counting the costs: Estimating the impact of domestic violence in the London Borough of Hackney*, London: Children's Society/Hackney Safer Cities.

Steele, A. (1997) *Young, drifting and black*, Nottingham: Homeless Support Centre, Nottingham City Council.

Stewart, A. (1981) *Housing action in an industrial suburb*, London: Academic Press.

Stewart, G. (1998) 'Housing, poverty and social exclusion', in I. Shaw, S. Lambert and D. Clapham (eds) *Social care and housing*, Research Highlights in Social Work 32, London: Jessica Kingsley, pp 47-61.

Stewart, J., Harris, J. and Sapey, B. (1998) 'Truth or manipulation? The politics of government-funded disability research', *Disability and Society*, vol 13, no 2, pp 297-300.

Stewart, M. and Taylor, M. (1995) *Empowerment and estate regeneration: A critical review*, Bristol: The Policy Press.

Stones, R. (1996) *Sociological reasoning: Towards a past-modern sociology*, Basingstoke: Macmillan.

Sykes, R. (1994) 'Older women and housing - prospects for the 1990s', in R. Gilroy and R. Woods (eds) *Housing women*, London: Routledge, pp 75-100.

Taylor, D. (1998) 'Social identity and social policy: engagements with postmodern theory', *Journal of Social Policy*, vol 27, no 3, pp 329-50.

Tennyson, R. (1991) 'An experiment in community care', *Housing Review*, vol 40, no 5, pp 101-3.

Third, H. (1995) *Affordable childcare and housing: A case study of tenants of a black housing association*, Research Report, Centre for Housing Policy, York: University of York.

Third, H., Wainwright, S. and Pawson, H. (1997) *Constraint and choice for minority ethnic home owners in Scotland*, Edinburgh: Scottish Homes.

Thomas, C. (1999) 'Understanding health inequalities: the place of agency', ESRC, *Health Variations*, Newsletter 3, January, pp 10-11.

Thomas, C. (1999a) *Female forms: Experiencing and understanding disability*, Buckingham: Open University Press.

Thomas, H. (2000) *Race and planning: The UK experience*, London: UCL Press.

Thomas, H. and Krishnarayan, V. (eds) (1994) *Race equality and planning: Policies and procedures*, Aldershot: Avebury.

Thompson, S. and Hoggett, P. (1996) 'Universalism, selectivism and particularism: towards a postmodern social policy', *Critical Social Policy*, 16, 1; 46, pp 21-43.

Timms, P. (1998) 'Partnership and conflict: working relationships between voluntary and statutory agencies providing services for homeless people', in D. Cowan (ed) *Housing: Participation and exclusion*, Aldershot: Ashgate, pp 68-83.

Tinker, A., Wright, F. and Zeilig, H. (1995) *Difficult to let sheltered housing*, London: HMSO.

Titmuss, R. (1958) 'The social division of welfare: some reflections on the search for equity', in R. Titmuss, *Essays on 'the welfare state'*, London: Unwin University Books, pp 34-55.

Tomas, A. and Dittmar, H. (1995) 'The experience of homeless women: an exploration of housing histories and the meaning of home', *Housing Studies*, vol 10, no 4, pp 493-515.

Tomlins, R. (1999) 'Race equality initiatives in housing provision: organisational change and the role of gatekeepers', *Journal of Ethnic and Migration Studies*, vol 25, no 1, pp 113-32.

Tomlins, R. (1999a) *Housing experiences of minority ethnic communities in Britain: An academic literature review and annotated bibliography*, CRER Bibliographies in Ethnic Relations No. 15, Coventry: University of Warwick.

Tomlins, R. (2000) 'Room to improve', *Housing Today*, 193, 20 July 2000, supplement, pp 4-5.

Tucker, J. (1966) *Honourable estates*, London: Victor Gollancz.

Turkington, R. and Dixon, A. (1997) *Thinking ahead: Housing, care and the future for black elders*, Birmingham: Nehemiah Housing/School of Housing, University of Central England.

Twine, F. (1994) *Citizenship and social rights: The interdependence of self and society*, London: Sage Publications.

Veit-Wilson, J. (2000) 'States of welfare: a conceptual challenge', *Social Policy and Administration*, vol 34, no 1, pp 1-25.

Vernon, A. (1996) 'A stranger in many camps', in J. Morris (ed) *Encounters with strangers*, London: The Women's Press, pp 48-68.

Vincent-Jones, P. and Harries, A. (1998) 'Tenant participation in contracting for housing management services: a case study', in D. Cowan (ed) *Housing: participation and exclusion*, Aldershot: Ashgate, pp 41-67.

Waddington, M. (1998) 'Too poor to stay here: "illegal immigrants" and housing officers', in D. Cowan (ed) *Housing: participation and exclusion*, Aldershot: Ashgate, pp 213-33.

Walby, S. (1997) *Gender transformations*, London: Routledge.

Walker, R. (1998) 'New public management and housing associations: from comfort to competition', *Policy & Politics*, vol 26, no 1, pp 71-87.

Walker, R. (2000) 'The changing management of social housing: the impact of externalisation and managerialisation', *Housing Studies*, vol 15, no 2, pp 281-99.

Ward, C. (1974) *Tenants take over*, London: The Architectural Press.

Ward, H. and Lupton, L. (1998) 'Resident involvement in housing associations and other "registered social landlords"', in C. Cooper and M. Hawtin (eds) *Resident involvement and community action: Theory to practice*, Chartered Institute of Housing Policy and Practice Series in collaboration with the Housing Studies Association, Coventry: CIH, pp 179-200.

Wardhaugh, J. (1999) 'The unaccommodated woman: home, homelessness and identity', *The Sociological Review*, vol 47, no 1, pp 91-109.

Warnes, T. (1996) 'The age structure and ageing of the ethnic groups', in D. Coleman and J. Salt (eds) *Ethnicity in the 1991 Census*, Volume 1, Demographic characteristics of the ethnic minority populations, London: HMSO, pp 151-77.

Wasoff, F. (1998) 'Women and housing', in I. Shaw, S. Lambert and D. Clapham (eds) *Social care and housing*, Research Highlights in Social Work 32, London: Jessica Kingsley, pp 127-44.

Watson, L. (1997) *High hopes: Making housing and community care work*, York: Joseph Rowntree Foundation.

Watts, V. and Galbraith, C. (1998) 'Living independently', in R. Bull (ed) *Housing options for disabled people*, London: Jessica Kingsley, pp 203-35.

Weaver, M. (1998) 'Charity begins at home', *Housing Today*, 89, 25 June, p 12.

Weaver, M. (2000) 'Not the Field good factor', *Housing Today*, 179, 13 April, pp 16-17.

Welsh Women's Aid (1986 and revised 1989) *The answer is maybe ... and that's final!*, Cardiff: Welsh Women's Aid.

Whitehouse, L. (1998) 'The impact of consumerism on the home owner', in D. Cowan (ed) *Housing: participation and exclusion*, Aldershot: Ashgate, pp 126-46.

Wilcox, S. (ed.), (1997) *Housing finance review 1997/98*, York: JRF.

Wilcox, S. and Ford, J. (1997) 'At your own risk', in S. Wilcox (ed) *Housing finance review 1997/98*, York: JRF, pp 23-9.

Wilkinson, M. (1993) 'British tax policy 1979-90: equity and efficiency', *Policy & Politics*, vol 21, no 3, pp 207-17.

Williams, F. (1996) 'Postmodernism, feminism and the question of difference', in N. Parton (ed) *Social theory, social change and social work*, London: Routledge, pp 61-76.

Williams, F. (1999) 'Good-enough principles for welfare', *Journal of Social Policy*, vol 28, no 4, pp 667-87.

Williams, P. (1997a) 'Getting the foundations right: housing organisations and structures', in P. Williams (ed) *Directions in housing policy: Towards sustainable housing policies for the UK*, London: Paul Chapman, pp 120-37.

Williams, P. (1999) 'A commentary on "housing policy: does it have a future?"', *Policy & Politics*, vol 27, no 2, pp 231-32.

Williams, P. (ed) (1997) *Directions in housing policy: Towards sustainable housing policies for the UK*, London: Paul Chapman.

Williamson, K. (1993) 'Race and housing in London's docklands', *Housing Review*, vol 42, no 3, p 53.

Wistow, G. (1999) 'Community care in the twenty-first century', in F. Spiers (ed) *Housing and social exclusion*, London: Jessica Kingsley, pp 43-62.

Withers, P. and Randolph, B. (1994) *Access, homelessness and housing associations*, London: NFHA.

Women's Unit, Cabinet Office/Home Office (1999) *Living without fear: an integrated approach to tackling violence against women*, London: Central Office of Information.

Woods, R. (1996) 'Women and housing', in C. Hallett (ed) *Women and social policy: An introduction,* London: Prentice Hall/Harvester Wheatsheaf, pp 65-83.

Woodward, K. (1997) 'Feminist critiques of social policy', in M. Lavalette and A. Pratt (eds) *Social policy: A conceptual and theoretical introduction,* London: Sage Publications, pp 83-100.

Wootton, B. (assisted by Seal, V. and Chambers, R.) (1959) *Social science and social pathology,* London: George Allen and Unwin.

Yinger, J. (1995) *Closed doors, opportunities lost: The continuing costs of housing discrimination,* New York: Russell Sage Foundation.

Young, I. (1990) *Justice and the politics of difference,* Princeton, NJ: Princeton University Press.

Index